Armoured
Fighting Vehicles
of the
World

Armoured Fighting Vehicles of the World

CHRISTOPHER F. FOSS

CHARLES SCRIBNER'S SONS
NEW YORK

To our Parents

Printed in Great Britain

Library of Congress Catalog Card Number 74-11927

ISBN 0-684-14113-2

Contents

Abbreviations

AA	Anti-Aircraft
AFV	Armoured Fighting Vehicle
AMX	Atelier des Constructions d'Issy-les-Moulineaux
AP	Armour Piercing
APC	Armoured Personnel Carrier
APDS	Armour Piercing Discarding Sabot
APG	Aberdeen Proving Ground (United States)
APHE	Armour Piercing High Explosive
API	Armour Piercing Incendiary
APS	Armour Piercing Shot
ARV	Armoured Recovery Vehicle
ATGW	Anti-Tank Guided Weapon
AVLB	Armour Vehicle Launched Bridge
AVRE	Armoured Vehicle Royal Engineers
BAC	British Aircraft Corporation
BAOR	British Army of the Rhine
BARV	Beach Armoured Recovery Vehicle
BHP	Brake Horse Power
C & R	Command and Reconnaissance
CEV	Combat Engineer Vehicle
FVRDE	Fighting Vehicles Research & Development Establishment (now the Military Vehicles and Engineering Establishment)
G/Clearance	Ground Clearance
GMC	General Motors Corporation
G/Pressure	Ground Pressure
GPO	Gun Position Officer
HE	High Explosive
HEAT	High Explosive Anti-Tank
HEI	High Explosive Incendiary
HEP	High Explosive Plastic
hp	Horse Power
HVAP	High Velocity Armour Piercing
ICBM	InterContinental Ballistic Missile
inc	Including
IR	Infra-Red
kg	Kilogramme
kg.cm^2	Kilogramme per square centimetre
km	Kilometre
km/ph	Kilometre per hour
LVT	Landing Vehicle, Tracked
max	Maximum
MBT	Main Battle Tank
MICV	Mechanised Infantry Combat Vehicle
min	Minimum
mg	Machine Gun
m	Metre
mm	Millimetre
MVEE	Military Vehicles and Engineering Establishment
NATO	North Atlantic Treaty Organisation
NBC	Nuclear, Biological, Chemical
ROF	Rate of Fire *or* Royal Ordnance Factory
rpm	Revolutions per minute *or* Rounds per minute
SPG	Self-Propelled Gun
SPH	Self-Propelled Howitzer
SPRR	Self-Propelled Recoilless Rifle
USMC	United States Marine Corps
V/Obstacle	Vertical Obstacle
W/O	With-out

Introduction

The first edition of *Armoured Fighting Vehicles of the World* was published in 1971. Since then revised editions have appeared in both Germany and Italy.

In the last three years many developments have taken place in the field of armoured fighting vehicles. Vehicles such as the Fox and Scorpion that were then still under development have now entered service. Others, such as the American Mechanised Infantry Combat Vehicle and the Armoured Reconnaissance Scout Vehicle, were then only projects and they are now being built in prototype form. Some vehicles such as the French Light Fighting Unit and the American SWAT have been abandoned all together, other vehicles have been phased out of service upon the introduction of more modern vehicles.

Recent conflict in the Middle East has focused attention on armoured fighting vehicles again. Once again, certain people have been saying that the tank is dead, people have been saying this on and off for some forty years. The tank is far from dead and the tanks that are at present under development, for example the American XM-1 and the new German/British MBT, will ensure that tanks will be around for a good many years yet.

More recent tanks are now being fitted with superior day and night vision devices, stabilised armament, laser rangefinders, radar and a wide range of other sensors, more reliable engines and transmissions. Future AFVs will see improved mobility, improved weapons systems and new types of vehicle construction.

Armoured personnel carriers are now giving way to the new generation of vehicle, called the mechanised infantry combat vehicle. Most artillery is now self-propelled, as are a growing number of anti-aircraft missile systems. More wheeled armoured vehicles are being developed both for the internal security and load carrying roles.

This book contains data, development history, variants and a list of user countries of all tanks, reconnaissance vehicles, armoured personnel carriers, self-propelled guns (including anti-aircraft missile systems that will be found in the immediate battle area) and armoured load carriers that are at present in service or under development.

None of the photographs in this edition appeared in the first edition of *Armoured Fighting Vehicles of the World*. All data is now in metric and it is hoped that this will be of assistance to the many overseas readers of this book. The text has been fully revised and updated and many new vehicles have been included.

The author would like to thank the many governments, manufacturers and individuals all over the world who have provided material for this book. In addition special thanks are due to John F. Milsom, Geoff Tillotson and C. W. Moggridge for their most valuable assistance.

Additional material, including photographs, for future editions of *Armoured Fighting Vehicles of the World* should be forwarded to Ian Allan Limited, Terminal House, Shepperton TW17 8AS, England.

January 1974   **Christopher F. Foss**

Acknowledgements

The author would like to thank the following companies and individuals for their most valuable assistance during the preparation of this book.

Aérospatiale (France)
Alvis Limited (Great Britain)
Associated Press (London)
Australian Army
Austrian Army
Belgian Army
Berliet Company (France)
Bowen-McLaughlin-York Company (United States)
British Aircraft Corporation—GW Division (Great Britain)
British Information Service
British Ministry of Defence (ARMY)
Bundesgrenzschutz (Federal German Border Police)
Cadillac Gage Company (United States)
Canadian Armed Forces
Chrysler Corporation (United States)
Creusot-Loire Company (France)
DAF Company (Holland)
E.C.P.Armées (France)
E.M.I. Limited (Great Britain)
F.F.V. (Sweden)
FIAT Company (Italy)
F.M.C. Corporaton (United States)
F.N. (Belgium)
Finnish Army
French Army
G.K.N. Sankey Limited (Great Britain)
General Electric Company (United States)
German Army
Groupement Industriel des Armements Terrestres (France)
Hägglund and Söner (Sweden)
Hotchkiss-Brandt (France)
Indian Army
Irish Army
Israeli Army
Japanese Self-Defence Forces
Krauss-Meffei (Germany)
Lockheed Missiles and Space Company (United States)
Mercedes-Benz (Germany)
Mitsubushi Heavy Industries (Japan)
Messerschmitt-Bölkow-Blohm (Germany)
Normalair-Garrett Limited (Great Britain)
Oto Melara (Italy)
Panhard and Levassor (France)
Philco-Ford Corporation (United States)
Rheinstahl (Germany)
Royal Armoured Corps Tank Museum
Royal Danish Army
Royal Netherlands Army
Saviem (France)
Short Brothers and Harland Limited (Great Britain)
Soltàm Company (Israel)
Steyr-Daimler-Puch (Austria)
Swedish Ministry of Defence
Thomson CSF (France) ´
United States Army including :
  United States Army Audio Visual Agency
  United States Army Europe
  United States Army Material Command
  United States Army—Office of the Chief of Information
  United States Army Tank-Automotive Command
United States Marine Corps
Vickers Limited (Great Britain)
Volvo Company (Sweden)

T. Bell (Great Britain)
R. M. Bennett (Great Britain)
Robert J. Icks (United States)
George Von Rauch (United States)
Stephen Tunbridge (Switzerland)
J. I. Taibo (Spain)
Susuma Yamada (Japan)

Below : *Panzerjäger K 4KH6FA, FL-12*

Panzerjäger K 4KH6FA, FL–12 — Austria

Armament: 1 × 105mm gun, elevation + 13°, depression −6°
1 × 7.62mm co-axial machine gun
2 × 3 smoke dischargers
26 rounds of 105mm ammunition carried
Crew: 3
Length: 7.778m (including gun)
5.58m (excluding gun)
Width: 2.50m
Height: 2.355m (w/o cupola)
G/Clearance: .40m
Weight: 17,000kg (loaded)
G/Pressure: .65kg.cm²
Engine: Steyr Model 6FA 6 cylinder diesel
10 litres, developing 300hp at 2300rpm
Speed: 65km/ph (road)
Range: 530km
Fuel: 400 litres
Fording: 1.00m
V/Obstacle: .80m
Trench: 2.40m
Gradient: 70%
Armour: 8mm–40mm

Development/Variants
Development of this vehicle started in 1965 and the first prototype was completed by Saurer in 1967. It basically consists of a modified Saurer chassis on which has been fitted a French FL-12 turret with a 105mm gun, in fact the same as that fitted to AMX-13 tanks. The turret is of the oscillating type and has two magazines each holding six rounds and fires spin stabilised rounds with a m/v of 800 m/s. The modifications to the chassis have been quite extensive and include moving the engine and transmission to the rear, the drive sprocket now being at the rear, the suspension has been modified and there are now three return rollers, the APC having two.
A German infra-red/white light searchlight can be fitted to the top of the turret towards the rear to assist in locating targets at night. A laser rangefinder is under development.
Trials of the prototype and five pre-production vehicles were carried out by the Austrian Army. It is expected that a production order will shortly be given to Steyr-Daimler-Puch to produce these. The turrets will be produced in Austria or purchased from France.
Employment
Trials with the Austrian Army.

Saurer 4K 4FA Armoured Personnel Carrier   Austria

Armament: 1×12.7mm machine gun
Crew: 2+8
Length: 5.40m
Width: 2.50m
Height: 2.10m (including mg)
1.65m (hull top)
G/Clearance: .42m
Weight: 12,500kg (loaded)
11,200kg (empty)
G/Pressure: .51kg.cm²
Engine: Saurer Model 4FA 6 cylinder diesel
9.981 litres, developing 250hp at 2400rpm
Speed: 61.7km/ph (road)
Range: 370km
Fuel: 184 litres
Fording: 1.00m
V/Obstacle: .80m
Trench: 2.20m
Gradient: 75%
Armour: 8mm–20mm

Development

Development of an APC was started by Saurer in 1956, the first prototype was completed in 1958 this being the 3K3H which was powered by a 3H 200hp Saurer diesel. This was followed by the 4K3H in 1959 and the 4K2P. The 4K4F was built in 1961 and the latest models are the 4K 3FA and 4K 4FA all with more powerful engines. Production has now been completed

and the vehicles were built by Saurer, although Saurer was taken over by Steyr-Daimler-Puch in 1970.

Variants

There are two basic armoured personnel versions. One is armed with a 12.7mm machine gun, this being provided with front and side armour; in addition the crew can mount a total of four MG42 7.62mm machine guns on sockets around the top of the hull. The second model is fitted with an Oerlikon GAD AOA turret armed with a 20mm 204 GK gun with 100 ready rounds. This turret can be elevated from −12° to +70°, and has armour of 15mm–35mm.

Other versions include an ambulance (Sanitätspanzer San), multiple rocket launcher with 2×80mm launching systems, 4K 3FA-FU (command vehicle), 4K 3FA-FU/A (artillery command vehicle), 4K 3FA-FU/FIA (anti-aircraft command vehicle), 4K 3FA-FS2 (radio vehicle), 81mm mortar carrier (GrW 1), 120mm mortar carrier (GrW 2).

Employment

Used only by the Austrian Army.

Saurer APC with Oerlikon Turret and 20mm Cannon

FN 4 RM/62F AB Armoured Car   Belgium

	Machine gun version	Gun version
Length Overall:	4.50m	5.42m
Length Hull:	4.50m	4.50m
Width:	2.26m	2.26m
Height Overall:	2.37m	2.52m
G/Clearance:	.324m	.324m
Weight Loaded:	8660kg	7880kg

Data the same for both vehicles includes:
Crew: 3
Wheelbase: 2.45m
Track: 1.62m
Gradient: 60%
Armour: 6.5mm–13mm
Engine: FN 652, 6 cylinder, in-line, OHV petrol engine developing 130hp at 3500rpm
Speed: 110km/ph (road)
Range: 550/600km
Fuel: 180 litres
Fording: 1.10m

Development
This armoured car was designed by Fabrique Nationale d'Armes de Guerre of Herstal, Belgium, and uses many components of the FN 4RM Ardennes truck. The first prototype was built in 1962, followed by the second prototype in 1965. Production was completed in 1971 and 62 were built, all being delivered to the Belgian Gendarmerie.

Variants
Machine gun version: This is armed with a 60mm mortar, 2 × 7.62mm machine guns and 12 smoke dischargers. The turret has a traverse of 360°, and the machine guns can be elevated from −10° to +55° and the mortar from −10° to +75°. Ammunition carried is: 46 mortar rounds, 4850 machine gun rounds, 36 smoke grenades and 12 anti-personnel grenades.

Gun version: This is armed with a 90mm CATI gun, 1 × 7.62mm co-axial machine gun, 1 × 7.62mm anti-aircraft machine gun and 12 smoke dischargers. The turret has a traverse of 360° and the gun has an elevation from −12° to +27°. Ammunition carried is: 40 rounds of 90mm, 3680 machine gun rounds, 36 smoke grenades and 12 anti-personnel grenades.

Armoured Personnel Carrier: Only one of these was built. It was armed with a 7.62mm machine gun, height to hull top was 1.78m and height to cupola was 2.11m, other data was the same as for the armoured car version. Large doors were provided either side for the crew to leave the vehicle quickly.

Employment
Used only by the Belgian Gendarmerie.

FN 4 RM/62F AB Armoured Car with a 90mm gun

Brazilian Armoured Fighting Vehicles
ENGESA Armoured Vehicles

	CTRA	CRR
Crew:	1+14	3
Length:	5.76m	4.90m
Width:	2.44m	2.26m
Height Overall:	2.45m	2.34m
G/Clearance:	.50m	.50m
Weight Loaded:	10,500kg	9000kg
Speed Road:	95km/ph	95km/ph
Speed Water:	12km/ph	
Range:	700km	700km
Fording:	Amphibious	1.00m
Vertical Obstacle:	.60m	.60m
Trench:	1.50m	1.50m
Gradient:	70%	70%

CTRA (EE-11 Urutu)
Armoured Personnel Carrier
Design commenced in January 1970 and the first prototype was completed by Engesa in July 1970. In 1972 a production order for this vehicle was awarded to Engesa, these vehicles will be supplied to the Brazilian Army (non amphibious models) and the Brazilian Marines (amphibious models and powered by Chrysler 318, 8 cylinder petrol engines).
The first CTRA was powered by a Mercedes-Benz 352A, 6 cylinder diesel developing 150hp. The vehicle is of all welded construction, there are doors in each side of the vehicle and a large single door at the rear, roof hatches are provided. Armament can be installed, for example a simple mounting for a 7.62mm or 12.7mm machine gun, or a turret, similar to that fitted to the Commando armoured car armed with a 12.7mm and a 7.62mm machine gun. The vehicle is fully amphibious being propelled in the water by two propellers at the rear of the vehicle.

CRR (EE-9 Cascavel) Armoured Car
Design commenced in July 1970 and the first prototype was completed by Engesa in November 1970. This vehicle uses some of the components of the EE-11 including engine, transmission, gearbox and axles. The prototype was armed with a 37mm gun (as fitted to the M-8 Greyhound armoured car), a co-axial 7.62mm machine gun and a 12.7mm anti-aircraft machine gun. Production vehicles, however, will probably have a more up to date gun fitted. This vehicle is not amphibious. A small production order has been awarded to Engesa for this vehicle.

Cutia–Vete T1 A1

Design of this vehicle is reported to have commenced in 1966 and according to reports over 100 of these vehicles have been built. It is an armoured, full tracked vehicle and is armed with at least one machine gun. Provisional data is given below.

Length: 3.66m
Width: 1.83m
Height: 1.00m
Weight: 2720kg (loaded)
Crew: 4+
Speed: 80km/ph (road)
Range: 370km
Engine: 4 cylinder petrol

VBB Vehicle
The 4×4 VBB was built by the Brazilian Army in 1966, it did not progress beyond the prototype stage.

Cutia-Vete T1 A1 Armoured Vehicle, note the very narrow tracks

Sexton Self-Propelled Gun

Canada

Armament: 1×25 pounder (88mm) gun elevation +40°, depression −9°, traverse 25° left and 15° right
2× Bren LMGs with 1500 rounds
25 pounder ammunition—112 cartridges, 87 HE and 18 AP projectiles
Crew: 6
Length: 6.12m
Width: 2.717m
Height: 2.870m (inc. canvas top)
2.438m (w/o canvas top)
G/Clearance: .431m
Weight: 25,855kg
G/Pressure: .80kg.cm²
Engine: Continental R975-C1 petrol engine, 400hp at 2400rpm OR
Continental R975-C4 petrol engine, 475hp at 2400rpm
Speed: 40km/ph (road)
Range: 290km (road)
Fuel: 682 litres
Fording: .914m
V/Obstacle: .609m
Trench: 1.879m
Gradient: 60%
Armour: 13mm–32mm

Development
The Sexton, full designation 25 pounder, self-propelled, tracked, Sexton, was developed in Canada. The first prototype was built late in 1942, production commenced early in 1943 at the Montreal Locomotive Works. A total of 2150 were built before production was completed late in 1945. The vehicle had an open roof although a cover was provided for use in bad weather. The Sexton served with the British Army until the 1950s.
Variants
The Sexton GPO was a Sexton without its armament and was used as a Gun Position Officer vehicle. It has additional communications equipment as well as tables and seats.
Employment
The Sexton is still used by India, Italy and South Africa.

Sexton Self-Propelled Gun (World War II photograph)

¾ Ton Truck 4 x 4

Canada

Armament: Crew weapons only
Crew: 8
Length: 4.749m
Width: 2.336m
Height: 2.27m
G/Clearance: .241m
Weight: 4887kg (loaded)
Engine: General Motors 6 cylinder petrol engine developing 104bhp at 3000rpm
Speed: 72km/ph (road)
Range: 713 km
Fuel: 181 litres
Fording: .457m

Gradient: 60%
Armour: 8mm–12mm
Development/Variants/Employment
The ¾ ton armoured truck was designed and built in Canada during World War II. The chassis was made by General Motors of Canada and the hull by the Hamilton Bridge Company Limited. The vehicle could be used as an armoured personnel carrier, load carrier or as an ambulance. It is reported that the vehicle is still used in South Vietnam. A turreted version of this vehicle was known as the Otter.

Chinese Armoured Fighting Vehicles

Type 55 Armoured Personnel Carrier:
This is the Soviet BTR-40 built in China.
Type 56 Armoured Personnel Carrier:
This is the Soviet BTR-152 built in China.
M-1967 (or M-1970) Armoured Personnel Carrier: This is a Chinese designed and built APC and was first seen in 1967. It has a weight of 10,000kg and is armed with a 12.7mm machine gun. It can carry ten men. Running gear is similar to that used on the T-60 light tank. Some have been delivered to Tanzania.
T-60 Light Tank: This is a development of the PT-76. It has six road wheels with the driving sprocket at the rear and the idler at the front. The turret is similar in shape to the T-59. It is armed with a turret mounted 85mm gun and a co-axial 7.62mm machine gun, a 7.62mm anti-aircraft machine gun can also be fitted. It is fully amphibious being propelled in the water by waterjets. It is also used by North Vietnam, Pakistan and Tanzania. Many have been captured by the South Vietnamese.

T-62 Tank: This is said to look rather like a mini-T-59 and to be armed with an 85mm gun loaded weight is about 21,000kg, it has five large road wheels. Some have been supplied to Albania and Sudan.
T-63 Tank: This is armed with an 85mm gun, it has 5 small road wheels and 4 support rollers.
T-59 Medium Tank: This is the Chinese copy of the Soviet T-54 tank and it has been in production since 1961. The original vehicle had no infra-red equipment, no stabiliser for the main armament and the turret only had hand traverse. Later models may have infra-red systems and improved turret traverse and stabiliser for the gun. This tank has also been exported to Albania, North Vietnam, Pakistan, Tanzania and Sudan.

Above: *A T-59 of the Pakistani Army knocked out during the Indian/Pakistan campaign of 1971*

SKOT, OT–64 Model 2A
Armoured Personnel Carrier

Czechoslovakia

Armament: 1 × 14.5mm machine gun, elevation +29°, depression —4°
1 × 7.62mm machine gun co-axial with 14.5mm machine gun
Crew: 2+18
Length: 7.44m
Width: 2.55m
Height: 2.71m (including turret)
G/Clearance: .40m
Weight: .40m
Weight: 12,800kg

Armour: 10mm
Engine: Tatra T-928-14, V-8 diesel developing 180hp at 2000rpm
Speed: 95km/ph (road)
8.9km/ph (water)
Range: 650/750km
Fording: Amphibious
V/Obstacle: .50m
Trench: 2.00m
Gradient: 60%

Development
The OT-64, also known as SKOT (Czechoslovakian designation is Střední Kolový Obojživelny Transporter), is based on the Tatra 813 truck, development started in 1959. The 8×8 vehicle is fully amphibious being propelled in the water by two propellers; a trim board is erected at the front of the vehicle before entering the water. The vehicle is also fitted with a tyre pressure regulation system enabling the tyre pressures to be adjusted to suit the ground conditions. The infantry are at the rear of the vehicle and are provided with overhead hatches, rear exit doors and firing ports. The vehicle has an NBC system.

Variants
Model 1: The Polish Army has some Model 1s with a single 7.62mm machine gun in an unprotected mount. The Czechoslovakian Army Model 1s have no armament.

Model 2: This model is used by the Polish Army and has either a single 12.7mm or 7.62mm machine gun with a curved shield, this is mounted in the forward part of the vehicle.

Model 3: This model is called the Model 2A by the Czechs. It has a turret armed with a 14.5mm and a 7.62mm machine gun, the turret has a traverse of 360°, elevation +29° and depression −4°. The turret is situated just to the rear of the vehicle. The same turret is fitted to the Soviet BTR-60PB and BTR-40P-2 vehicles.

Model 4: This model has the same armament as the above but has a new turret which is higher than the Model 3, the Czechoslovakian designation of this model is the Model 2AP. The machine guns have an elevation of $+89\frac{1}{2}°$ and a depression of −4°. This turret is also fitted to some late model BTR-50PKs.

Model 5: This model is a Model 1 with two Sagger anti-tank missiles mounted over the rear of the infantrymen's compartment.

Employment
Czechoslovakia, Egypt, Hungary, India (inc Model 3s), Morocco (inc Model 3s), Poland, Sudan, Syria, Uganda (inc Model 3s).

Right: *OT-64 Model 5 with Sagger Anti-Tank missiles*

Below: *OT-64 Model 1*

OT–62, TOPAS, Model 2   Czechoslovakia

Armament: 1×82mm Recoilless Gun T-21 (outside of turret)
1×7.62mm machine gun M-59 (inside of turret)
Crew: 2+18
Length: 7.08m
Width: 3.14m
Height: 2.35m (inc turret)
2.038m (w/o turret)
G/Clearance: .364m
Weight: 15,000kg
G/Pressure: .53kg.cm²
Engine: Model PV-6, 6 cylinder, in-line diesel developing 132hp at 1100/1200rpm
Speed: 62km/ph (road)
11km/ph (water)
Range: 450km
Fording: Amphibious
V/Obstacle: 1.10m
Trench: 2.80m
Gradient: 70%
Armour: 10mm

Development
The OT-62 TOPAS (Transporter Obojzivelńy Ṕasov́y Stredni) is the Czechoslovakian version of the Soviet BTR-50PK APC. It is however a more powerful vehicle and the Czechs have adapted the vehicle to their own requirements. The vehicle is fully amphibious being propelled in the water by waterjets; it is also fitted with an NBC system.

Variants
Model 1: This has two projecting bays (similar to the Soviet BTR-50PU Model 2), side doors in the troop compartment and two rectangular overhead hatches. No armament is fitted although an 82mm recoilless rifle M59 may be carried and fired on the rear decking.
Model 2: This is similar to the above model but in addition has a small turret on the right bay. This is armed with a 7.62mm M59 mg, a T-21 recoilless rifle can be mounted on the outside of the turret.
Model 3: This model is fitted with the same turret that is fitted to the OT-64 Model 4, it is armed with a 14.5mm and a 7.62mm machine gun, turret has a traverse of 360°. The turret is mounted over the rear troop compartment, in the centre of the vehicle. This model has a crew of 3+12 and a height of 2.73m. Its Czech designation is TOPAS Model 2AP. Command and ambulance versions of the OT-62 are believed to be in service.

Employment
Czechoslovakia, Egypt, Hungary, India, Poland.

Above: OT-62, TOPAS Model 1, note the side door of this model

OT–810 Armoured Personnel Carrier   Czechoslovakia

This is a Czechoslovakian copy of the World War II German Sd.Kfz.251/1 half-track. Early models of this vehicle had a petrol engine and no overhead armour. Later models had overhead armour and were powered by a Tatra 912-2 diesel. This vehicle is used both as an armoured personnel carrier and as a tractor for towing 82mm M59 recoilless guns. Some vehicles have been seen fitted with a 7.62mm M59 machine gun on the roof. The vehicle is only used by the Czechoslovakian Army.

M53/59
Self-Propelled Anti-Aircraft Vehicle   Czechoslovakia

Armament: 2×30mm M-53 cannon, elevation +90°, depression −10°, traverse 360°
Crew: 3
Length: 6.984m
Width: 2.383m
Height: 2.50m (w/o magazines)
2.74m (with magazines)
G/Clearance: .40m
Weight: 9500kg
Engine: Tatra T912-2 6 cylinder, in-line, water cooled diesel developing 110hp at 2200rpm
Speed: 60km/ph (road)
Range: 500km
Fording: .80m
V/Obstacle: .46m
Trench: .69m
Gradient: 60%
Armour: 10mm

Development/Variants
The M53/59 twin 30mm self-propelled anti-aircraft system is based on the Praga V3S 6×6 truck chassis. The guns have a vertical feed for loading whereas the towed version of these guns have a horizontal feed system. The guns have a cyclic rate of fire of 450/500 rounds per gun per minute but the practical rate of fire is 150 rounds per minute. It fires HEI or API rounds, in clips of 10, these have an effective anti-aircraft range of 2000m. The guns can be used both against ground and air targets.

The vehicle has a crew of three, the driver, the commander, who sits next to the driver and is provided with a transparent observation cupola on the right of the superstructure, and the gunner with the guns. There is no provision for deep wading or radar control.

Employment
In service with Czechoslovakia and Yugoslavia.

Below: M53/59 with guns forward, the magazines for the 30mm guns can be clearly seen in this photograph

AMX–30 Main Battle Tank   France

Armament: 1×105mm gun, elevation +20°
depression – 8°
1×12.7mm mg or 20mm cannon co-axial with
main armament, it can however be elevated to
+40°
1×7.62mm machine gun on commander's
cupola
2×2 smoke grenade launchers
50 rounds of 105mm ammunition, 600 rounds
of 12.7mm ammunition, 1600 rounds of
7.62mm ammunition
Crew: 4
Length: 9.48m (gun forward)
6.59m (hull only)
Width: 3.10m
Height: 2.85m (top of cupola)
2.28m (turret roof)
G/Clearance: .44m
Weight: 36,000kg (loaded)
G/Pressure: .77kg.cm²
Engine: Hispano-Suiza HS-110, 12 cylinder
multi-fuel, water cooled engine developing
700hp at 2400rpm. Engine is built in France
by Saviem.
Speed: 65km/ph (road)
Range: 650km (road)
Fording: 2.00m
4.00m (with schnorkel)
Fuel: 970 litres
V/Obstacle: .93m
Trench: 2.90m
Gradient: 60%

Development

In 1956. France, Germany and Italy decided to
build a common tank. This idea did not work
out and France decided to build the AMX-30.
The first prototype AMX-30 was completed in
1960, this being followed by the second
prototype in 1961. These were followed by a
further seven models in 1963 and pre-
production tanks in 1965. In 1966 the tank
entered production and the first French M-47
units were re-equipped with AMX-30s in the
summer of 1967.
The vehicle is fitted with infra-red driving and
fighting equipment, it also has an NBC system
and can be fitted with a schnorkel. Under
development is a laser rangefinder. The 105mm
gun can fire either hollow charge rounds
(m/v 1000 m/s) or HE rounds (m/v 700 m/s),
maximum rate of fire is 8rpm.

Variants

AMX-30 Export Model: This has no NBC
system, no schnorkel or infra-red equipment
and a simple cupola.
AMX-30S: This model has been developed
for use in hot climates; it is fitted with sand-
shields and its engine develops only 620hp at
2400rpm; the gearbox has been modified. It
can be fitted with air conditioning.
AMX-30 Anti-Aircraft Tank: This is simply
an AMX-30 chassis with the turret of the
AMX-13 A/A tank. It is armed with 2×30mm
guns. It has not been placed in production,
trials only.
AMX-30 155mm GCT: This 155mm self-
propelled gun is at present under test. For full
details see separate entry.
AMX-30 ACRA: An AMX-30 tank is being
used to test the new 142mm ACRA anti-tank
system. It was reported in 1973 however that
the ACRA system had been cancelled or scaled
down.
AMX-30 Recovery Tank: This is designed
to carry out repairs in the field and to carry out
this role it is fitted with a crane (can lift
13/20,000kg), main winch (35,000kg with
120m of cable), auxiliary winch (4000kg and
120m of cable) and a dozer blade at the front.
It is armed with a 7.62mm machine gun and
smoke dischargers. In production and service.
AMX-30 Bridgelayer Tank: This tank can
lay a class 50 bridge across a 20m ditch. The
bridge is 22m long, 3.15m wide (w/o widening
panels) and 3.95m wide (with widening
panels), when laid out. It is entering service.
AMX-30 Roland Anti-Aircraft Tank: This
is under test. It has two Roland missiles in the
ready to fire position, with a further eight in
reserve. It is a complete weapons system
having its own radar.
Pluton Weapon System: This is an AMX-30
chassis fitted with a Pluton tactical nuclear
missile with a range of over 100km.
AMX-30 Training Tank: This is an AMX-30
on which the turret has been replaced by an
observation cupola.
AMX-30 with TSE 6000 Javelot: This is a
close-air defence system under development
by Thomson-CSF.
AMX-30 with RAPACE radar: An AMX-30
has been fitted with the EMD Rapace tank
detection radar for trials pusposes.

Employment

The AMX-30 is used by Chile, France, Greece,
Iraq, Libya, Peru, Saudi-Arabia, Spain,
Venezuela. This includes those on order.

	155mm SPG	ARV	Bridgelayer	Roland
Length Overall:	10.40m	7.18m	11.40m	6.65m
Width Overall:	3.115m	3.14m	3.95m	3.10m
Height Overall:	3.30m	2.65m	4.29m	3.02m
Weight Loaded:	41,000kg	40,000kg	42,500kg	33,000kg
Crew:	4	4	3	3

AMX-30 fitted with a Schnorkel for deep fording

AMX-30 Main Battle Tank

The AMX-30 Anti-Aircraft Tank, this is still in the trials phase

The AMX-30 Armoured Recovery Vehicle

The AMX-30 Bridgelayer Tank in the travelling position

The AMX-30 fitted with the Roland Anti-Aircraft System

The AMX-30 Training Tank has no turret

AMX–13 Light Tank   France

Armament: 1 × 90mm gun, elevation +12½°, depression −5½°
1 × 7.62mm machine gun co-axial with main armament
1 × 7.62mm machine gun on commander's cupola (optional)
2 × 2 smoke dischargers. (Some AMX-13s have 7.5mm mgs.)
34 rounds of 90mm and 3600 rounds of 7.62mm ammunition
Crew: 3
Length: 6.36m (with gun)
4.88m (w/o gun)
Width: 2.50m
Height: 2.30m (cupola)
G/Clearance: .37m
Weight: 15,000kg (loaded)
13,000kg (empty)
G/Pressure: .76kg.cm²
Engine: SOFAM 8GXb 8 cylinder water cooled, 8.25 litres petrol engine developing 270hp at 3200rpm (built by Saviem)
Speed: 60km/ph (road)
Range: 350km/400km (road)
Fuel: 480 litres
Fording: .60m
V/Obstacle: .65m
Trench: 1.60m
Gradient: 60%
Armour: 10 mm 40mm

Development
The design of the AMX-13 started shortly after the end of World War II. AMX standing for the design centre (Atelier des Constructions d'Issy-les-Moulineaux) and 13 for the original requested weight. The first prototype was built in 1949 and deliveries to the French Army started in 1952. The AMX-13 tank chassis has been used for a whole range of AFVs, a few of which are described below, the rest later in the book. The AMX-13 has been constantly modified to keep it an effective weapon.

Variants
AMX-13 Model 51: This was the first model to enter service. It was armed with a 75mm gun in an FL-10 turret. It was armed with a 75mm gun and a 7.5mm or 7.62mm machine gun and four smoke dischargers. 37 rounds of 75mm ammunition are carried, of these 12 rounds were in two revolver type magazines with 6 rounds each. This enabled the tank to fire 12 rounds very quickly. The drawback being that these magazines then had to be re-loaded again from outside of the vehicle.

AMX-13 with FL-11 turret: This was

Note. *The data left relates to the AMX-13 with the new 90mm gun.*

Below: *AMX-13 Bridgelayer*

designed in the mid-1950s for use in Algeria. It is armed with a short 75mm gun in an FL-11 turret.

AMX-13 Model 58 with FL-12 turret: This is armed with a 105mm gun that fires fin-stabilised, non-rotating hollow charge rounds. These rounds have a m/v of 800 m/s and will penetrate 360mm of armour. 32 rounds of 105mm ammunition are carried.

AMX-13 with 90mm gun: This is the latest model of the AMX-13. The barrel is a 75mm barrel which has been rebored and an insulating jacket fitted. The gun fires 90mm hollow charge rounds with a m/v of 950 m/s and will penetrate 320mm of armour; 34 rounds of ammunition are carried.

AMX-13 Model 51 with SS-11 missiles: This retains its gun armament but also has four SS-11 ATGW, these are mounted two either side of the gun. The missiles have an effective range of 3000m. This system is in service with the French Army. A later version, still under test, is fitted with the TCA optical/infra-red guidance system for the missiles, a similar guidance system is fitted to the AMX-13 with HOT.

AMX-13 with HOT ATGW: This version is not yet in service, being still under development. It is a basic AMX-13 fitted with 3 HOT ATGW either side of the turret. These have an effective range of 75m–4000m.

AMX Armoured Recovery Vehicle (Char de Dépannage Model 55): This has spades at the rear, 15 ton capacity winch, an auxiliary winch, 5 ton "A" frame, lighting equipment and tools. The French ARVs are armed with a 7.5 or 7.62mm mg, the Netherlands ARVs have six smoke dischargers and a 7.62mm mg.

Basic data is similar to the AMX-13 except:
Crew: 3
Width: 2.60m
Length: 5.515m
Weight: 15,000kg
Height: 2.682m

AMX-13 Bridgelayer: Called Poseur de Pont by the French. It is a modified AMX-13 chassis fitted with a scissors bridge. When opened out this is 7.15m in length and can take tanks up to class 25, two of these bridges used together can take class 50 tanks. Basic data is similar to the AMX-13 except:
Weight: 19,700kg (with bridge)
Length: 7.75m (with bridge)
Width: 3.05m
Height: 4.30m (with bridge)

AMX-13 Training Tank: This is an AMX tank without its turret and used for driver training. The French also have some vehicles with M-24 Chaffe turrets.

Employment

Used by Algeria, Argentina (including bridge-layers) Austria (including ARV), Cambodia, Chile, Dominican Republic, Ecuador, Egypt, France, India, Indonesia, Ivory Coast, Jordan, Kenya, Lebanon, Morocco, Netherlands (including ARV), Nepal (from Israel), Peru, Saudi Arabia, Singapore (from Israel), South Vietnam, Switzerland (called Pz-51), Tunisia, Venezuela. Argentina has assembled AMX-13s, the first one being completed late in 1969.

AMX-13 Model 1951 with four SS-11 Anti-Tank missiles

AMX-13 Model 51
mounting a 75mm Gun
in a FL-10 turret

AMX-13 Armoured
Recovery Vehicle

AMX-13 Model 58
mounting a 105mm Gun
in FL-12 turret, this
vehicle belongs to the
Netherlands Army, note
the Infra-Red/White
light searchlight on the
right of the turret

AMX-13 with a 90mm
Gun

EBR 75 Heavy Armoured Car France

Armament: See below
Length: 7.33m (o/a FL-10 turret)
6.15m (o/a FL-11 turret)
5.56m (vehicle only)
Width: 2.42m
Height: 2.32m (FL-11 on 8 wheels)
2.24m (FL-11 on 4 wheels)
G/Clearance: .41m (on 8 wheels)
.33m (on 4 wheels)
Weight: 15,200kg (loaded FL-10)
13,500kg (loaded FL-11)
G/Pressure: .75kg.cm² (on 8 wheels)
Engine: Panhard 12 cylinder petrol engine,
developing 200hp at 3700rpm.
Crew: 4
Speed: 105km/ph (road)
Range: 650km
Fuel: 370 litres
Fording: 1.20m
V/Obstacle: .40m
Trench: 2.00m
Gradient: 60%+
Armour: 10mm–40mm

Development
In 1937 Panhard started to design an 8×8
armoured car for the French Army. A prototype
was completed in December 1939 and the
vehicle was given the Panhard No. Model 201.
The vehicle, together with its drawings, were
lost during the war. Development work started
again after the war and the first post-war
prototype was completed in July 1948. This
had an FL-11 turret and was called the EBR 75
(Engin Blindé Reconnaissance), its Panhard
designation being Model 212. The vehicle
entered production in August 1950 and production was completed in 1960 by which
time 1200 had been built.
The EBR has a number of unusual features.
It has a crew of four which consists of a
commander, gunner and two drivers (one at
the front and one at the rear). All eight wheels

are powered and when crossing rough country
its centre four wheels, which have steel treads,
can be lowered into position. All of the turrets
used, the FL-10 and FL-11, are of the
oscillating type.
Variants
EBR 75 with FL-11 turret: Also known as
type B, has a 75mm gun, elevation +15°,
depression −10°, with 56 rounds of ammunition. This was the first model to enter service.
Other data see below.
EBR 75 with FL-10 turret: This has a
75mm gun with an elevation of +13° and a
depression of −6°. A total of 38 rounds of
ammunition are carried. The gun has automatic loading, ie two revolver type magazines
hold 6 rounds each. Three 7.5mm mgs are
fitted, one co-axial with the main gun and one
fixed for the use of each driver. Two smoke
dischargers are fitted either side of the turret.
It is also known as the Model A.
EBR 75 with 90mm gun in FL-11 turret:
This is the latest version and mounts a 90mm
gun that fires fin-stabilised ammunition, all
earlier versions will be re-fitted with this new
gun. It is also called Model C.
EBR Anti-Aircraft Vehicle: One of these
was built in 1952. It consisted of an EBR
chassis on which was mounted a turret armed
with 2×30mm cannon.
EBR ETT Armoured Personnel Carrier:
This had the Panhard No. Model 238, the first
vehicle was built in 1957 and a total of 30
were built. There were two models—one had
a single large mg turret and the other had two
small turrets, one at each end of the vehicle.
Some vehicles had their metal centre wheels
replaced by conventional wheels with tyres.
Employment
Used by France, Morocco and Portugal.

Above: *EBR 75 with FL-11 turret mounting
a 75mm gun*

Panhard AML Light Armoured Car   France

Armament: 1×60mm mortar, elevation +76°, depression −15°
1×12.7mm machine gun, elevation +75°, depression −11°
41 rounds of 60mm mortar ammunition
1200 rounds of 12.7mm machine gun ammunition
Crew: 3
Length: 3.79m
Width: 1.97m
Height: 2.12m (over searchlight)
1.885m (turret top)
G/Clearance: .33m
Weight: 4800kg (loaded)
Track: 1.62m
Wheelbase: 2.50m
Engine: Panhard Model 4 HD, 4 cylinder air-cooled petrol engine developing 90hp at 4700rpm
Speed: 100km/ph (road)
Range: 600km (road)
Fuel: 150 litres
Fording: 1.10m
V/Obstacle: .30m
Trench: .80m (one channel)
3.10m (four channels)
Gradient: 60%
Armour: 8mm–12mm

Note. *The above data relates to the AML with the HE 60-12 turret.*

Development
The AML-245 is manufactured by Panhard in Paris. The first prototype was completed in 1959 followed by the first production vehicle in 1961. Since then the vehicle has been built in large numbers and exported all over the world, in addition a production line has been established in South Africa, this, however, is not run by Panhard. AML means Automitrailleuse Légère, or light armoured car. The AML can be fitted with a variety of night fighting and night driving equipment and is airportable by aircraft and helicopters (ie the SA 321 Super Frelon). The AML has been continuously developed over the last 10 years and a full list of variants is listed below. Many components of the AML are used in the Panhard M-3, which is described later in this book.

Variants
AML with HE 60-7 turret (also known as Model A): This is armed with a 60mm mortar (Model CS DTAT or Hotchkiss Brandt CM 60A1) with an elevation of +76°, depression −15°, this has a range of 300m–1700m and 2×7.62mm machine guns. These have an elevation of +60° and a depression of −15°. 53 rounds of 60mm and 3800 rounds of 7.62mm ammunition are carried. Four ENTAC missiles can be fitted as required, this then becomes the Model D.

AML with HE 60-20 turret (also known as Model E): This is armed with a 60mm breach-loaded mortar with an elevation of +76° and a depression of −15° and a 20mm M621 cannon. This has an elevation of +50° and a depression of −8°. 39 rounds of 60mm and 300 rounds of 20mm ammunition are carried. A 7.62mm anti-aircraft machine gun is fitted

The AML with H-90 turret mounted 90mm gun

to the roof of the vehicle and 1000 rounds of 7.62mm ammunition are carried.

AML with H-90 turret (also known as Model C): This is armed with a 90mm gun with an elevation of $+15°$ and a depression of $-8°$ and a co-axial 7.62mm machine gun. The 90mm gun has an effective range of 1500m when firing HE rounds (m/v 650 m/s) or 2400m when firing fin-stabilised hollow charge rounds (m/v 760 m/s). Twenty rounds of 90mm and 2400 rounds of 7.62mm ammunition are carried. In addition there are two smoke dischargers either side of the turret. If required 2 ENTAC or SS-11 ATGW can be mounted either side of the 90mm gun.

AML-30: This has a new turret mounting a 30mm HS 831A cannon and a co-axial 7.62mm machine gun. A 7.62mm anti-aircraft machine gun is mounted on the turret roof. There are two smoke dischargers mounted either side of the turret. 200 rounds of 30mm and 2200 rounds of 7.62mm ammunition are carried.

AML with NA 2 turret: This was an experimental vehicle and was a basic AML fitted with a NA 2 turret mounting 4 SS-11 ATGW ($+2$ reserve) or 2 SS-12 ($+2$ reserve) ATGW. Also fitted were 2 ACL 89mm anti-tank rockets or 2×7.62mm machine guns.

AML S 530 anti-aircraft vehicle: The prototype was completed in 1969 and the first production vehicle in 1971. It is a basic AML, fitted with a new turret designed by SAMM (Société d'Applications des Machines Motrices). This mounts 2×20mm 621 automatic cannon, with powered traverse and elevation from $+75°$ to $-10°$, traverse being 360°, Effective range is 1300m and rate of fire is 740rpm per barrel. 600 rounds of 20mm ammunition are carried. In addition there are two smoke dischargers either side of the turret.

Amphibious kit

An amphibious kit has been developed that can be fitted to any of the AML series. This kit consists of thin steel sheets around the hull of the vehicle, these are filled with a self-extinguishable non-spongy synthetic matter. A propeller kit is available, this gives the vehicle a speed of 6–7km/ph in the water. Loaded weight of an AML 90 with the amphibious kit is 5750kg.

Employment

The AML is used by Algeria, Burundi, Cambodia, Congo, Ecuador, Eire, Ethiopia, France, Iraq, Israel, Ivory Coast, Kenya, Libya, Mauritania, Morocco, Malaysia, Nigeria, Portugal, Rhodesia (from South Africa), Rwanda, Saudi Arabia, Senegal, South Africa, Spain, Tunisia.

The AML-30 with a 30mm HS 831A cannon

*The AML with an
HE 60-7 turret*

*The AML S 530 Anti-
Aircraft Vehicle with twin
20mm cannon*

*The AML with the
HE 60-20 turret*

AMX–10P Family
Mechanised Infantry Combat Vehicle

France

Armament: 1×20mm cannon M-693 and 1×7.62mm machine gun in a mount with a traverse of 360°, elevation +50° and depression −8°. 800 rounds of 20mm ammunition (of which 350 are for ready use) and 2000 rounds of 7.62mm ammunition (of which 900 are for ready use) are carried.
4 smoke grenade launchers mounted on the rear of the vehicle.
Crew: 2+9
Length: 5.778m
Width: 2.780m
Height: 2.54m (overall)
1.87m (hull top)
G/Clearance: 0.45m
Weight: 13,800kg (loaded)
11,300kg (empty)
Engine: Hispano-Suiza HS 115-2, V-8 water-cooled engine developing 276hp at 3000rpm.
8.21 litres
Speed: 65km/ph (road)
7.92km/ph (water)
Range: 600km
Fording: Amphibious
V/Obstacle: 0.70m
Trench: 1.60m
Gradient: 60%
G/Pressure: .53kg.cm²

Development
The prototype was called the AMX-10A and was shown at the 1969 French Satory exhibition. The first vehicle in the series is the AMX-10P, from this has been developed a whole new range of armoured fighting vehicles for the French Army, both tracked and wheeled. The vehicles are fully amphibious being propelled in the water by water jets, they are fitted with NBC systems and/or infra-red/image intensifier driving and fighting equipment.

Variants—Tracked
AMX-10P: This is now in production. It is an infantry combat vehicle and has started to replace the AMX Model 56 APC. It carries nine infantry men and these are provided with overhead hatches, periscopes and firing ports in the rear. Under development is a version with Milan ATGW, also being developed is a stabilisation system for the gun turret.
AMX-10TM: This version is also in production and tows the Hotchkiss-Brandt 120mm mortar, the vehicle has a crew of six and carries 60 mortar rounds.
AMX-10C: This version is under development and will have a turret mounted gun similar to that fitted to the AMX-10RC.
AMX-10D: This is a recovery version under development.
AMX-10M: There were to have been two

versions, one armed with the ACRA anti-tank system and the other with four HOT ATGW launchers and a 20mm cannon. Development of ACRA has stopped so there is some doubt about the first version.
AMX-10PC: This is a command vehicle and is in production. It has a crew of six. Various types of radio can be installed and the vehicle has been provided with an additional generator. Additional working space can be provided by erecting awnings at the rear and side of the vehicle.

Variants—Wheeled
The wheeled vehicles have also been developed to a French Army requirement to replace vehicles used by their Armoured Light Cavalry Regiments. They use many components of the tracked versions but offer increased road speed, increased range and better strategic mobility. The versions announced so far are:
AMX-10RP: This is an AMX-10P with wheels and the prototype, designated AMX-10R has been under test for three years.
AMX-10RM: This will be armed with HOT ATGW and a 20mm cannon.
AMX-10RC: This was first shown at the Satory display in June 1973. It is a 6×6 vehicle with hydro-pneumatic suspension, it has a maximum speed of 85km/ph and a range of 800km. It is fully amphibious. Armament consists of a 105mm gun, 7.62mm mg and four smoke dischargers. The turret has a traverse of 360°, elevation being +20° and depression −8°. A complete range of fighting and driving aids are fitted including a laser rangefinder, image intensification equipment and an NBC system. Basic data is:
Length: 6.243m (hull)
G/Clearance: .30m
Gradient: 60%
Width: 2.78m
Weight: 15,000kg (loaded)
Trench: 1.60m
Height: 2.565m (o/a)
V/Obstacle: 0.70m
Employment
The AMX-10P is in service with the French Army.

Top: *An early model of the AMX-10P vehicle*

Centre: *The AMX-10R was first shown at Satory in 1971*

Bottom: *The AMX-10RC is armed with a 105mm turret mounted gun*

AMX VCI
France
Armoured Personnel Carrier/Infantry Combat Vehicle

Armament: 1 × 7.5mm or 7.62mm or 12.7mm machine gun
Crew: 1+12
Length: 5.544m
Width: 2.51m
Height: 2.32m (with turret)
1.92m (w/o turret)
G/Clearance: .48m
Weight: 14,000kg (loaded)
11,700kg (empty)
G/Pressure: .70kg.cm²
Engine: SOFAM 8 GXb 8 cylinder petrol engine developing 250hp at 3200rpm
Speed: 65km/ph (road)
Range: 350/400km (road)
Fuel: 410 litres
Fording: .60m
V/Obstacle: .65m
Trench: 1.60m
Gradient: 60%
Armour: 10mm–30mm

Note. *Above dimensions can vary according to date built.*

Development/Variants
The specification for the AMX APC was issued in 1954 and production commenced in 1956. It is based on the AMX tank chassis which has been lengthened and vehicles can be seen with three or four return rollers. It was originally called the AMX-VTP (Véhicule Transport de Personnel) or TT.CH.Mle.56 (Transport de Troupe Chenillé Model 56) but it is now referred to as the AMX VCI (Véhicule de Combat d'Infanterie). The machine gun can be mounted in a turret (7.5mm or 7.62mm) or on a ring mount (12.7mm mg). The infantry carried can fire their weapons through firing ports in the sides and rear of the vehicle.

The vehicle has an NBC system and can be fitted with infra-red driving lights. A number of these vehicles were built in Belgium. The vehicle has no amphibious capability.
Command Vehicle: This is known as the 'Véhicule de Commandement', and has been fitted with additional radios, map boards and so on. It has a crew of 4–9 men and is recognisable by its three radio aerials.
Ambulance: Known as the 'Véhicule Sanitaire Model 56', no armament is fitted. It has a crew of four and can carry four seated and three stretcher patients. Basic data is similar to the APC except that its loaded weight is 13,500kg.
Dozer Vehicle: This is simply an AMX APC with a dozer blade fitted at the front, known as the 'Char AMX Dozer'. Loaded weight is 16,200kg.
Battery Command Vehicle: This has been developed for use with artillery, for example the 155mm SPG. Equipment fitted includes additional radios, map boards and fire control equipment. Under development is an electronic fire control computer. Data similar to the APC except for its crew of seven.
Mortar Vehicles: These are called AMX-VCPM (Véhicule Chenillé Porte-Mortier) and there are two versions:
81mm mortar with elevation of +43° to +80°, traverse 40°, 128 rounds carried, crew of 6. Mortar can also be fired away from the vehicle
120mm mortar with an elevation of +45° to +77°, traverse 46°, 60 rounds carried, crew of five. Mortar can also be fired away from the vehicle.
Pioneer Vehicle: Known as the AMX-VCG (Véhicule de Combat du Génue). This is fitted

with a dozer blade, winch, 'A' frame, search-light and other equipment. It has a crew of 10, armed with a 12.7mm mg, weight 17,800kg, length 6.37m and height 3.46m.

Cargo Vehicle: When used as a cargo vehicle the AMX VCI can carry 3,170kg of cargo.

Missile Launcher Vehicle: This is a standard AMX VCI fitted with two missile launchers at the rear, each launcher having two missiles. A total of 26 ENTAC missiles are carried and it has a crew of five. Another version has two SS-11 missiles, one either side of the commanders cupola.

Artillery Support Vehicle: This is used to support the AMX 155mm SPG. It has a crew of eight and carries 25 shells, 25 cartridge bags and 24 fuses. It can also tow an ammunition trailer. Loaded weight is 13,700kg.

Roland Anti-Aircraft Missile Vehicle: This was a trials vehicle and mounted 2 Roland SAMs in the ready to fire position.

TOW Launcher Vehicle: DAF have fitted an AMX VCI of the Netherlands Army with a launcher system for the American TOW ATGW.

Employment

Used by Argentina, Belgium, France, Italy and the Netherlands.

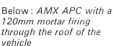

Right: *AMX-VCG fitted with its Dozer Blade and 'A' Frame*

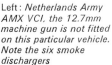

Below: *AMX APC with a 120mm mortar firing through the roof of the vehicle*

Left: *Netherlands Army AMX VCI, the 12.7mm machine gun is not fitted on this particular vehicle. Note the six smoke dischargers*

Panhard M-3 Armoured Personnel Carrier   France

Armament: See below, according to requirements
Crew: 2+10
Length: 4.457m
Width: 2.40m
Height: 2.48m (turret)
2.0m (w/o turret)
G/Clearance: .35m
Weight: 6100kg (loaded)
Track: 2.05m
Wheelbase: 2.70m
Engine: Panhard Model 4 HD, 4 cylinder, air cooled petrol engine developing 90hp at 4700rpm
Speed: 100km/ph (road)
4km/ph (water)
Range: 600km (road)
Fuel: 165 litres
Fording: Amphibious
V/Obstacle: .30m
Trench: .80m (with 1 channel)
Gradient: 60%
Armour: 8mm–12mm

Development

The Panhard M-3 armoured personnel carrier is based on components of the AML family, 95% of the components of the M-3 are interchangeable with those of the AML. The prototype M-3 was built in 1969 and the first production model in 1971. The prototype was rather square in appearance. In recent years the vehicle has been sold in large numbers all over the world. The hull of the M-3 is of all welded construction. There are doors on either side of the vehicle and twin doors at the rear. A circular opening in the front part of the roof can be fitted with a variety of turrets or mounts. There is also a hatch on the rear part of the roof allowing use of a machine gun mounted on a rail. There are flaps in the sides of the vehicle and firing ports in the rear door. The M-3 is fully amphibious without preparation; it is propelled in the water by its wheels.

Variants

The basic vehicle can be used as an armoured personnel carrier, load carrier, ambulance, riot control vehicle, mortar carrier, repair vehicle, command post, radio vehicle or missile vehicle. A wide range of armament can be fitted, some of which is listed below:
Turret TL.2.1.80 with twin 7.62mm machine guns.
Turret MAS T.20.13.621 with AME 621 20mm cannon.
Turret TL 52 S with one 7.62mm machine gun and 1 Strim rocket launcher.
Turret TL 52 3S with one 7.62mm machine gun and 3 Strim rocket launchers.
Mount CB.20 M621 with 20mm cannon.
Mount CB.60.HB with 60mm mortar.
Mount CB.127 with 12.7mm machine gun.
Mount CB.80 and CB.52 with 7.62mm machine gun.
Mount STB.80, STB.52, STB.MG with 7.62mm machine gun.
Mount STB.80, STR.52 and STR.B with 7.62mm machine gun.
Panhard M-3 VDA: This is currently under development and was shown for the first time at Satory in June 1973. It has been designed by Panhard in association with EMD, CNMP, Galileo and Oerlikon. It is basically an M-3 chassis with a turret mounting 2×20mm HS 820 SL guns with an elevation of $+85°$ and a depression of $-5°$, these have power traverse and elevation. A total of 600 rounds of 20mm ammunition are carried. In addition there is a 7.62mm machine gun on the roof of the vehicle. It has a crew of three men. There are two stabilisers either side of the hull, which can be let down to provide a stable firing platform. The vehicle is fitted with a radar scanner and a computer sight.

Employment

Used by Abu-Dhabi, Congo, Iraq, Eire, Kenya, Lebanon, Malaysia, Saudi-Arabia.

Below: Panhard M-3 with single 7.62mm machine gun mounts

A Panhard M-3
Armoured Personnel
Carrier of the Irish Army.
This particular vehicle is
armed with the TL.2.1.80
turret which has twin
7.62mm machine guns

A Panhard M-3 with
60mm Hotchkiss-Brandt
mortar

Panhard M-3 VDA
Anti-Aircraft Vehicle

Panhard M–4

France

Armoured Car/Personnel Carrier

Armament: Various types of armament can be fitted
Crew: 10 (maximum)
Length: 5.305m
Width: 2.50m
Height: 1.986m (high)
1.866m (road)
1.725m (low)
G/Clearance: .214m (low)
.354m (road)
.474m (high)
Weight: 9500kg (loaded)
7000kg (empty)
Engine: Berliet V-800 8 cylinder diesel developing 170hp at 3000rpm. (Two other engines are available.)
Speed: 90km/ph (road)
7km/ph (water)
Range: 1000km+ (road)
Fording: Amphibious
V/Obstacle: .60m
Trench: 1.10m
Gradient: 60%
Track: 2.12m
Wheelbase: 2.95m
G/Pressure: 1.6kg.cm²
Armour: 8mm–25mm

Development
The Panhard M-4 has been designed and built by Panhard of Paris. It is a 4×4 vehicle of all welded construction, is fully amphibious, being propelled in the water by two propellers at the rear. The M-4 is fitted with an NBC system and has hydropneumatic suspension allowing the height of the vehicle to be adjusted to suit the type of ground being crossed.

Variants
The M-4 can be used for a wide variety of roles including armoured car, armoured personnel carrier, command vehicle, load carrier, ambulance and anti-aircraft vehicle. Many types of armament can be fitted including all of the turrets fitted to the AML armoured car (including the 90mm gun version), also single 7.62mm and 12.7mm machine guns.

Employment
Trials with the French Army. The M-4 has been developed under a programme of the French Army, the Saviem 4×4 and 6×6 VAB vehicles have been built under the' same programme. The earlier Panhard M-2 8×8 vehicle has not been developed further than the prototype stage. It did however play a valuable part in the development of the M-4, M-6 and M-8 vehicles.

Below: One of the prototypes of the new Panhard M-4 Armoured Vehicle

Panhard M–6 and M–8

France

Armoured Car/Personnel Carrier

The Panhard M-6 (6×6) and M-8 (8×8) armoured vehicles are at present under development by Panhard. They use many components of the Panhard M-4. A wide range of armament can be fitted to these vehicles, the most powerful of which will be a turret-mounted 105mm gun on the M-8.

Berliet VXB 170
Multi-Role Vehicle

France

Armament: See below
Crew: 1+12
Length: 5.99m
Width: 2.50m
Height: 2.05m (w/o turret)
G/Clearance: .45m (transfer box)
Weight: 12,700kg (loaded)
9800kg (empty)
Engine: Berliet V8 diesel, 6.92 litres, developing 170hp at 3000rpm
Speed: 85km/ph (road)
4km/ph (water)
Range: 750km
Fuel: 220 litres
Fording: Amphibious
Trench: nil
Gradient: 60%
Armour: 7mm (maximum)

Development
This vehicle was originally known as the Berliet BL 12. The first of two prototypes was built in March 1968. One of these was tested by the French Army in 1969 and the other retained by Berliet. The first of five VXBs was built in May 1971 and tested by the French Gendarmerie. In 1973 a production order was given to Berliet for 50 vehicles for the French Gendarmerie; production commenced in 1973 at the Berliet factory at Bourg.

The VXB is a 4×4 vehicle and its hull is of all-welded construction. Firing ports are provided in the hull and the crew can enter and leave the vehicle by way of side, rear and roof hatches. It is fully amphibious being propelled in the water by its wheels. A 3500/4500kg winch is fitted at the front. Optional extras are many and include heater, radios, NBC system, night driving equipment and a dozer blade.

Variants
The VXB can be used for the following five basic roles: armoured personnel carrier, load carrier, light combat vehicle, light reconnaissance vehicle and an anti-riot vehicle. Many types and combinations of armament can be fitted including the following: 90mm gun, 2×20mm cannon, 1×20mm cannon, 1×12.7mm machine gun, 2×7.62mm machine guns, 2 single 7.62mm machine guns, 81mm mortar, various anti-tank missile systems and anti-aircraft missile systems. The vehicle can also be used as a command vehicle or ambulance.

Employment
Used by the French Gendarmerie.

Below: A Berliet VXB with turret mounted 20mm cannon

Saviem VAB

France

Armament: 1 × 12.7mm machine gun
Crew: 2
Length: 5.855m
Width: 2.48m
Height: 2.06m (w/o armament)
G/Clearance: .40m
Engine: 6 cylinder water-cooled diesel developing 240hp
Speed: 90km/ph (road)
Range: 1000km (road)
Fording: Amphibious
Gradient: 70%
Track: 2.07m
Wheelbase: 3.00m

Development

Details of the Saviem VAB (Vehicule de L'Avant Blindé), or front armoured vehicle were first released in June 1973. At the present time a total of five prototypes are undergoing comparative tests with the Panhard built M-4 vehicle. The vehicle is designed to transport 12 men or 2000kg of cargo in the immediate battle area. The vehicle is fully amphibious being propelled in the water by two hydrojets at the rear, there is a trim board at the front of the vehicle. The hull is of all welded construction and there are hatches in the roof. At the rear are two large doors, each of which has a small flap, and in addition there are three small flaps either side, which allow the crew to fire their small arms. Other features include a front-mounted winch, NBC system, power steering, air brakes and the engine is provided with a fire-fighting system.

Variants

The VAB could be adopted for a wide variety of roles including armoured personnel carrier armed with a 20mm cannon, missile vehicle, mortar carrier, command vehicle, ambulance, radio vehicle and recovery vehicle.

Employment

Trials with the French Army.

Below: *The Saviem 6 × 6 VAB armed with a 12.7mm machine gun*

Bottom: *The Saviem 4 × 4 VAB*

Hotchkiss Carriers

France

	A	B	C	D
Crew:	5	5	4/5	3/5
Length:	4.51m	4.51m	4.66m	4.66m
Width:	2.28m	2.28m	2.28m	2.28m
Height:	1.97m	1.69m	1.84m	1.84m
G/Clearance:	.35m	.35m	.35m	.35m
Weight Loaded:	8200kg	7500kg	8200kg	8000kg
G/Pressure:	.58kg,cm²	.55kg.cm²	.58kg.cm²	.57kg.cm²
Speed Road:	58km/ph	58km/ph	58km/ph	58km/ph
Range:	390km	400km	375km	350km
Fuel:	330 litres	345 litres	320 litres	295 litres
Armament:	20mm	7.62mm	7.62mm	7.62mm

Data similar to all vehicles: **Fording:** 1m, **V/Obstacle:** .60m, **Trench:** 1.50m, **Gradient:** 60%, **Armour:** 8mm–15mm. All are powered by a Hotchkiss 6 cylinder, OHV, water-cooled petrol engine developing 164hp at 3900rpm. In the above table:

A Reconnaissance Vehicle SP.1A
B Observation & Command Veh. SP.111
C Mortar Carrier SP.1B
D Armoured Ambulance SP.IV

Development
These vehicles were developed from the earlier Hotchkiss TT6 series of carriers. They were built in France for the German Army, although some were also assembled in Germany. All of the above vehicles share the same engine, transmission, track and so on.

Variants
Reconnaissance Vehicle SP.1A: This is armed with a turret-mounted 20mm Hispano-Suiza cannon with a 360° traverse, elevation is +75°, depression −10°. Five hundred rounds of 20mm ammunition are carried. This vehicle is designated SPZ 11-2 in the German Army, a similar vehicle is the SPZ 31-2 radio vehicle.

Observation and Command Vehicle SP.111: This is similar to the above vehicle but without the turret. It is armed with a 7.62mm machine gun and carries three radios. The vehicle is designated SPZ 22-2 in the German Army.

Mortar Carrier SP.1B: This has an 81mm mortar firing through the roof, this has an elevation of +45° to +90°, and a traverse of 30° left and 30° right, 50 rounds of mortar ammunition are carried. The vehicle also has a 7.62mm machine gun and 500 rounds of ammunition. It is designated SPZ 51-2 by the German Army. Some have had their mortars removed and an AN/TPS-33 tractical radar system fitted. This model is often called the SPZ 2.

Ambulance SP.1V: This has a crew of three and can carry two stretchers and one sitting patient inside and a further two stretcher patients can be carried on the roof. No armament is fitted. It is designated SPZ 2-2 in the German Army.

Open Cargo Version: This is used by the German Army. It is powered by a 4 cylinder petrol engine and has only four road wheels each side instead of the five per side on the other models. Only the front of the vehicle is armoured (engine and driver's compartment).

Experimental Models: Many experimental models were developed to the prototype stage including: 120mm mortar carrier, 90mm tank destroyer, enclosed cargo carrier. armoured personnel carrier and various rocket models.

Employment
These are used only by the German Army. The SPZ 11-2 is being replaced by the new 8×8 Spähpanzer 2.

SPZ 11-2 of the German Army

AMX–30 155mm GCT

France

Armament: 1×155mm gun, elevation +66°, depression −5°, traverse 360°
1×7.62mm (or 12.7mm) anti-aircraft machine gun, elevation +50°, depression −20°, traverse 360°
2 smoke dischargers mounted either side of turret
42 rounds of 155mm ammunition
2000 rounds of machine gun ammunition
Crew: 4
Length: 10.40m (gun forward)
9.50m (gun rear)
6.485m (hull only)
Width: 3.150m (turret)
3.115m (over hull)
Height: 3.30m (including machine gun)
2.295m (turret top)
G/Clearance: .42m
Engine: Hispano-Suiza HS-110, 12 cylinder multi-fuel, water-cooled engine developing 700hp at 2400rpm. This is built in France by Saviem.
Speed: 60km/ph (road)
Range: 450km (road)
Fuel: 970 litres
Fording: 2.20m
V/Obstacle: .93m
Trench: 2.90m
Gradient: 60%
Weight: 41,000kg (loaded)
37,000kg (empty)

Development
The 155mm GCT was shown for the first time at Satory in June 1973. The chassis is a standard AMX-30 with the following modifica-
tions: installation of a cool air ventilation system, artillery communications equipment has been installed and the whole chassis is 2000kg lighter than the standard AMX-30 chassis.

The 155mm gun has an automatic loading mechanism which allows the gun to fire a maximum of 8 rounds a minute. It takes three men about half an hour to reload the magazine with a further 42 complete rounds (ie 42 projectiles and 42 cartridges). Its maximum range with TA68 rounds is 23,500m (m/v 810 m/s), or 30,000m using rocket-assisted projectiles currently under development.

The elevation and traverse of the turret is hydraulic, the breech block is of the vertical wedge type and is also hydraulically operated. The vehicle is equipped with an NBC system.

Variants
A German Leopard chassis has also been fitted with the same turret and, according to the GIAT, other MBTs could be fitted with this turret.

Employment
By the end of 1973 two prototypes had been built using an AMX-30 chassis, one prototype with the Leopard chassis and a further ten pre-production 155mm GCTs on AMX-30 chassis were being built. The first trials battery of six guns are being formed early in 1974 with production vehicles entering service in 1976/1977.

The AMX 30 155mm GCT with turret traversed to the left

155mm Self-Propelled Gun MK F3 France
Self-Propelled Howitzer

Armament: 1×155mm howitzer, 33 calibre barrel
Crew: 2 (on weapon)
Length: 6.22m (gun forward)
4.88m (chassis only)
Width: 2.72m
Height: 2.10m
G/Clearance: .47m
Weight: 17,400kg (loaded)
G/Pressure: .80kg.cm²
Engine: SOFAM 8GXb 8 cylinder water-cooled petrol engine developing 250hp at 3200rpm
Speed: 60km/ph (road)
Range: 300km (road)
Fuel: 450 litres
Fording: .65m
V/Obstacle: .60m
Trench: 1.50m
Gradient: 50%
Armour: 10mm–40mm

Development/Variants
This weapon consists of a modified AMX chassis on which has been mounted an OB 155-50-BF weapon. The chassis has five road wheels, three return rollers and the driving sprocket at the front; there is no idler at the rear. There are two spades at the rear of the chassis, which are lowered for firing and anchored in the ground by reversing the vehicle.

The gun can have either a 23 calibre or 30 calibre barrel, the latter being the model most found in service. The weapon has a range of 18,500m–21,500m depending on the type of ammunition used. Under development is a round with additional propulsion; this has a range of 25,300m. Types of ammunition available include HE, smoke, illuminating and hollow base. It has a maximum rate of fire of 4 rounds a minute.

Elevation limits are 0° to +67°, traverse being 20° left and 30° right (elevation 0° to +50°) and 16° left and 30° right (elevation 50° to 67°). When travelling the gun is located 8° to the right.

Trials commenced in 1966 and the vehicle is built by Creusot-Loire. It is fitted with infra-red driving lights.

This weapon is supported in action by an AMX-13 VCI. This carries the rest of the crew of eight men and also carries 25 shells, 25 cartridges and 39 fuzes. In addition this vehicle can tow the ARE 2T F2 ammunition trailer with a further 30 shells and 30 cartridge bags. Another AMX VCI acts as a battery command post and controls four guns.

Employment
Used by Argentina, France, Venezuela.

155mm Self-Propelled Gun MK F3 is based on the AMX 13 chassis

AMX–13 DCA
Self-Propelled Anti-Aircraft Gun System

France

Armament: 2×30mm Hispano-Suiza HSS 831A guns, elevation +85°, depression −8°, traverse 360°
2×2 smoke dischargers either side of turret
600 rounds of 30mm ammunition, 300 rounds per barrel
Crew: 3
Length: 5.373m
Width: 2.50m
Height: 3.794m (radar up)
3.00m (radar down)
G/Clearance: .37m
Weight: 17,200kg (loaded)
G/Pressure: .84kg.cm²
Engine: SOFAM 8GXb 8 cylinder water-cooled petrol engine developing 250hp at 3200rpm
Speed: 60km/ph (road)
Range: 300km (road)
Fuel: 450 litres
Fording: .60m
V/Obstacle: .65m
Trench: 1.90m
Gradient: 50%
Armour: 10mm–40mm

Development

Development of the AMX-13 DCA (Défence Centre Avions) started in 1960, the first prototype being completed in 1962. The system entered production in 1964 and went into service with the French Army in 1965.
The system consists of an AMX chassis on which has been mounted a turret with 2×30mm cannon. These cannon have a rate of fire of 600 rounds per minute per barrel and an effective range of 3000m. The guns can fire either single, 5, or 15 round bursts, or continuous fire. The guns have a maximum traverse speed of 80° a second and 45° a second in elevation.
Mounted on the rear of the turret is RD 515 Oeil Noir 1 (Black Eye) radar system. This scans through 360° and can pick up targets at a range of 12km and an altitude of 3000m. Sight corrections are controlled by an electric servo-motor and determined by an analogue computer. In addition two periscope sights are provided for use against ground targets.
The system was developed by DTAT, SAMM (turret), Hispano-Suiza (guns) and Thomson-CSF (radar).

Variants

Other anti-aircraft systems on an AMX chassis include:
1. A single 40mm anti-aircraft gun in an armoured turret.
2. 4×20mm cannon in an armoured turret with a radar ranging system developed in 1956/1958 by Oerlikon. Only one was built for trials purposes.
3. AMX-13 DCA but without the radar system.

Employment

In service with the French Army.

Above: *AMX-13 DCA with its radar retracted*

105mm Self-Propelled Howitzers France

	Model A (fixed)	Model B (turret)
Crew:	5	5
Length:	6.40m	5.90m
Width:	2.65m	2.50m
Height:	2.70m	2.70m
G/Clearance:	.275m–.32m	.37m
Weight Loaded:	16,500kg	17,000kg
G/Pressure:	.80kg/cm²	.82kg.cm²
Speed Road:	60km/ph	60km/ph
Range Road:	350km	300km
Fuel:	415 litres	450 litres
Fording:	.80m	.60m
V/Obstacle:	.66m	.66m
Trench:	1.90m	1.90m
Gradient:	60%	60%
Main Armament Calibre:	105mm	105mm
Anti-Aircraft Calibre:	7.5mm or 7.62mm (2)	7.5mm or 7.62mm (2)
Ammunition 105mm:	56	80
Engine:	Both are powered by a SOFAM 8GXb 8 cylinder water-cooled petrol engine developing 250hp at 3200rpm	
Armour:	10mm–20mm	10mm–20mm

Development/Variants

Self-Propelled Howitzer Mk 61: This was the first model built and is also known as the Model 'A' or Obusier de 105 Model 1950 sur Affût Automoteur by the French. It entered service with the French Army in 1952. It consists of an OB-105-61-AU weapon on a modified AMX chassis. The 105mm howitzer has an elevation of +70° and a depression of −4½°, traverse being 20° left and 20° right. It has a maximum range of 15,000m using the Mk 63 French ammunition, projectile weight being 16kg and m/v 220/670 m/s. Of the 56 rounds carried 6 are anti-tank rounds. Two machine guns are carried, one inside the vehicle and another on top of the vehicle. The latter machine gun can be either on a pintle mount or in a cupola. A total of 2000 rounds of machine gun ammunition are carried. There are both 23 and 30 calibre barrels available.

Self-Propelled Howitzer (turret): This is known as the Model 'B'. The prototype was built in 1961 and so far it has not entered production, although Switzerland has purchased some for trials. It is armed with a 105mm howitzer with a traverse of 360°, the gun can be elevated from −7° to +70°. Of the 80 rounds of ammunition carried 6 are anti-tank rounds. It has a range of 15,000m. Also mounted is an anti-aircraft machine gun, this can be on a pintle mounting or in a cupola. If in a cupola it has a traverse of 360°, elevation being +45° and depression −15°.

Employment

France (23 calibre barrels), Israel, Morocco Netherlands (30 calibre barrels).

105mm Self-Propelled Howitzer of the French Army (Model A)

Crotale   France
Self-Propelled Anti-Aircraft System (Missile)

Armament: 4× Crotale surface to air missiles
Crew: 3
Length: 6.22m
Width: 2.65m
Height: 2.04m
G/Clearance: .45m (road)
Weight: 14,800kg (launcher)
12,500kg (acquisition)
Wheelbase: 3.60m
Engine: Each of the four wheels has its own electric motor
Speed: 70km/ph (road)
Range: 500km
Fuel: not applicable
Fording: .68m
V/Obstacle: .30m
Trench: not applicable
Gradient: 40%
Armour: 3mm–5mm

Development/Variants
The Crotale anti-aircraft missile system has been developed by Thomson-CSF, Engins Matra (missiles) and Hotchkiss-Brandt (vehicle). The system was developed from 1964 at the request of the South African Government, who paid a large part of the initial development costs. By 1970 the system was in limited production.

The system comprises two basic vehicles. First the acquisition vehicle with its surveillance radar (range 18km), it also identifies the target and second the firing vehicle. This has four missiles in the ready to fire position, and also tracks the target, launches the missile and guides the missile to its target. Additional launcher vehicles can be added (to a maximum total of three) without needing additional acquisition vehicles. The missile itself has an effective range of over 8.5km and is designed to combat aircraft flying below 3000m. A normal Crotale battery would consist of one acquisition vehicle and two launcher vehicles.

Employment
Crotale is in service with the French Air Force and the South African armed forces where it is known as Cactus. Possible future orders could come from Australia, Norway, Switzerland and the United States. Extensive trials have been conducted in the United States of the Crotale missile system by the United States Army. The Lebanon did order Crotale but this order has now been cancelled.

The Crotale firing unit in position

Leopard A2 and A3 Main Battle Tank   Germany

Armament: 1 × 105mm L-7A3 gun, elevation
+ 20°, depression − 9°
1 × 7.62mm co-axial machine gun
1 × 7.62mm anti-aircraft machine gun
4 smoke dischargers mounted either side of
turret
60 rounds of 105mm ammunition
5500 rounds of 7.62mm machine gun
ammunition
Crew: 4
Length: 9.54m (gun forward)
6.94m (hull only)
Width: 3.25m (3.40m with skirts)
Height: 2.64m (top of cupola)
2.40m (turret roof)
G/Clearance: .44m
Weight: 42,400kg (loaded)
40,400kg (empty)
G/Pressure: .90kg.cm^2
Engine: MTU MB 838 Ca.M500, 10 cylinder,
multi-fuel engine developing 830hp at
2200rpm
Speed: 65km/ph (road)
Range: 600km (road)
450km (cross country)
Fuel: 985 litres
Fording: 2.25m
4.00m (with schnorkel)
V/Obstacle: 1.15m
Trench: 3.00m
Gradient: 60%
Armour: 10mm–60mm (estimate)

Development

The development of the Leopard can be
traced back as far as 1956 when France,
Germany and Italy formulated requirements
for a standard tank. In the end France built
the AMX-30, Germany the Leopard and Italy
the M-60A1 (only to purchase the Leopard
in 1970). Prototypes were completed by two
groups in Germany, Group 'A' in June 1960
and Group 'B' in August 1960. After extensive
evaluation the contract was awarded to
Group 'B' and the prime contractor was
Krauss-Maffei AG. The first production
Leopard was completed on 9th September
1965. There are the following models of the
basic gun tank: Leopard A1 (series 1 through
4), Leopard A2, Leopard A3 with a new turret
of welded construction and numerous other
modifications (5th production batch, 110
being built) and the Leopard A4 (6th production batch, 250 being built), the Leopard
A4 is similar to the A3 but has an integrated
fire control system and a fully automatic
gearbox. The Leopard has a NBC system and
a full range of night fighting and night driving
aids, in addition it can be fitted with a
schnorkel for deep wading.

Variants

Armoured Recovery Vehicle: This is

basically a Leopard chassis fitted with a
superstructure, dozer blade, winch with 100m
of cable and a maximum capacity of 35,000kg,
and a crane with a traverse of 270° and a
maximum lifting capacity of 20,000kg.
Armament consists of a 7.62mm A/A machine
gun and a 7.62mm bow machine gun, and
smoke dischargers. Data is similar to the
Leopard MBT except:
Length: 7.57m (travelling)
Width: 3.25m
Height: 2.69m (inc. A/A mg)
G/Clearance: .44m
G/Pressure: .815kg.cm^2
Weight: 39,800kg (loaded)
37,800kg (empty)
Range: 800km (road)
Fuel: 1570 litres
Fording: 2.10m
Armoured Pioneer Vehicle: This is very
similar to the armoured recovery vehicle but
it has an earth boring tool and the dozer blade
can be fitted with excavating teeth. Data is
similar to the ARV except that it has a loaded
weight of 40,800kg and an empty weight of
38,800kg.
Anti-Aircraft Vehicle: See separate entry.
Bridgelayer: Two models of this were built
in 1969. These were known as the Model 'A'
and Model 'B'. The production version is the
Model 'B' and this entered service in 1973
with the German Army. It has a loaded weight
of 45,300kg and its bridge is 22m long when
in position. Other data is similar to the MBT
except:
Crew: 2
Length: 11.40m (with bridge)
10.30m (w/o bridge)
Width: 4.00m (with bridge)
Height: 3.50m (with bridge)
2.56m (w/o bridge)
G/Pressure: .96kg.cm^2
Bridge Capacity: 50,000kg
Training Tank: This is simply a Leopard
MBT with its turret removed and a cab fitted.
It is used for training drivers. Loaded weight is
about 40,000kg.
Self-Propelled Gun: Under test in 1973
was a Leopard Chassis fitted with the turret
mounting a 155mm gun as fitted to the
AMX-30 155mm GCT self-propelled gun.

Employment

Used by Germany (and ARV, Pioneer,
Bridgelayer), Belgium (and ARV, Pioneer,
Training), Norway (and ARV), Netherlands
(ARV and Training), Italy (ARV and Pioneer—
600 Leopards are being built in Italy and 200
have been purchased from Germany).
Switzerland and Australia are also testing
Leopards. By late 1973 3250 Leopard MBTs
and 648 ARV and Pioneer Leopards had been
built, production is continuing.

Left: *Leopard MBT of the 4th production batch for the German Army*

Centre left: *Leopard A2*

Bottom left: *Leopard A3 has a chassis similar to that of the Leopard A2 but has a new turret with spaced armour*

Right: *Leopard Armoured Recovery Vehicle of the Belgian Army lifting a Leopard engine. Note the spade at the front of the vehicle*

Below: *Leopard Engineer Tank, the auger on the rear deck is making holes in the ground*

HWK 10 Series   Germany

Armament: 1×7.62mm or 1×12.7mm machine gun
Crew: 2+10
Length: 5.05m
Width: 2.58m
Height: 1.585m (w/o machine gun)
G/Clearance: .435m
Weight: 11,000kg (loaded) 9,000kg (empty)
G/Pressure: .55kg.cm^2
Engine: Chrysler 361B, 8 cylinder petrol engine developing 211hp at 4000rpm
Speed: 65km/ph (road)
Range: 320km (road)
Fuel: 300 litres
Fording: 1.20m
V/Obstacle: .68m
Trench: 2.00m
Gradient: 60%
Armour: 8mm–14.5mm
Note. *The data relates to the HWK 11 APC.*

Development
The HWK 10 series of light tracked vehicles were designed in the early 1960s as a private venture by Henschel-Werke (now Rheinstahl). The first prototypes of the HWK 11 were built in 1963 and these were followed by 40 production vehicles for export, in 1964. Only two HWK 13s were built. The hull of the HWK 11 is of all-welded construction and is proof against 7.62mm ammunition. The driver and commander have individual hatches, the crew have overhead hatches enabling them to fire their weapons from within the vehicle and there are two large doors at the rear of the vehicle. The vehicle is not fitted with an NBC system and it can be fitted with infra-red driving lights. It is not amphibious, capable only of fording.

Variants
HWK 10 Armed with 10 anti-tank guided missiles.
HWK 11 Armoured personnel carrier.
HWK 12 Anti-tank vehicle armed with a turret-mounted 90mm gun.
HWK 13 Reconnaissance vehicle armed with a turret-mounted 20mm cannon.
HWK 14 Mortar carrier with an 81mm or 105mm mortar.
HWK 15 Wireless, command or artillery fire control vehicle.
HWK 16 Ambulance, no armament fitted.

Employment
Used only by Mexico.

The HWK 11 Armoured Personnel Carrier

HWR 42   Germany

Henschel-Werke did have a project for a whole range of 4×4 armoured cars designated HWR 40 to 46. None have, however, been built.

Schützenpanzer, Neu Marder
Mechanised Infantry Combat Vehicle
Germany

Armament: 1×20mm Rh 202 cannon, elevation +65°, depression −17°
1×7.62mm MG 3 co-axial machine gun
1×7.62mm MG 3 machine gun at rear of vehicle
6 smoke dischargers on the turret
1250 rounds of 20mm ammunition
5000 rounds of 7.62mm ammunition
Crew: 10
Length: 6.79m
Width: 3.24m
Height: 2.95m (inc. searchlight)
2.86m (turret top)
G/Clearance: .44m
Weight: 28,200kg (loaded)
G/Pressure: .80kg.cm²
Engine: MTU MB 833 Ea-500, 6 cylinder diesel developing 600hp at 2200rpm
Speed: 75+km/ph (road)
Range: 520km (road)
Fuel: 652 litres
Fording: 1.50m
2.50m (with kit)
V/Obstacle: 1.00m
Trench: 2.50m
Gradient: 60%

Development

The requirements for a new infantry combat vehicle for the German Army were drawn up in 1959. The first contracts for the construction of prototype vehicles were awarded in 1960 to Rheinstahl, Henschel and Mowag (Switzerland). These were the first prototype series. They were followed by the second prototype series in 1961/1963. In 1967 a further 10 prototypes were built, these being known as the third series. In October 1969 a contract was awarded to Rheinstahl for the production of 1926 vehicles, of which Atlas MaK of Kiel would build 875 vehicles. The first vehicle was handed over on 7th May 1971 and production is scheduled to continue until the end of 1974. The Marder can also be used as a load carrier or ambulance.

The Marder, is without doubt, the most advanced Infantry Combat Vehicle in the West. It is fitted with an NBC system and a full range of night driving and night fighting equipment. Under development is an amphi-

The Marder chassis with the Roland 11 Anti-Aircraft Missile System

bious kit enabling the vehicle to cross rivers that are too deep to ford.

The crew are provided with roof hatches and there is a single ramp at the rear of the vehicle. Either side of the hull are two ball type mountings that allow the crew to fire their weapons from inside the vehicle. The two turrets can be used against both ground and air targets.

Variants

Schützenpanzer, Neu, Mörserträger: This has a crew of 4/5 men and is armed with a 120mm Tampella mortar and 2×7.62mm machine guns. One hundred rounds of mortar ammunition and 6000 rounds of machine gun ammunition are carried. Performance figures are similar to those of the Marder. It has a loaded weight of 25,500kg. This vehicle completed its trials in 1970 but no production order has been given. Rheinstahl have, however, converted over 500 M-113 APCs to carry the 120mm mortar.

Schützenpanzer, Neu, Waffenträger ROLAND: This is still in the development stage and no large production order has yet been given. It consists of a Marder chassis on which has been mounted the Roland anti-aircraft missile system developed by Germany and France. Roland 1 is a clear-weather system and Roland II an all weather system. Two missiles are carried in the ready to fire position with a further eight missiles in the hull. Roland has also been tested in the United States. So far four prototypes have been built and another eight prototypes are being built.

Marder with Rapier: Shown at Farnborough air display in 1970 was a model of the Marder fitted with the British Aircraft Corporation Rapier anti-aircraft missile system. It is a project only.

Radarpanzer: This is still under development.

Marder with new turret: Undergoing trials is a Marder with a three axis stabilised turret. This is hydraulically operated and electronically controlled.

Employment

Used only by the German Army.

Below: The Marder chassis has also been adopted to carry a 120mm Tampella Mortar. This model is not yet in service

Bottom: The Marder Mechanised Infantry Combat Vehicle

Schützenpanzer, SPZ 12–3
Armoured Personnel Carrier

Germany

Armament: 1×20mm Hispano-Suiza 820 gun, elevation +75°, depression −10°
1×7.62mm machine gun (optional)
2×4 smoke grenade launchers
2000 rounds of 20mm ammunition
Crew: 2+6
Length: 6.31mm (including gun)
5.56m (hull only)
Width: 2.54m
Height: 1.85m (including turret)
1.63m (without turret)
G/Clearance: .40m
Weight: 14,600kg (loaded)
G/Pressure: .75kg.cm²
Engine: Rolls-Royce B 81 Mk 80F, 8 cylinder petrol engine developing 235hp at 3800rpm
Speed: 58km/ph (road)
Range: 270km
Fuel: 340 litres
Fording: .70m
V/Obstacle: .60m
Trench: 1.60m
Gradient: 58%
Armour: 8mm–30mm

Development

The SPZ 12-3 (or Hispano-Suiza 30) was originally developed as a private venture by Hispano-Suiza of Switzerland. The chassis started off as an anti-aircraft vehicle. For a number of reasons production of the vehicle was undertaken in England (by Leyland Motors) and Germany (Henschel and Hanomag). It was in production from 1958 to 1962. All models have a British built engine, the 20mm cannon was made in Germany by Rheinmetall. The SPZ 12-3 does not have an NBC system, the vehicle is however fitted with infra-red driving lights. In 1971 there were still over 1800 of these vehicles in service. Hispano-Suiza projects included a 90mm tank destroyer, light tank with a 90mm gun various anti-aircraft

vehicles and a rocket launcher vehicle. Variants used by the German Army are listed below.

Variants

SPZ 12-3 with 106mm Recoilless Rifle: This is a standard SPZ 12-3 fitted with the American M-40A1 106mm recoilless rifle over the rear of the vehicle. It retains its 20mm gun turret. Weight is 14,300kg.

Jagdpanzer Rakete (JPZ 3-3): This has similar data to the basic APC and has a crew of three, loaded is weight is 13,100kg. No turret is fitted on this model. Armament consists of two launching rails for SS 11 ATGW, only one launcher rail is visible at any one time.

SPZ 52-3 Panzermörser: This vehicle is armed with a French 120mm mortar firing through the roof of the vehicle. The turret has been removed and the only armament fitted is a 7.62mm machine gun which is provided with a shield. It has a crew of four, height is 2.13m including the mortar.

SPZ 51-3 Morserträger: This is armed with an 81mm mortar firing through the roof of the vehicle, no turret is fitted although a 7.62mm machine gun can be fitted. It has a crew of four men.

SPZ 21-3 Funkpanzer: This is a command and radio vehicle.

SPZ 81-3 Feuerleitpanzer: This is an artillery fire control vehicle and can also be used as a command post.

SPZ 12-3 with TOW system: In 1971 tests were started of an SPZ 12-3 with its turret removed and a TOW ATGW system installed. The installation being called PARS-3.

Employment

Used only by the German Army.

A Schützenpanzer, SPZ 12-3 of the German Army

Jagdpanzer Rakete
(JPZ 3-3)

SPZ 51-1 is armed with
an 81mm mortar

SPZ 12-3 fitted with an
M-40A1 106mm
Recoilless Rifle

UR–416 Armoured Personnel Carrier   Germany

Armament: 1 × 7.62mm machine gun, elevation + 75°, depression − 10°
Crew: 2 + 8
Length: 4.99m
Width: 2.26m
Height: 2.24m (w/o machine gun)
2.18m (hull top)
G/Clearance: .44m (differential)
Weight: 6300kg (loaded)
5300kg (empty)
Track: 1.616m
Engine: DB OM-352, 6 cylinder, water-cooled, in-line, diesel developing 110hp at 2800rpm
Speed: 80km/ph (road)
Range: 700km (road)
Fuel: 150 litres
Fording: 1.00m
V/Obstacle: .55m
Trench: nil
Gradient: 70%
Armour: 9mm
Wheelbase: 2.90m

Development
The UR-416 has been designed by Rheinstahl primarily for internal security duties and border patrols. The first prototype was completed in 1965 and series production commenced in 1969. The chassis used is that of the famous Daimler-Benz Unimog; this is a 4 × 4 (cross country) or 4 × 2 (road) vehicle. The hull can be easily separated from the chassis for maintenance purposes. The hull is of all welded construction and doors are provided on the sides and rear of the vehicle, in addition there are hatches in the roof and firing ports are provided at the sides and rear of the vehicle. Optional extras include radios, various types of tyres and a winch.

Variants
The following versions of the basic armoured personnel carrier have been developed by Rheinstahl:
Ambulance: Carrying 8 sitting, or 4 stretcher, or 4 sitting and 2 stretcher patients.
Command: Crew of 4 with various radios, mapboards etc.
Scout Car: Various versions armed with:
single turret mounted 7.62mm machine gun
twin turret mounted 7.62mm machine guns
single turret mounted cannon (two versions)
single turret mounted 90mm recoilless rifle.
Missile: Two versions: COBRA anti-tank missile vehicle
TOW anti-tank missile vehicle.
Maintenance: Has a jib at the front, welding equipment, benches and tools.
Police: Three types of police vehicle have been designed:
Fitted with obstacle clearing blade at the front
Fitted with observation Cupola Model I
Fitted with observation Cupola Model II.

Employment
Over 300 UR-416s have been built for customers in Europe, South America, Africa and Asia.

A UR-416 armed with turret mounted twin 7.62mm machine guns and smoke dischargers

Jagdpanzer Kanone (JPZ 4–5)   Germany
Self-Propelled Anti-Tank Gun

Armament: 1×90mm gun, elevation +15°, depression −8°, traverse 15° left and 15° right
1×7.62mm co-axial machine gun
1×7.62mm anti-aircraft machine gun
8 smoke dischargers
51 rounds of 90mm ammunition
4000 rounds of 7.62mm ammunition
Crew: 4
Length: 8.75m (including gun)
6.238m (hull only)
Width: 2.98m
Height: 2.085m (w/o A/A machine gun)
G/Clearance: .45m (front)
.44m (rear)
Weight: 25,700kg (loaded)
G/Pressure: .75kg.cm² (loaded)
Engine: Daimler-Benz, MB 837, 8 cylinder diesel developing 500hp at 2000rpm
Speed: 70km/ph (road)
Range: 400km (road)
Fuel: 470 litres
Fording: 1.40m
2.10m (with kit)
V/Obstacle: .75m
Trench: 2.00m
Gradient: 60%
Armour: 50mm (maximum)

Development
This vehicle uses the same chassis as the Jagdpanzer Rakete. Design of the JPZ 4-5 started in the late 1950s and the first prototypes were built by Hanomag (1 RU 3/1, 1 RU 3/2), Henschel (1 HK 3/1, 1 HK 3/2) and Mowag (HM 3), these were known as the first series. They were followed by the second series built by Hanomag and Henschel in 1963/64. Last came the third series from Hanomag (RU 331-333) and Henschel (RU 334-336). The vehicle was then ordered in quantity. A total of 750 vehicles have been built for the German Army by Rheinstahl-Hanomag and Rheinstahl-Henschel, production ran from 1965 to 1967. In 1972 Belgium ordered 80 of these to be assembled in Belgium for the Belgian Army. The Belgian vehicles will have modernised transmission and suspension system (using Marder components) and an improved fire control system.

The vehicle has a hull of all welded steel. An NBC system is fitted and infra-red driving and fighting lights can be fitted. The 90mm gun has an effective combat range of 2000m and fires HEAT-T and HEP-T rounds, maximum stated rate of fire is 12 rounds a minute. The gun is elevated and traversed by hand, a double baffle muzzle brake is fitted.

Variants
The Jagdpanzer Rakete has the same hull. Other variants that have not reached production include a multiple rocket launcher system, an anti-aircraft vehicle and a reconnaissance tank (Spähpanzer).

Employment
Used by the Belgian and German Armies.

The Jagdpanzer Kanone (JPZ 4-5). Note the 7.62mm machine gun on the roof of the vehicle

Jagdpanzer Rakete with SS-11 ATGW on one of its launchers

A Jagdpanzer Rakete with the new Hot ATGW is undergoing trials

Jagdpanzer Rakete (RJPZ–2)
Germany
Missile Armed Anti-Tank Vehicle

Armament: 2× launchers for SS 11 ATGW
1×7.62mm bow machine gun
1×7.62mm anti-aircraft machine gun
8 smoke dischargers
14 SS 11 ATGW carried
3200 rounds of 7.62mm ammunition
Crew: 4
Length: 6.43m
Width: 2.98m
Height: 2.60m (with missiles)
1.98m (hull top)
G/Clearance: .43m
Weight: 23,000kg (loaded)
G/Pressure: .63kg.cm²
Engine: Dailmer-Benz, 8 cylinder diesel, Model MB-837 developing 500hp at 2000rpm
Speed: 70km/ph (road)
Range: 400km (road)
Fuel: 470 litres
Fording: 1.40m
2.10m (with kit)
V/Obstacle: .75m
Trench: 2.00m
Gradient: 60%

Development
The hull of the Jagdpanzer Rakete is almost the same as that of the Jagdpanzer Kanone. The hull is of all welded construction and an NBC system is fitted. Infra-red driving lights are fitted. The first prototype was the RU 234 by Hanomag, this was followed by the RU 341, 342 and 343 (all by Hanomag) and the RU 344, 345 and 346 (all by Henschel). Production started in 1967 and 370 have been built for the German Army. The left launcher can be traversed from 270° to 360° and the right launcher from 0° to 90°, thus covering a 180° arc at the front of the vehicle. Elevation is from 0° to +20°. The SS 11 missiles are re-loaded from within the vehicle and have an effective range of 3000m. The 7.62mm machine gun mounted in the bow of the vehicle has a traverse of 15° left and 15° right, elevation is +15° and depression −8°.

Variants
Under development is a model fitted with the German/French HOT ATGW, this has a range of 75m–4000m. This has two launcher shoes and a single periscope, the empty tubes are ejected after the missile has been fired.

Employment
In service only with the German Army.

Flakpanzer 1 (Gepard)   Germany

Armament: 2×35mm Oerlikon cannon, elevation +85°, depression −5°, traverse 360°
4 smoke dischargers mounted either side of the turret
700 rounds of 35mm ammunition are carried
Crew: 3
Length: 7.70m (including guns)
7.27m (excluding guns)
Width: 3.25m
Height: 3.00m (without radar)
G/Clearance: .44m
Weight: 45,100kg (loaded)
43,500kg (empty)
G/Pressure: .97kg.cm²
Engine: MTU MB 838 Ca.M500, 10 cylinder, multi-fuel engine developing 830hp at 2200rpm
Speed: 65km/ph (road)
Range: 600km (road)
450km (cross country)
Fuel: 985 litres
Fording: 2.25m
V/Obstacle: 1.15m
Trench: 3.00m
Gradient: 60%

Development/Variants

In 1968 two German firms each built prototypes of a new anti-aircraft gun system on a Leopard chassis. The Rheinmetall vehicle was armed with 2×30mm guns. It had a Siemens surveillance radar and the fire control radar and computer by AEG-Telefunken. The Oerlikon vehicle was armed with 2×35mm cannon. This was known as the 5PZF-A. The Oerlikon vehicle was found to be the

better of the two models and development of this model continued.
In 1969 a further 4 prototypes were ordered. These were designated 5PZF-B. At about the same time the Netherlands Army became interested in the vehicle and they ordered a Model known as the 5PZF-C. These Models differ only in their make and type of radar equipment. After very successful trials, 12 pre-production 5PZF-Bs were ordered by Germany in 1970, followed by an order for 5 5PZF-Cs for the Netherlands.
The 5PZF-B has a fire control and radar system developed by Siemens AG whilst the 5PZF-C system has been developed by Hollandse Signaalapparaten of the Netherlands. Both of these systems have a search radar with a range of 15km. When travelling the radar scanner can be folded down behind the turret.
The guns fire at the rate of 550 rounds a minute per gun and can be fired either as single shots, controlled bursts or long bursts. Of the 700 rounds or ammunition carried, 660 are anti-aircraft rounds and are carried inside the vehicle and 40 are for ground use, these being in an external armoured magazine. Types of ammunition available includes APHE, HEAT and API.

Employment

On order for Belgium, Germany and the Netherlands. Deliveries to the German Army are expected to commence in 1976.

The Flakpanzer 1

New Range of Wheeled Vehicles — Germany

	Spähpanzer 2	Spähpanzer 3	TPz 1	TPz 2
Type:	8×8	4×4	6×6	4×4
Crew:	4	4	2	2
Length:	7.34m	5.95m	6.74m	5.89m
Width:	2.98m	2.50m	2.94m	2.917m
Height:	2.50m	2.50m	2.30m	2.15m
G/Clearance:	.405m	.405m	.405m	.405m
Weight Loaded:	19,000kg	10,600kg	14,500kg	12,000kg
Speed Road:	100km/ph	90km/ph	100km/ph	100km/ph
Speed Water:	11km/ph	10km/ph	9km/ph	9km/ph
Range:	800km	800km	800km	800km
Fording:	Amphibious	Amphibious	Amphibious	Amphibious
Gradient:	60%	60%	60%	60%
Track:	2.50m	—	2.50m	2.50m

Development

In 1964 the German Ministry of Defence approached German Industry with proposals for a new range of wheeled vehicles. In 1965 a Joint Project Office was formed with the following companies: Büssing, Klockner-Humboldt-Deutz, Krupp, MAN and Rheinstahl, in addition Daimler-Benz went ahead on their own and developed a range of new vehicles. In 1971 it was decided that Daimler-Benz would be responsible for all the armoured vehicles in the range and the Joint Project Office for all the un-armoured vehicles in the range.

All of these vehicles have a large number of similar components and have rapidly exchangeable power packs, rigid axles with control rods in conjunction with coil springs and telescopic shock absorbers.

Variants

Spähpanzer 2: This is an 8×8 amphibious armoured reconnaissance vehicle which is now in production for the German Army. It will replace the old Hotchkiss Spz 11-2 that are currently used for reconnaissance purposes. The vehicle is fully amphibious being propelled in the water by two propellers at the rear; a trim vane is erected at the front of the vehicle before it enters the water. It is fitted with an NBC system and has a crew of four which consists of commander, gunner and two drivers, one at the front and one at the rear. Armament consists of a 20mm cannon, a 7.62mm anti-aircraft machine gun and four smoke dischargers mounted either side of the

The Spähpanzer 2, 8×8 Amphibious Reconnaissance Vehicle

turret. It is powered by a Mercedes-Benz Model OM 403 VA, 10 cylinder multi-fuel engine that produces 390hp.

Spähpanzer 3: This is a 4 × 4 reconnaissance vehicle at present in the development stage. The data in the above table should therefore be taken as provisional. The vehicle will be fully amphibious being propelled in the water by two propellers. It will have the same turret as fitted to the Spähpanzer 2 and will have a crew of three consisting of commander, gunner and driver.

Transportpanzer 1 (TPz 1): This is a 6 × 6 armoured, amphibious load carrier and is fitted with an NBC system. It can carry 12 soldiers or 2030/3050kg of cargo; the cargo can be loaded through doors at the rear of the vehicle. It is powered by a Mercedes-Benz Model OM 403 VA 10 cylinder multi-fuel engine developing 390hp. The engine is mounted behind the driver. A 7.62mm machine gun can be fitted if required.

Transportpanzer 2 (TPz 2): This is a 4 × 4 armoured, amphibious load carrier. It is fitted with an NBC system. It is propelled in the water by two propellers at the rear of the vehicle. It can carry 10 soldiers in addition to its crew of two, and is powered by a Mercedes-Benz Model OM 402 VA 8 cylinder, multi-fuel engine developing 310hp. It can carry 2030kg of cargo. A 7.62mm machine gun can be fitted if required.

The TPz 1 and TPz 2 are designed to transport men, fuel, ammunition and food in the immediate front line area. It is interesting to note that the French Army has a similar range of so-called 'front armoured vehicles' under development.

Employment

The Spähpanzer 2 is in production for the German Army and it is expected that the TPz 1 and TPz 2 will be entering service in the future.

Below: *The Transportpanzer 1, 6 × 6 Armoured Amphibious Load Carrier*

Bottom: *The Transportpanzer 2, 4 × 4 Armoured Amphibious Load Carrier*

Chieftain Mk 3 Main Battle Tank   Great Britain

Armament: 1×120mm gun L 11A2, elevation +20°, depression −10°
1×12.7mm ranging machine gun
1×7.62mm L8 A1 co-axial machine gun
1×7.62mm L37 A1 machine gun (commander's cupola)
2×6 barrelled smoke dischargers
53 rounds of 120mm ammunition
600 rounds of 12.7mm ranging machine gun ammunition
6000 rounds of 7.62mm ammunition
Crew: 4
Length: 10.79m (gun forward)
7.52m (hull only)
Width: 3.66m (inc searchlight)
3.50m (over skits)
Height: 2.89m (inc commander's mg)
G/Clearance: .51m
Weight: 54,100kg (loaded)
51,460kg (empty)
G/Pressure: .843kg.cm²
Engine: Leyland L60 No. 4 Mk 5A, 6 cylinder, multi-fuel engine developing 730bhp at 2100rpm
Speed: 48km/ph (road)
Range: 500km (road)
300km (cross country)
Fuel: 950 litres
Fording: 1.07m
4.57m (schnorkel)
V/Obstacle: .914m
Trench: 3.15m
Gradient: 60%
Armour: 150mm (estimate)

Development
The Chieftain (FV 4201) was developed to replace the Centurion MBT. The first prototype Chieftain was completed in 1959, and was first shown to the public in 1961. In May 1963, the Chieftain was accepted for service and two production lines were set up, one at the Royal Ordnance Factory, Leeds, and the other at Vickers Elswick Works. Vickers are the design parents of the Chieftain. The Chieftain is fitted with an NBC system, a full range of night vision devices, a dozer kit is available and a schnorkel can be fitted. A ranging machine gun is fitted, although more recent models have in addition a laser rangefinder. The gun is stabilised and can be fired accurately whilst on the move; types of ammunition carried are APDS and HESH, with bagged charges.

Variants
Mk 1: This was introduced in 1965 for training purposes, 585bhp engine.
Mk 1/2: This is a Mk 1 modified to Mk 2 standards for training purposes.
Mk 1/3: This is a Mk 1 with a new power pack, for training purposes.
Mk 1/4: This is a Mk 1/2 with a new power pack, modified ranging mg, used for training.
Mk 2: This was the first model to enter service in 1966, 650bhp engine.
Mk 3: This entered service in 1969 and has an improved auxiliary generator, improved engine and a No. 15 Mk 2 cupola with L37 machine gun.
Mk 3/G: Prototype with turret air breathing.
Mk 3/2: This is a modified Mk 3/G.
Mk 3/S: Modified Mk 3/G (production), turret air breathing.
Mk 3/3: This is a Mk 3 with extended range ranging machine gun (2500m), laser rangefinder, improved engine and a new air cleaner system.
Mk 3/3(P): This is a Mk 3/3 with a number of modifications for Iran.
Mk 4: Prototype only, had additional fuel and less ranging mg ammunition.
Mk 5: This is a Mk 3/3 with many improve-

The Chieftain Armoured Recovery Vehicle

ments including an improved engine and gearbox, increased ammunition stowage (64 rounds carried).

Mk 5/5(P): This is a Mk 5 for Iran with modifications.

Mk 6: This is the Mk 2 with new powerpack and modified ranging machine gun.

Mk 7: This is Mk 3, Mk 3/G, Mk 3/2 and Mk 3/S with modified ranging machine gun and improved powerpack.

Mk 8: This is the Mk 3/3 with above modifications.

Chieftain Armoured Recovery Vehicle (FV 4202): Prototype built in 1971, now in production. It is armed with a 7.62mm machine gun (cupola mounted) and 12 smoke dischargers. It has a crew of four. The vehicle has two winches, each of the double capstan type to give sustained pulls to the front of the vehicle of 30 tonnes and 3 tonnes respectively. A hydraulic operated dozer blade is fitted at the front of the vehicle. Basic data is as follows:

Length: 8.256m
Width: 3.518m (over blade)
Height: 2.746m
Fuel: 955 litres
Weight: 52,000kg (loaded)

50,250kg (empty)
Speed: 41.5km/ph (road)
Range: 322km (road)

Chieftain Bridgelayer (FV 4205): This is a Chieftain chassis fitted with a 24.40m long class 60 scissors bridge. This can cover a span of 22.9m, under development is a 13.4m bridge. This bridge is launched hydraulically and takes about three minutes to lay in position. The vehicle has a crew of three men. Basic data is as follows:

Length: 13.73m
Width: 4.16m
Height: 3.93m
Weight: 53,300kg

Chieftain Armoured Vehicle Royal Engineers (FV 4203): This is a project only. It is not in service.

Employment

Chieftains have now replaced all Centurion gun tanks in the British Army. Chieftains are also in service with the Iranian Army. The ARV is on order for Britain and Iran. The AVLB is in service with the British Army and on order for Iran.

The Chieftain Armoured Vehicle Launched Bridge in travelling order

A Chieftain Mk 3 of the Queen's Royal Irish Hussars

Vickers MBT Mk 1 Main Battle Tank   Great Britain

Armament: 1×105mm L7A1 gun, elevation
+20°, depression −7°
1×12.7mm ranging machine gun
1×7.62mm co-axial machine gun
1×7.62mm anti-aircraft machine gun
2×6 barrelled smoke dischargers
44 rounds of 105mm ammunition
600 rounds of 12.7mm ammunition
3000 rounds of 7.62mm ammunition
Crew: 4
Length: 9.728m (gun forward)
7.920m (hull only)
Width: 3.168m
Height: 2.640m (w/o A/A machine gun)
2.438m (turret roof)
G/Clearance: .406m
Weight: 38,600kg (loaded)
36,000kg (empty)
G/Pressure: .90kg.cm²
Engine: Leyland L60 Mk 4B, 6 cylinder,
water-cooled multi-fuel engine developing
650bhp at 2670rpm   OR
General Motors 12V 71T turbo-charged
diesel, developing 800bhp at 2500rpm
Speed: 56km/ph (road)
Range: 480km (road)
Fuel: 1000 litres
Fording: 1.143m
V/Obstacle: .914m
Trench: 2.438m
Gradient: 60%
Armour: 25mm–80mm (estimate)

Development

In August 1961 an agreement was signed
between Vickers Limited and the Indian
Government. Under this agreement Vickers
undertook to design an MBT and also set up
a production line in India; some tanks were
also to be built in Britain. The first prototype
was completed early in 1963. The tank uses
the engine and transmission of the Chieftain,
gun of the late Centurion (also used in the
Leopard, Pz 61 and so on), and a suspension
based on the cancelled FV 300 series. Production commenced at Vickers Elswick works
in 1964 and the first British-built tank was
delivered to India in 1965. In the meantime a
factory was built at Avadi, near Madras, and
the first Indian-built tank was completed in
1966. Early Indian tanks used many components from the UK. The Vickers MBT is
called VIJAYANTA by the Indians. According
to reports from India, 66 had been built by
mid-1968 and 300 by 1971, the production
target being 200 tanks a year.

The tank is fitted with a gun control and
stabilisation system developed by GEC-AEI.
This enables the tank to fire on the move.

The vehicle can be fitted with a flotation
screen. This takes about 15-20 minutes to be
erected and enables the vehicle to cross rivers,
being propelled by its tracks at about 6km/ph.
Other optional equipment includes an NBC
system and infra-red driving and fighting
equipment.

Variants

Mk 2: This was a project only and was
basically a Mk 1 with two BAC Swingfire
ATGW missiles mounted either side of the
turret rear.

Mk 3: This is at present under development.
The improvements over the Mk 1 include a
new turret and mantlet, gun has a depression
of −10°, new and improved glacis plate,
increased ammunition stowage (50 rounds),
it can also be fitted with passive night
fighting and night driving equipment. Under
development is a laser rangefinder. ARV and
Bridgelayer versions of the Vickers MBT are
under development.

Employment

The Vickers MBT Mk 1 is in service with
India and Kuwait.

*Vickers MBT Mk 1 firing
its main 105mm gun*

Centurion Main Battle Tank

Great Britain

Armament: 1×105mm L7A2 gun, elevation +20°, depression −10°
1×12.7mm ranging machine gun
1×7.62mm co-axial machine gun
1×7.62mm anti-aircraft machine gun
2×6 barrelled smoke dischargers
64 rounds of 105mm ammunition
600 rounds of 12.7mm ammunition
4750 rounds of 7.62mm ammunition
Crew: 4
Length: 9.854m (including gun)
7.823m (excluding gun)
Width: 3.39m
Height: 3.009m (w/o A/A machine gun)
G/Clearance: .51m
Weight: 51,820kg (loaded)
G/Pressure: .95kg.cm²
Engine: Rolls-Royce Meteor Mk IVB, 12 cylinder, liquid cooled petrol engine developing 650bhp at 2550rpm
Speed: 34.6km/ph (road)
Range: 190km (road)
Fuel: 1037 litres
Fording: 1.45m
2.74m (with kit)
V/Obstacle: .914m
Trench: 3.352m
Gradient: 60%
Armour: 17mm–152mm

Note. *The above data relates to the Mk 13 Centurion.*

Development

The Centurion was developed during World War II as a cruiser tank. The first prototype was completed in 1945. This was called the A-41. Later this was changed to Centurion Mk 1. AEC were the original design parents. First production vehicles were the Mk 2s which entered service after the end of the war. Centurions were built by Vickers, Leyland Motors and the ROF at Leeds. The Centurion chassis has been used as a basis for many prototype vehicles including the FV 4004 Conway, FV 4005 Tank Destroyer, FV 4019 Flame-thrower, FV 3802 25 Pounder and FV 3805 5.5in self-propelled guns. The British Aircraft Corporation (GW Division) did have a project to fit Swingfire ATGW to the vehicle, but this only reached mock-up stage. Centurions can be fitted with a dozer blade on the front of the vehicle. A summary of Centurion tanks still in service is listed below.

Variants

Mk 3: 20 pounder (83.4mm) gun with 65 rounds, 7.92mm Besa co-axial machine gun, Meteor Mk 1VB engine. Most were re-built to Mk 5 standards.
Mk 5: Based on Mk 3 hull but with 7.62mm co-axial machine gun. Vickers were design parents. Could tow a trailer with additional fuel.

Mk 5/1: Is Mk 5 up armoured, designated FV 4011.
Mk 5/2: Is Mk 5 up gunned with 105mm gun.
Mk 6: Is Mk 5 up gunned and up armoured, also has additional fuel in hull rear.
Mk 6/1: Is Mk 6 with infra-red driving and fighting equipment, stowage basket on rear of turret.
Mk 6/2: Is Mk 6 with 12.7mm ranging machine gun for 105mm gun.
Mk 7: Designated FV 4007, design parents were Leyland Motors. Armamant is a 20 pounder gun with 61 rounds, 7.62mm co-axial machine gun, fume extractor on barrel, additional fuel.
Mk 7/1: Is Mk 7 up armoured, designated FV 4012.
Mk 7/2: Is Mk 7 up gunned with 105mm gun.
Mk 8: Based on Mk 7 hull, 20 pounder gun with 63 ready rounds, fume extractor on barrel. Meteor IVC engine, contra-rotating cupola with raisable roof for commander, resilient gun mantlet. New elevating gear.
Mk 8/1: Is Mk 8 up armoured.
Mk 8/2: Is Mk 8 up gunned with 105mm gun.
Mk 9: Is Mk 7 up gunned and up armoured, designated FV 4015.
Mk 9/1: Is Mk 9 with infra-red driving and fighting equipment, stowage basket on rear of the turret.
Mk 9/2: Is Mk 9 with ranging machine gun for 105mm gun.
Mk 10: Is Mk 8 up gunned and up armoured, designated FV 4017. Armed with 105mm L7A1 gun with 70 rounds, new control equipment for gun, impact resisting trunions, automatic stabilisation when vehicle exceeds 6.43km/ph.
Mk 10/1: Is Mk 10 with infra-red driving and fighting equipment and stowage basket on rear of turret.
Mk 10/2: Is Mk 10 with ranging machine gun for 105mm gun.
Mk 11: Is Mk 6 with ranging machine gun, infra-red driving and fighting equipment and a stowage basket on the rear of the turret.
Mk 12: Is Mk 9 with infra-red driving and fighting equipment, ranging machine gun and stowage basket on the rear of the turret.
Mk 13: Is Mk 10 with ranging machine gun and infra-red driving and fighting equipment.

Vickers Modified Centurions (1973): In May 1973 Vickers Limited demonstrated a Centurion MBT which had been fitted with a new powerpack based on a GM 12V-71 diesel engine with a power output of 720bhp and a new gun control and stabilisation system. Under development is a laser range-finder, new cupola, passive nightfighting equipment, revised ventilation system and new final drives. Thus resulting in a highly effective MBT at low outlay. This vehicle also has a larger radius of action and a higher maximum speed.

Armoured Recovery Vehicle, Centurion Mk 2 (FV 4006): This is a Mk 3 Centurion with an armoured superstructure, its equipment includes a winch (maximum capacity 90,000kg pro rata), spades at the rear, jib crane, tools and so on. Armament is a 7.62mm machine gun and smoke dischargers.
Length: 8.96m
Width: 3.39m
Height: 2.88m
Weight: 50,200kg (loaded)
47,250kg (empty)
Crew: 4

Tank, Beach, ARV, Centurion (BARV) (FV 4018): This is basically a Centurion with no turret and fitted with a superstructure. It is capable of operating in 2.74m of water.
Length: 8.08m
Width: 3.39m
Height: 3.45m
Weight: 40,500kg (loaded)
37,800kg (empty)
Crew: 4

Tank, Armoured Vehicle, Royal Engineers (AVRE) Mk 5 (FV 4003): This is armed with a 165mm demolition charge projector as well as a co-axial machine gun. At the front of the vehicle is a hydraulically operated dozer blade and it can also carry a fascine. It can tow a trailer fitted with the Giant Viper mine clearance equipment.
Length: 8.70m (including blade)
Width: 3.39m (without blade)
3.95m (with blade)
Height: 2.50m
Weight: 51,800kg (loaded)
49,500kg (empty)

Tank, Bridgelayer, Centurion Mk 5 (FV 4002): This is fitted with a single span bridge that can be laid across gaps up to 13.72m wide, this takes only two minutes to lay. Data of the vehicle with bridge is:
Length: 16.3m
Width: 4.26m
Height: 3.88m
Weight: 50,400kg (loaded)
48,700kg (empty)
Crew: 2–3

Tank ARK Centurion Mk 5 (FV 4016):
This is used for spanning gaps up to 22.86m wide. The vehicle itself enters the ditch and then opens out. Data with the trackways in travelling position is:
Length: 10.37m
Width: 3.96m
Height: 3.88m
Weight: 51,800kg (loaded)

Employment
Australia: Centurion Mk 5 and Mk 7 (some with 105mm guns, Mk 5s have ranging machine gun for 20 pounder), ARV Mk 2 Bridgelayer Mk 5.
Canada: Centurion Mk 2, Mk 5, Mk 5/2 and ARV Mk 2.
Denmark: Centurions with 20 pounders, 105mm, ARV Mk 2. Centurion MBTs have German-built AEG dual purpose IR/White Light searchlight type XSW 3OU (E) and IR sighting device B8V (ELTRO).
Egypt: Has a few Mk 3s, doubtful if still in service.
Great Britain: Last MBTs phased out 1973, all Mks still in use for training, plus ARVs, bridgelayers and AVREs.
India: Centurion Mk 5 and Mk 7.
Iraq: Centurion Mk 5.
Israel: Various Mks, including ARV Mk 2. See Israel section.
Jordan: Centurion Mk 5 and Mk 10.
Lebanon: Centurion Mk 5.
Libya: Has a few Centurion Mk 5s, probably non-operational.
Netherlands: Centurion Mk 5, Mk 5/2, Mk 5 with special dozer, Mk 5 with scissors bridge, ARV Mk 2.
Kuwait: Centurion Mk 5 and Mk 10.
South Africa: Mk 5 and Mk 7.
Sweden: Mk 3 and Mk 5 (originally called Strv 81, when up gunned to 105mm=Strv 102), Mk 10 is Strv 101, ARV Mk 2 is Bgbv 81, monowheel fuel trailers used, Strv 101 and Strv 102 have new radios and 7.62mm machine guns.
Switzerland: Centurion Mk 3 (Pz 55), Mk 5 (Pz 60), Mk 7 (Pz 57), ARV Mk 2 (Entpannungspanzer 56), some MBT have 105mm guns.

Centurion Mk 5 Armoured Vehicle Royal Engineers (AVRE)

Left: *Centurion Mk 5/2
of the Netherlands Army*

Below left: *Centurion
MBT modified by Vickers
Limited, modifications
include a new engine and
a new gun control and
stabilisation system*

Right: *Centurion Mk 2
ARV of the Netherlands
Army*

Right: *Centurion
Bridgelayer*

Below: *Centurion
Scissors Bridgelayer of
the Netherlands Army*

Charioteer Tank Destroyer
Great Britain

Armament: 1×84mm gun, elevation +10°, depression −5°
1×7.62mm co-axial machine gun
2×6 barrelled smoke dischargers
25 rounds of 84mm ammunition
3375 rounds of 7.62mm ammunition
Crew: 4
Length: 8.71m (including gun)
6.324m (excluding gun)
Width: 3.067m
Height: 2.59m
G/Clearance: .406m
Weight: 28,958kg
G/Pressure: .98kg.cm²
Engine: Rolls-Royce Meteor Mk 3, 12 cylinder (V-12), water-cooled petrol engine developing 600hp at 2500rpm

Speed: 51.5km/ph (road)
Range: 241km (road)
Fuel: 526 litres
Fording: 1.04m
V/Obstacle: .914m
Trench: 2.362m
Gradient: 40%
Armour: 10mm–64mm
Development/Employment
In 1952/1954 a large number of Cromwells were modified by fitting a new turret, mounting the 84mm gun as used in the Centurion. The hull machine gun was removed and there were a number of other modifications. This tank then became the Charioteer. The vehicle is still used by Finland, Jordan and the Lebanon.

Churchill Infantry Tank
Great Britain

A small quantity of these are still used by Eire and there are unconfirmed reports that there are some in Iraq and India. Also unconfirmed are reports of Valentines in the Sudan and Portugal.

Comet Cruiser Tank
Great Britain

Armament: 1×77mm gun, elevation +20°
depression −12°
1×7.92mm co-axial machine gun
1×7.92mm bow mounted machine gun
2×6 barrelled smoke dischargers
61 rounds of 77mm ammunition
5175 rounds of 7.92mm ammunition
Crew: 5
Length: 7.66m (including gun)
6.55m (excluding gun)
Width: 3.073m
Height: 2.67m
G/Clearance: .40m
Weight: 33,250kg
G/Pressure: .97kg.cm²
Engine: Rolls-Royce Meteor Mk 3, 12 cylinder (V-12), water-cooled petrol engine developing 600hp at 2500rpm
Speed: 51.5km/ph (road)

Range: 241km (road)
Fuel: 526 litres
Fording: 1.04m
V/Obstacle: .914m
Trench: 2.438m
Gradient: 60%
Armour: 14mm–101mm

Development/Employment
The Comet was a complete re-design of the Cromwell tank. This was undertaken by Leyland Motors in 1943/1944. The vehicle saw action in the closing months of World War II and postwar in Korea. The vehicle is still used by a number of countries including Burma, Eire, Finland and South Africa.

A Comet Tank of the Finnish Army

FV 601 Alvis Saladin Mk 2 Armoured Car

Great Britain

Armament: 1×76mm gun, elevation +20°, depression −10°, 43 rounds of ammunition. carried
1×7.62mm machine gun co-axial with main armament
1×7.62mm machine gun for commander (A/A role)
2×6 barrelled smoke dischargers
2750 rounds of 7.62mm ammunition are carried
Crew: 4
Length: 5.284m (including gun)
4.93m (excluding gun)
Width: 2.54m
Height: 2.39m (w/o machine gun)
G/Clearance: .426m
Weight: 11,590kg (loaded)
10,500kg (empty)
G/Pressure: 1.12kg.cm²
Engine: Rolls-Royce B.80 Mk 6A, 8 cylinder petrol engine developing 170hp at 3750rpm
Speed: 72km/ph (road)
Range: 400km (road)
Fuel: 241 litres
Fording: 1.07m
2.13m (with kit)
V/Obstacle: .46m
Trench: 1.52m
Gradient: 42%
Armour: 8mm–32mm

Development

Design of the Saladin dates to 1947 but it was not until 1954 that the prototype vehicle was completed, the first production models followed in 1958, production of the Saladin was completed in 1972. Production being undertaken by Alvis Limited of Coventry.
The Saladin uses many components of the FV 603 Saracen APC, one of the differences being that the Saracen has its engine in the front, and the Saladin has its engine in the rear.

Variants

The production vehicle was the Mk 2, its full designation being FV 601(C) Armoured Car 76mm (Alvis Saladin Mk 2 6×6). BAC and Alvis modified a Saladin to carry a single Swingfire anti-tank missile either side of the turret and two reserve missiles at the rear of the vehicle. This, however, was a project only. Also tested in 1966 was a Saladin fitted with a flotation screen, this enabled the vehicle to cross rivers, being propelled in the water by its wheels. It did not progress further than trials.
The German Border Police use the FV 601(D). This has no co-axial machine gun and has German type lights and six German smoke grenade launchers either side of the turret. Its German designation is SW-111 Kfz-93, Geschützer Sonderwagen 111.

Employment

Used by Abu Dhabi, Bahrain, Great Britain (being replaced by Scorpion), German Border Police, Ghana, Indonesia, Jordan, Kuwait, Libya, Muscat and Oman, Nigeria, Qatar, South Yemen, Sudan, Tunisia, Uganda, Portugal.

Other British Armoured Cars Still in Service

Daimler: Still used by some countries including India.
AEC: Still used by the Lebanon.
Humber: Still used by Burma, Ceylon, Cyprus, India, Mexico.
Dingo: The Daimler scout car is still used by Cyprus and Portugal.

Above: *Alvis Saladin FV 601 (D) of the Federal German Border Police*

Scorpion Family
Combat Vehicle (Reconnaissance) Tracked
Great Britain

	FV 101	FV 102	FV 103	FV 104	FV 105	FV 106	FV 107
Crew:	3	3	3+4	3+4	5/6	3	3
Length:	4.388m	4.759m	4.839m	4.991m	4.991m	4.934m	4.388m
Width:	2.184m	2.184m	2.184m	2.184m	2.184m	2.184m	2.184m
Height:	2.096m	2.210m	2.250m	2.016m	2.016m	2.023m	2.115m
G/Clearance:	.356m	.356m	.356m	.356m	.356m	.356m	.356m
Weight Loaded:	7960kg	8221kg	8172kg	7710kg	7918kg	8002kg	7900kg
G/Pressure:	.35kg.cm²	.35kg.cm²	.35kg.cm²	.35kg.cm²	.35kg.cm²	.35kg.cm²	.35kg.cm²
Speed Road:	87km/ph	87km/ph	87km/ph	87km/ph	87km/ph	87km/ph	87km/ph
Range Road:	644km	644km	644km	644km	644km	644km	644km
Fuel:	391 litres	364 litres	364 litres	364 litres	364 litres	364 litres	391 litres
Fording:	1.07m	1.07m	1.07m	1.07m	1.07m	1.07m	1.07m
V/Obstacle:	.508m	.508m	.508m	.508m	.508m	.508m	.508m
Trench:	2.057m	2.057m	2.057m	2.057m	2.057m	2.057m	2.057m
Gradient:	70%	70%	70%	70%	70%	70%	70%
Engine:	All are powered by Jaguar 6 cylinder water-cooled petrol engine developing 195bhp at 4750rpm						

Development

The Scorpion was preceded by a vehicle known as the TV 150000 and a Mobile Test Rig (MTR). In September 1967, Alvis of Coventry was awarded a contract to build the prototype Scorpions. The first prototype was completed in January 1969, and in September 1969, prototypes were shown to the Public and Press. The first production order was awarded to Alvis in May 1970, and the vehicle entered production in 1971, the first production Scorpion being completed early in 1972. In 1970 a co-production order was signed between Great Britain and Belgium. Belgium will receive a total of 700 members of the Scorpion family

The basic role of the Scorpion is that of reconnaissance and for this reason the vehicle is equipped with a complete range of day and night observation, driving and fighting systems. An NBC system is fitted. The vehicle can be made amphibious in several minutes by erecting a flotation screen carried around the top of the hull, the vehicle is propelled in the water by its tracks at 6.5km/ph. A propeller kit is under development and this will increase the vehicle's water speed to 9.6km/ph. The Scorpion is of all welded aluminium armour construction and uses the same engine as the Fox CVR(W). Scorpion can also be fitted with the ZB 298 Radar System, Radiac system and navigational aids. The vehicle is air-portable by such aircraft as the C-130 (2 vehicles) or CH-53A helicopter.

Variants

FV 101 Scorpion: This is armed with a 76mm gun with an elevation of +35° and a depression of −10°, a 7.62mm machine gun is fitted and this can also be used as a ranging gun, 2 three barreled smoke dischargers are fitted. Forty rounds of 76mm and 3000 rounds of 7.62mm ammunition are carried.

FV 102 Striker: This is an anti-tank guided weapons vehicle. Mounted on the top of the hull, towards the rear is a launching box

containing five BAC Swingfire ATGW with a range of 4000m, a further five missiles are carried inside of the vehicle. A 7.62mm machine gun is cupola mounted and there are two Lyran launchers for launching flares, thus giving the vehicle day and night capability, smoke dischargers are mounted on the front of the vehicle.

FV 103 Spartan: This is a small armoured personnel carrier and would be used to carry assault troops or engineers. It could also be used to support other members of the family for example carrying spare missiles or ammunition. It is armed with a cupola mounted 7.62mm machine gun and smoke dischargers.

FV 104 Samaritan: This is an ambulance and has a raised roof, no armament is fitted. It can carry four stretcher patients, six sitting patients or three sitting and two stretchers, in addition to its crew.

FV 105 Sultan: This is a command vehicle and has a similar hull to that of the FV 104.

Additional radios are fitted as are mapboards. A penthouse can be erected at the rear of the vehicle to give additional working space. It is armed with a pintle mounted 7.62mm machine gun.

FV 106 Samson: This is a recovery vehicle and has an internally mounted winch with a capacity of 20,000kg and 229m of wire rope. This is driven from the main engine and has a variable speed. Anchors are provided at the rear of the vehicle.

FV 107 Scimitar: This has the same hull and turret as the Scorpion but is armed with a 30mm Rarden cannon and a 7.62mm machine gun. The gun has an elevation of $+40°$ and a depression of $-10°$. One sixty-five rounds of 30mm and 3000 rounds of 7.62mm ammunition are carried. Two three-barrelled smoke dischargers are fitted either side of the turret front.

Employment
In service with Abu Dhabi, Belgium and Great Britain. On order for Canada and Iran.

Right: *FV 102 Striker, Anti-Tank Guided Weapon Vehicle, with the launcher box containing 5 BAC Swingfire missiles in the elevated position, ready for firing*

Below left: *FV 101 Scorpion, Combat Vehicle Reconnaissance (Tracked)*

Below: *FV 107 Scimitar is armed with a 30mm Rarden cannon, as fitted to the Fox Armoured Car*

Fox
Combat Vehicle Reconnaissance (Wheeled)

Great Britain

Armament: 1×30mm Rarden cannon, elevation +41°, depression −14°
1×7.62mm machine gun co-axial with main armament
2×3 barrelled smoke dischargers
96 rounds of 30mm ammunition in clips of 3
2600 rounds of 7.62mm ammunition
Crew: 3
Length: 5.359m (gun forward)
4.242m (hull)
Width: 2.134m
Height: 2.20m (overall)
1.98m (turret top)
G/Clearance: .30m
Weight: 6386kg (loaded)
5733kg (empty)
G/Pressure: .46kg.cm²
Engine: Jaguar 4.2 litre, 6 cylinder petrol engine developing 195hp at 5000rpm
Speed: 104km/ph (road)
5km/ph (water)
Range: 434km (road)
Fuel: 145 litres
Fording: 1.01m
V/Obstacle: .50m
Trench: 1.22m (with channels)
Gradient: 50%
Track: 1.753m
Wheelbase: 2.464m

Development
The Fox is a development of the Ferret scout car. Design work on the Fox (FV 721) started in 1965/1966. Prototypes were built by the Daimler Company at Radford, Coventry, the first prototype being completed in November 1967. The vehicle was first shown to the public in October 1969. The production contract was awarded to the Royal Ordnance Factory at Leeds and the first production vehicle was completed in May 1973.

A flotation screen is carried around the top of the hull. This can be quickly erected and enables the vehicle to cross streams and rivers. The vehicle is propelled in the water by its wheels at about 6km/ph.

The hull and turret of the Fox are constructed of welded aluminium armour. Equipment includes an NBC system, navigation system and a full range of day and night vision and fire control devices. The engine of the Fox is also used in the CVR(T) Scorpion and the 30mm Rarden cannon is also used in the Scimitar vehicle. This 30mm cannon can fire a British developed APDS round or standard Hispano HE, AP or Practice rounds. Rate of fire is 90 rounds per minute, and maximum range is about 4000m. Single shots or bursts can be fired and the spent ammunition cases are ejected outside of the vehicle.

The ZB 298 Radar System can be fitted to the vehicle if required.

Variants
Under development is the FV 722 Vixen, Combat Vehicle Reconnaissance (Wheeled) Liason. This has a similar hull to that of the Fox and has a crew of four. It is armed with a turret-mounted 7.62mm machine gun and eight smoke dischargers. Loaded weight is about 6350kg and height is 2.008m, other data is similar to the Fox.

Employment
Fox is in service with the British Army and on order for Iran.

One of the first Fox production vehicles

Ferret Family Light Scout Cars — Great Britain

	Mk 1/1 FV 701	Mk 1/2 FV 704	Mk 2/3 FV 701	Mk 2/6 FV 703	Mk 4 FV 711	Mk 5 FV 712
Crew:	2–3	2–3	2	2	2–3	2
Length:	3.84m	3.84m	3.84m	3.84m	3.96m	3.96m
Width:	1.91m	1.91m	1.91m	1.91m	2.13m	2.13m
Height:	1.45m	1.65m	1.88m	1.88m	2.03m	2.08m
G/Clearance:	.33m	.33m	.33m	.33m	.41m	.41m
Weight Loaded:	4210kg	4370kg	4395kg	4560kg	5400kg	5890kg
Weight Empty:	3510kg	3660kg	3684kg	3680kg	4725kg	4980kg
Speed Road:	93km/ph	93km/ph	93km/ph	93km/ph	80km/ph	80km/ph
Range Road:	300km	300km	300km	300km	300km	300km
Fuel:	96 litres	96 litres	96 litres	96 litres	96 litres	96 litres
Fording (w/o kit):	.914m	.914m	.914m	.914m	.914m	.914m
V/Obstacle:	.406m	.406m	.406m	.406m	.406m	.406m
Trench (with channels):	1.22m	1.22m	1.22m	1.22m	1.22m	1.22m
Gradient:	46%	46%	46%	46%	46%	46%
Wheelbase:	2.286m	2.286m	2.286m	2.286m	2.286m	2.286m
Track:	1.55m	1.55m	1.55m	1.55m	1.75m	1.75m
Engine:	All have Rolls-Royce B60 Mk 6A 6 cylinder, water-cooled petrol engine developing 129bhp at 3750rpm					

Development

Development started shortly after the end of World War II. The first prototype, the Mk 1, was completed by Daimler in 1949 and delivered in 1950. Production was undertaken by Daimler at Coventry and the first production vehicle was completed in 1952. Production continued until 1971. The Ferret was further developed into the Fox.

The hull of the Ferret is of all welded construction, armour thickness is 6mm–16mm. The vehicle does not have an NBC system All Ferrets have two 3-barrelled smoke dischargers.

Variants

Mk 1/1 FV 701 (J) Scout Car Liaison: This is the basic open topped version and is armed with a Bren LMG or a 7.62mm machine gun. A trials version existed with a flotation screen.

Mk 1/2 (FV 704) Scout Car Liaison: This is a Mk 1/1 with a small turret with a flat roof and it is armed with a Bren LMG.

Mk 2/2: This is a Mk 2 with an extension collar between the top of the vehicle and the machine-gun turret. The Mk 2 has a 2-door machine gun turret and the Mk 2/1 is a Mk 1 with a 2-door machine-gun turret.

Ferret Mk 2/3 armed with a turret mounted 7.62mm machine gun. Note the sand channels on the front of the vehicle

Mk 2/3 FV 701 (H) Scout Car Reconnaissance: This is similar to the Mk 1/1 except that it has a 7.62mm machine gun in a turret with an elevation of +45° and a depression of −15°, traverse being 360°. Two thousand five hundred rounds of 7.62mm ammunition are carried. This vehicle can also be fitted with the ZB 298 Radar System. The Ferret Mk 2/4 and Mk 2/5 have additional armour.

Mk 2/6 FV 703 Scout Car Reconnaissance (Guided Weapon): This is the Mk 2/3 but with a VIGILANT wire guided anti-tank missile mounted either side of the turret with a common elevating mechanism. Two spare missiles are carried in place of the spare wheel. The missiles can be controlled from within the vehicle or away from the vehicle with the aid of a combined sight/controller and seperation cable. The missiles have a range of 200m to 1375m.

Mk 2/7: This is a Mk 2/6 but with its missile equipment removed and used as a reconnaissance vehicle.

Mk 3 Scout Car Liaison: This is a Mk 1/1 but with modified suspension, larger wheels and a flotation screen. Trials only.

Mk 4 FV 711 Scout Car Reconnaissance: This is a re-built Mk 2 and has stronger suspension units, disc brakes, larger wheels and tyres. A flotation screen can be quickly erected and the vehicle is propelled in the water by its wheels at a maximum speed of 3.8km/ph.

Mk 5 FV 712 Scout Car Reconnaissance/ Guided Weapon: Only a small number of these were built and they were re-builds of earlier vehicles. It has a turret with a 7.62mm machine gun and two launcher boxes (elevated to fire), each containing two BAC Swingfire ATGW. A further two missiles are carried under armour. The missiles can be fired from within the vehicle or away from the vehicle.

Employment

In service with Abu Dhabi, Bahrain, Brunei Burma, Cameroon, Canada, Ceylon, Gambia, Ghana, Great Britain, Iran, Indonesia, Iraq, Jamaica, Jordan, Kenya, Kuwait, Libya, Malaysia, Mali (from South Africa), Muscat and Oman, New Zealand, Nigeria, Qatar, Ras Al Khaimah, Rhodesia, Sierra Leone, Somali, South Africa, South Arabia, South Yemen, Sudan, Uganda, Zaire, Zambia.

Ferret Mk 2/6 firing a BAC Vigilant Anti-Tank Guided Missile

Early Ferret Mk 4 with flotation screen erected

Ferret Mk 4, note the larger wheels on this model

Ferret Mk 5 with its launcher boxes for Swingfire Anti-Tank Guided Weapons in the elevated position

Ferret Mk 1/1 armed with a 7.62mm machine gun

Shorland Mk 3 Armoured Patrol Car Great Britain

Armament: 1×7.62mm machine gun and 1500 rounds of ammunition
2×3 smoke dischargers (optional)
Crew: 3
Length: 4.597m
Width: 1.778m
Height: 2.286m
G/Clearance: .21m (minimum)
Weight: 3360kg (loaded)
2931kg (empty)
G/Pressure: 2.4kg.cm^2
Engine: Rover 6 cylinder petrol engine developing 91bhp at 4500rpm. 2.625 litres
Speed: 88.4km/ph (road)
Range: 257km (standard tank)
514km (long range tank)
Fuel: 64 litres (standard)
128 litres (long range)
V/Obstacle: .23m
Trench: not applicable
Armour: 8.25mm–11mm

Development

The Shorland was conceived, prototype built, and placed in production in 1965. It was designed by the General Engineering Division of Short Brothers and Harland, at their Newtownards factory. The vehicle is essentially a 2.77m modified Land Rover chassis with an armoured body, in addition the engine and radiator have been armoured. The Shorland was first used by the Royal Ulster Constabulary, since then however the British Army have taken over the vehicles. Shorland is recognised by the British Army as an Internal Security Vehicle.

Variants

The first model to enter production was the Mk 1. This had hull armour of 7.25mm and was powered by a 4 cylinder Rover petrol engine developing 67bhp at 4100rpm. This was followed by the Mk 2 which had a 4 cylinder petrol engine developing 77bhp at 4100rpm.

The latest production model is the Mk 3. This has a thicker hull armour of 8.25mm which is resistant to the standard 7.62mm NATO round, also it is powered by a 6 cylinder petrol engine developing 95bhp at 4500rpm.

Other variants have included a Shorland with two Vigilant ATGW, Shorland with water cannon, Shorland with tear gas projector and the Shorland Security Vehicle for carrying cash and bullion. A more recent version is the SB 301 armoured personnel carrier, a similar vehicle to the SB 301 is the Glover armoured personnel carrier.

Employment

To date over 200 Shorlands have been built and the vehicle is in service with 16 countries including Argentina, Brunei, Great Britain, Libya, Persian Gulf States, Thailand and Venezuela.

Shorland Armoured Patrol Car armed with a 7.62mm machine gun and smoke dischargers

FV 432 Series
Armoured Personnel Carrier

Great Britain

Armament: 1×7.62mm GPMG and 2×3 barrelled smoke dischargers
Crew: 2+10
Length: 5.251m (overall)
4.87m (hull)
Width: 2.80m (overall)
Height: 2.286m (including machine gun)
1.879m (hull roof)
G/Clearance: .406m
Weight: 15,280kg (loaded)
13,740kg (empty)
G/Pressure: .78kg.cm²
Engine: Rolls-Royce K60 No 4 Mk 4F, multi-fuel, 240bhp at 3750rpm
Speed: 52km/ph (road)
6.6km/ph (water)
Range: 580km (road)
Fuel: 454 litres
Fording: Amphibious
V/Obstacle: .609m
Trench: 2.05m
Gradient: 60%
Armour: 6mm–12mm

Development

The FV 432 was developed from the earlier FV 420 series. The first prototype FV 432 was completed in 1961 and production commenced in 1963. Production was undertaken by Joseph Sankey and has now been completed. Prototype FV 432s were powered by a B.81 petrol engine and were called Trojans.

First production FV 432s were the Mk 1 and Mk 1/1, followed by the Mk 2 and Mk 2/1. The FV 432 is made amphibious by erecting a screen and is propelled in the water by its tracks. It is fitted with an NBC system and has infra-red driving lights. The FV 433 Abbot uses components of the FV 432.

Variants

The FV 432 can be adopted for the following roles:

(a) **Mortar:** 81mm mortar with a traverse of 360°, 160 rounds of ammunition, crew of six, laden weight 16,400kg.

(b) **Command:** Has mapboards, additional radios. Crew of seven, laden weight 15,500kg. A large tent can be erected at the rear of the vehicle to give additional working space.

(c) **Recovery:** Fitted with a winch, winch sub-frame, earth anchor, 107m of cable, maximum line pull 2 part tackle 16,270kg. Winch is driven from the PTO on the engine transfer case.

(d) **Wombat:** Can be fired mounted or dismounted, 14 rounds of ammunition are carried, crew of four, weight 15,870kg.

(e) **Load Carrier:** Can carry 3670kg of cargo.

(f) **Minelayer:** Can tow the Bar minelaying equipment.

(g) **Ambulance:** Can carry four stretchers

Infantry dismount from their FV 432 APC

(two each side), or two stretchers on one side and five seated patients on the other side. Crew of two.

(h) **Carl Gustav:** Bar across fighting compartment on which is mounted a Carl Gustav anti-tank weapon.

(i) **Artillery Control:** Fitted with the FACE (Field Artillery Computer Equipment).

(j) **Radar:** Can be fitted with the ZB 298 ground surveillance radar.

(k) **Navigation:** Can be fitted with navigation equipment.

The following versions of the FV 432 are under test: FV 432 fitted with the CYMBELINE Mortar Locating Radar System, FV 432 fitted with twin 7.62mm GPMG, FV 432 fitted with 30mm Rarden turret, FV 432 fitted with RANGER anti-personnel minelaying equipment.

The following use a modified FV 432 hull:

FV 434 Carrier, Maintenance, Full Tracked: This version is fitted with an HIAB crane and carries special tools and equipment. Crew is four, data as for FV 432 except:

Length: 5.72m
Weight: 17,750kg (loaded)

15,040kg (empty)
Height: 2.83m (travelling)
Width: 2.84m
Its crane can lift 1250kg at 3.96m radius to 3050kg at 2.26m radius.

FV 436 Self-Propelled Mortar Locating Radar: The rear hull has been cut away to provide a mounting for the Green Archer Mortar Locating Radar. Crew of three and it retains its amphibious capability.

FV 437 Pathfinder Recovery Vehicle (Trials only): This is a much modified FV 432 whose job was to recover vehicles in water.

FV 438 Swingfire Launcher Vehicle: This version has two launcher boxes for the Swingfire ATGW. A total of 14 missiles are carried. It also carries a 7.62mm GPMG. It has a crew of three. Data is similar to the basic FV 432 except:

Height: 2.705m
Weight: 16,200kg (loaded)
14,520kg (empty)

Sonic Detection Vehicle: This is used by the Royal Artillery to locate enemy gun and mortar positions.

Employment
Used only by the British Army.

FV 432 fitted with the EMI Cymbeline Mortar Locating Radar System. In this photograph the radar is in the travelling position

The FV 438 launching a BAC Swingfire ATGW

FV 603 Alvis Saracen
Armoured Personnel Carrier

Great Britain

Armament: 1 × 7.62mm machine gun, elevation +45°, depression −15°
1 × 7.62mm machine gun on ring mount at rear of vehicle
2 × 3 barrelled smoke dischargers
3000 rounds of 7.62mm machine gun ammunition
Crew: 2+10
Length: 5.233m (overall)
Width: 2.539m
Height: 2.463m
G/Clearance: .432m
Weight: 10,170kg (loaded)
8640kg (empty)
G/Pressure: .98kg.cm²
Engine: Rolls-Royce B.80 Mk 6A, 8 cylinder petrol engine developing 170hp at 3750rpm
Speed: 72km/ph (road)
Range: 400km
Fuel: 200 litres
Fording: 1.07m
1.98m (with kit)
V/Obstacle: .46m
Trench: 1.52m
Gradient: 42%
Armour: 8mm–16mm

Development
Design work on the Saracen started shortly after the end of World War II. The first prototype was built in 1950, followed by the first production vehicle in 1952. The last Saracen was built in 1972. The Saracen uses many components of the Saladin armoured car and the Stalwart High Mobility Load Carrier.

Variants
The full designation of the Saracen is Carrier Personnel Wheeled APC Mk 2 (Alvis Saracen 6 × 6). The Mk 1 had a slightly different turret and other minor differences. The basic vehicle can be quickly adopted for use as an ambulance, load carrier or engineer vehicle. The FV 603(C) incorporates reverse flow cooling enabling the vehicle to operate in the Middle East. This is distinguishable from the basic vehicle by its different arrangement of engine covers and the large cover over the radiator.
FV 604 Command Post: This is a Saracen without its turret, modified to carry additional radios, extra batteries, auxiliary charging equipment, map boards, the seating arrangement have also been modified. Sometimes an LMG is fitted on a ring mount slightly forward to where the turret was. Some FV 603s have been converted to FV 604 standards but retaining their turrets.
FV 610 Command Post: This is similar to the FV 604 but its height has been increased to 2.36m as this is intended to be used in the static role for longer periods. Additional working space is obtained by erecting tentage at the rear of the vehicle (FV 604 is similar). This vehicle can be fitted with the Field Artillery Computer Equipment. Laden weight is 10,620kg.
Other Projects/Variants: There was a project to fit Swingfire ATGW to a Saracen but this progressed only as far as the mock up stage. An FV 610 vehicle was used as a test vehicle for the GS No 9 Mk 1 Radar called Robert, this did not, however, enter service. Some Saracens were built without roofs for operation in the Middle East.

Employment
In service with Abu Dhabi, Brunei, Great Britain, Hong Kong (Police), Indonesia, Jordan, Kuwait (open topped versions), Libya, Nigeria, South Africa, Sudan, Thailand, Uganda, Qatar.

FV 603 Saracen Armoured Personnel Carrier

FV 610 Command Post
Vehicle

FV 603 Saracen with
reverse flow cooling and
also fitted with a
Normalair-Garret Air-
conditioning System

FV 604 Command Vehicle

The AT Series
Armoured Security Vehicles

Great Britain

	AT-100	AT-104
Crew:	1+12	1+12
Length:	4.697m	5.283m
Width:	2.133m	2.434m
Height:	2.412m	2.434m
	(cupola)	(cupola)
	2.184m (hull)	2.209m (hull)
G/Clearance:	.559m (hull)	.508m (hull)
Weight		
Loaded:	7030kg	8074kg
Fuel:	122 litres	122 litres
Armour:	6mm-12.5mm	6mm-12.5mm
Wheelbase:	2.743m	3.302m

Development/Variants

In April 1972, GKN Sankey Limited, built prototypes of two armoured internal security vehicles. These are called the AT-100 and the AT-104. The AT-100 is a 4×2 vehicle and the AT-104 a 4×4 vehicle. The AT-104 is longer and wider than the AT-100 and has limited cross country capability. The vehicles are powered by standard Bedford 330 (100hp) or 466 six cylinder diesel engines, Allison AT 540 4 speed transmission is fitted. All mechanical components are standard Bedford commercial parts, thus keeping maintenance costs to a minimum.

The hull is of all welded construction and is proof against 7.62mm AP rounds, bullet proof glass vision blocks are fitted and provision is made for the crew to fire their weapons from within the vehicle. Both side and rear doors are provided. The tyres are 11.00×20 run flat tyres.

A wide range of optional extras are available including a winch, petrol engine in place of the diesel engine, left-hand drive, ventilation system, various types of machine-gun mount, push bar on the front of the vehicle and a range of radio installations including a loud speaker system.

A breakdown and recovery vehicle is under development. The basic vehicle can be easily adopted for use as a load carrier, ambulance, headquarters vehicle, airfield patrol vehicle and ammunition supply vehicle.

Employment

Prototypes have been built and tested by GKN and the British Ministry of Defence (Army). A small quantity of AT-104s have been purchased by the Danish State Police.

The GKN Sankey AT-104 Internal Security Vehicle (4×4)

The GKN Sankey AT-100 Internal Security Vehicle (4×2)

77

Humber 1 Ton Armoured Truck (FV 1611)
Great Britain

Crew: 2
Length: 4.93m
Width: 2.05m
Height: 2.12m
Weight: 5790kg (loaded)
4770kg (empty)
Speed: 64km/ph (road)
Range: 400km
Fuel: 145 litres
Wheelbase: 2.74m
Track: 1.72m

Development/Variants
The FV 1611 was developed from the earlier FV 1609A armoured truck which in turn was based on the chassis of the Humber FV 1601A one-ton cargo truck. The chassis was made by Humber and the body by J. Sankey Limited or the Royal Ordnance Factories. The basic vehicles are:

FV 1611: Used to transport personnel and stores, also used to tow the Green Archer Mortar Locating Radar system.

FV 1612: This is a radio vehicle and has a crew of three, driver, commander and radio operator.

FV 1613: Ambulance version. Crew of two, driver and medical orderly. Can carry three stretcher or eight sitting, or one stretcher and four sitting patients.

FV 1620: Hornet/Malkara vehicle is no longer in service having been replaced by the Ferret Mk 5.

Employment
Used by the British Army and Portugal. The vehicles are widely used in Northern Ireland. In 1972/1973 some 500 of these vehicles were fitted with additional armour.

The Humber 1 Ton Armoured 4×4 Truck

Abbot – Self-Propelled Gun   Great Britain
Falcon – Self-Propelled Anti-Aircraft System

	Abbot	V/E Abbot	Falcon
Crew:	4	4	3
Length Overall:	5.84m	5.714m	5.333m
Length Hull:	5.709m	5.333m	5.333m
Width:	2.641m	2.641m	2.641m
Height:	2.489m	2.489m	2.514m
G/Clearance:	.406m	.406m	.406m
Weight Loaded:	16,556kg	15,900kg	15,850kg
Weight Empty:	14,878kg	14,200kg	14,300kg
G/Pressure:	.89kg.cm²	.81kg.cm²	.81kg.cm²
Speed Road:	48km/ph	48km/ph	48km/ph
Range Road:	390km	390km	390km
Fuel:	386 litres	386 litres	386 litres
Fording:	1.219m	1.117m	1.117m
V/Obstacle:	.609m	.609m	.609m
Trench:	2.057m	2.057m	2.057m
Gradient:	60%	60%	60%
Main Armament Calibre:	105mm	105mm	—
Anti-Aircraft Calibre:	7.62mm	—	30mm
Ammunition Main:	40	36	—
Ammunition A/A:	1200	—	620
Armour:	6mm–12mm	6mm–12mm	6mm–12mm

Development
Development of the Abbot commenced in 1958, the design parents being Vickers Limited. The first of 12 prototypes was completed in 1961. After trials a production order was awarded to Vickers Limited. The Abbot was in production at Vickers Elswick Works from 1964 until 1967. The Abbot uses many components of the FV 432 series of armoured personnel carriers.

Variants
Abbot (FV 433): The Abbot is armed with a 105mm gun in a turret with a traverse of 360°, the gun has an elevation of +70° and a depression of −5°. Sustained rate of fire is 12 rounds a minute. The gun has a maximum range of 17,000m and six different types of shell are available. A 7.62mm anti-aircraft machine gun is mounted for the use of the commander and there are three smoke dischargers mounted either side of the turret. The Abbot is fitted with an NBC system and infra-red driving lights. A flotation screen is carried around the top of the hull, when erected this enables the vehicle to cross rivers. It is propelled in the water by its tracks at about 5km/ph. The Abbot is powered by a Rolls-Royce K60 Mk 4G, 6 cylinder, in line, multi-fuel engine developing 240bhp at 2750rpm.

Value Engineered Abbot: The first prototype was completed in 1971 and it has been built at Vickers Elswick Works for the Indian Army. The Value Engineered Abbot is basically a standard Abbot with non-essential equipment removed, more economical components have been used. It lacks such items as the NBC system and the flotation screen as a number of Armies have no requirement for these. Any of these components could be added at a later date. It must be emphasised that there has been no degradation of standards or materials. The Value Engineered Abbot is powered by a Rolls-Royce K60 Mk 60G/1, 6 cylinder, in line diesel engine developing 213bhp at 3750rpm.

Falcon: The Falcon anti-aircraft system is a Value Engineered Abbot chassis fitted with a turret designed by the British Manufacture and Research Company. The turret mounts two Hispano Suiza 831L guns, these have an elevation of +85° and a depression of −10°, traverse and elevation is powered. The 30mm guns fire a wide range of ammunition and have a maximum range in the anti-aircraft role of 3000m. They are also highly effective in the ground role, especially against lightly armoured vehicles such as APCs. Their combined rate of fire is 1300 rounds per minute. The vehicle is powered by a Rolls-Royce Mk 60G/2, 6 cylinder, in line, water-cooled diesel engine developing 213bhp at 3750rpm. Trials have been completed and the vehicle is ready for production.

Employment
Abbot is used by the British Royal Artillery. Value Engineered Abbot is used by the Indian Army.

The Value Engineered Abbot. Note the lack of flotation screen and no smoke dischargers

The Falcon Anti-Aircraft System uses the same chassis as the Value Engineerd Abbot

An Abbot Self-Propelled Gun of the 2nd Royal Horse Artillery

Fug M–1963 Amphibious Scout Car Hungary

Armament: 1 × 7.62mm SGMB machine gun
OR 1 × 7.62mm M-59 machine gun
1250 rounds of 7.62mm ammunition
Crew: 5
Length: 5.79m
Width: 2.362m
Height: 1.90m (w/o machine gun)
G/Clearance: .305m
Weight: 6100kg (loaded)
Track: 2.050m
Wheelbase: 3.20m
Engine: Csepel 4 cylinder, in-line, water-cooled diesel, Model D-414.44, developing 100hp at 2300rpm
Speed: 87km/ph (road)
9km/ph (water)
Range: 500km
Fording: Amphibious
V/Obstacle: .47m
Trench: 1.30m
Gradient: 60%
Armour: 10mm

Development
The FUG M-1963 (FUG = Felderítö Úszó Gépkocsi) is the Hungarian equivalent of the Soviet BTR-40P (BRDM) amphibious scout car. The FUG is fully amphibious being propelled in the water by two hydro jets (the Soviet vehicle has only one). The engine of the FUG is in the rear (on the Russian vehicle it is in the front). It also has four small wheels under the centre of the vehicle. These can be lowered when required. The tyre pressures can be adjusted as and when required. The FUG is fitted with infra-red driving lights and an NBC system. The FUG M-1963 is called the OT-65 by the Czechoslovakian Army.

Variants
The FUG M-1963 has also been used as an ambulance and a radiological-chemical reconnaissance vehicle.

Employment
Used by Czechoslovakia, Hungary and Poland.

Fug M–1966 Hungary

This was first seen in 1966. It is based on the M-1963 but has no belly wheels and a different glacis plate. It has a turret armed with a 23mm cannon and a 7.62mm machine gun. It is fully amphibious and has infra-red driving lights and an NBC system. Data is similar to the FUG M-1963 except that it has a weight of 6500kg and a height of 2.20m.

The FUG M-1966 is called the OT-66 by the Czechoslovakians.

Employment
Used by Czechoslovakia, Hungary and Poland.

The Fug M-1966 has a turret mounted 23mm cannon and a 7.62mm machine gun

Israel

Israel has been modifying and adapting armoured fighting vehicles to its own requirements for many years. Below is a resumé of some of these modifications

Ben-Gurion: This is the Centurion MBT fitted with the French 105mm gun. It would seem, however, that there are few of these, if any, in service, as most Israeli Centurions are armed with the British 105mm gun.

Super-Sherman: This is a Sherman fitted with a French 75mm gun similar to that used in the AMX-13 light tank. In addition the turret rear has been modified and two smoke dischargers fitted either side of the turret. Israel has captured a number of Shermans from the Egyptian Army fitted with the complete turret of the AMX-13 light tank. These have most probably been used as chassis for self-propelled guns.

Isherman: This is a Sherman fitted with a French 105mm gun and a new 500hp Pratt and Whitney R-1340-AN-1 petrol engine. This new engine gives the vehicle a higher speed. The steering and transmission have been replaced and a new exhaust installed. Some Ishermans have been fitted with wider tracks. Smoke dischargers are fitted to either side of the turret.

Sherman: Shermans used for the Super-Sherman and Isherman conversions include the M-4A1, M-4A2 and M-4A3. Some of these have vertical volute spring suspensions and some horizontal volute spring suspension. It would appear that all Sherman gun tanks will eventually be converted to either self-propelled artillery or self-propelled mortar roles.

Sherman-Flail: Israel used Sherman flail tanks for mine-clearing operations during the six-day war of 1967.

AMX-13: Israel has sold some, if not all, of her AMX-13s as these were found unsuitable for desert operations. The AMX 105mm self-propelled guns will probably be phased out in the near future as the standard Israeli SPG is now a 155mm weapon.

Centurion: First shown in 1973 was the new Israeli Centurion. The Israelis have fitted a new Continental 750hp diesel, GE hydraulic gearbox, 105mm gun, more fuel capacity, in all over 2000 modifications have been made. This gives the vehicle twice the range and increases its maximum speed to 43km/ph, as well as making the vehicle more reliable.

M-48: Israel has received M-48A1, M-48A2 and M-48A2Cs from the United States and Germany. The following modifications have been carried out which bring the vehicle up to M-60 standards: 105mm gun fitted, Continental diesel engine, wider tracks and an XENON searchlight. Some M-48s have a smaller commander's cupola and an open 12.7mm machine gun.

T-54 and T-55: Israel has rebuilt many captured Soviet T-54 and T-55 tanks. These are called TI-67 and are not liked by the Israelis. The modifications have included the fitting of an American diesel engine, the 100mm gun has been replaced by a 105mm British gun, a 12.7mm anti-aircraft machine gun has replaced the Soviet one, a fire control system has been installed as has a new electrical system and air-conditioning.

Sabra: Early in 1970 it was reported that Israel had a prototype of a new MBT under test, this being designed and built in Israel. Early reports indicated that it had a 120mm gun but later reports state that it has a 105mm gun, a laser rangefinder and an American Continental diesel engine. Unconfirmed reports say that ALL Israeli tanks have, or will have, a laser rangefinder.

155mm Self-Propelled Howitzer: This is simply an M-7 Priest or Sherman chassis fitted with the French 155mm M-1950 weapon. It was first seen in 1964. A more recent 155mm weapon is the L-33 (see separate entry).

160mm Self-Propelled Mortar Carrier: This is an M-7 or M-4 Sherman chassis on which has been mounted a 160mm Soltam mortar. When in action the sides and front of the vehicle can be folded horizontal thus providing space for the crew of 4–7 men to load the weapon. The mortar has a maximum range of 9600m and is breech loaded. A high rate of fire can be achieved. A 12.7mm anti-aircraft machine gun is fitted.

Half-Tracks: The Israeli Army has adopted many M-2 and M-3 half-tracks for various roles including ambulances, command vehicles, ammunition vehicles, load carriers and engineer vehicles. Other versions include:

Missile: This has four SS-11 ATGW mounted in the ready-to-fire position.

Anti-Aircraft: This is armed with 2×20mm cannon.

Mortar: This is armed with a Soltam 120mm mortar which has a range of 400m–6500m. Over 30 rounds of ammunition are carried. The mortar can also be moved from the vehicle for firing.

Anti-Tank: Armed with a 106mm recoilless-rifle.

Anti-Tank: Armed with a 90mm Mecar gun.

Soviet and Egyptian APCs: The Israeli Army have adopted BTR-40, BTR-50, BTR-152 and the Egyptian Walid APCs to their own requirements. The wheeled vehicles are used in the internal security role.

Above: *A modified Israeli M-48. This has been fitted with the British designed 105mm gun, new diesel engine, Xenon searchlight and a new fire control system*

Below: *A Sherman fitted with the Soltam 160mm mortar*

An Israeli Half-Track with a 90mm gun. This gun is mounted on a modified 6 pounder Anti-Tank carriage and shield. It is normally mounted in the rear of the vehicle with the carriage towed behind the vehicle

An Israeli Half-Track fitted with the Israeli built Soltam 120mm mortar

An Israeli Super-Sherman armed with a 75mm gun

L–33 Self-Propelled Gun/Howitzer   Israel

Armament: 1×155mm gun/howitzer, elevation +52°, depression −3°, traverse 30° left and 30° right
1×7.62mm anti-aircraft machine gun
Crew: 8
Length: 8.55m (overall)
6.40m (hull—estimate)
Width: 3.33m
Height: 3.46m
G/Clearance: .43m (estimate)
Weight: 41,500kg (loaded)
G/Pressure: .84kg.cm² (estimate)
Engine: Cummins diesel
Speed: 36.8km/ph (road)
Range: 260km
Fuel: 636 litres (estimate)
Fording: .914m (estimate)
V/Obstacle: .60m
Trench: 2.30m
Gradient: 60%
Armour: 64mm (hull front)

Development/Variants
The L-33 was first shown in 1973. It is basically a Sherman M-4A3E8 chassis (with horizontal volute suspension) fitted with a large superstructure. In this is mounted a SOLTAM M 68 155mm gun/howitzer. This has a 33 calibre barrel and is fitted with a fume extractor. It fires a projectile weighing 43.7kg (muzzle velocity 725 metres/second) to a maximum range of 21,500m. The vehicle is fitted with a pneumatic lifting-loading system, this combined with the semi-automatic breech mechanism, enables the weapon to achieve a high rate of fire. It can be used for both direct and indirect fire.
An internal communications system is fitted and the crew are all provided with seat belts. A 7.62mm remote-controlled machine gun is mounted on the roof of the vehicle and this can be used for both anti-aircraft and ground roles.
The L-33 saw extensive action on the Sinia front during the Middle East conflict of October 1973.
Employment
Israel.
Below: *The L-33 155mm Self-Propelled Gun/Howitzer*

Fiat 6614 Personnel Carrier/Armoured Car   Italy

Armament: 1 × 7.62mm light machine gun
Crew: 1+6
Length: 5.16m
Width: 2.25m
Height: 1.71m (hull top)
G/Clearance: .375m
Weight: 5900kg (loaded)
5200kg (empty)
Track: 1.85m
Engine: Fiat 6 cylinder, 122hp at 5000rpm, 3.048 litres. Petrol
Speed: 100km/ph (road)
5km/ph (water)
Fording: Amphibious
V/Obstacle: .50m
Trench: nil
Gradient: 60%
Wheelbase: 2.40m

Development/Variants

The Fiat 6614 has been developed and built by Fiat of Torino. Prototypes have been built and evaluated by both Italian and overseas military and police authorities. Production of the vehicle may start in 1974, this depending on orders received.

The Fiat 6614 is a 4 × 4 vehicle and is of all welded construction. The vehicle is fully amphibious being propelled in the water by its wheels.

There is a door each side of the vehicle and a single large downward opening ramp at the rear. In the roof is a hatch for the driver; the commander's cupola is provided with a light machine gun mounting. Other types of armament can be fitted, and there is another hatch at the rear. The crew are provided with three firing ports each side, each having a vision block. At the rear of the vehicle is a further vision block either side of the ramp. The engine is on the right side of the vehicle, the silencer is on the right side of the hull with the exhaust pipe running along the roof. The gearbox has five forward and one reverse gear.

Employment

Trials with the Italian military and police authorities.

The Fiat 6614 with no armament fitted

Fiat 6616 Armoured Car   Italy

This has been built as a prototype by Fiat. It is a 4 × 4 vehicle and is armed with a turret-mounted 20mm Rheinmetall Rh 202 cannon and a 7.62mm machine gun, smoke dischargers are mounted each side of the turret. The vehicle has a road speed of 96km/ph and is amphibious, water speed being 4.8km/ph.

It is powered by a six cylinder diesel engine developing 145hp at 3200rpm, range is about 700km and it will climb a 60% gradient. The Fiat 6616 has a crew of three men. Overall dimensions are length 5.33m, width 2.50m and height 2.44m.

STB Main Battle Tank

Japan

Armament: 1 × 105mm gun (L-7A1)
1 × 7.62mm co-axial machine gun
1 × 12.7mm anti-aircraft machine gun (M-2)
2 × 3 smoke dischargers either side of turret
Crew: 4
Length: 9.33m (gun forward)
8.30m (gun in lock)
6.60m (hull)
Width: 3.18m
Height: 2.25m (normal)
G/Clearance: .40m (normal)
Weight: 38,000kg (loaded)
Engine: Mitsubishi 10ZF Type 21 WT, 10 cylinder diesel, air-cooled, developing 720hp at 2200rpm
Speed: 53km/ph (road)
Fording: 1.00m
V/Obstacle: 1.00m
Trench: 2.70m
Gradient: 60%
G/Pressure: .85kg.cm²

Development/Variants
In 1962 Japan started to design a new tank for the 1970s. The first prototypes were built in 1968/1969, and these underwent trials from the end of 1969. The original prototypes were called STB-1s. These had a remote controlled machine gun towards the rear of the turret. Later models, the STB-3 have a 105mm L7A3 gun, the anti-aircraft gun has a simple open type mount between the

commander's and loader's hatch, also the turret rear has been altered and a stowage box added. The first models had a semi-automatic loading system for the 105mm gun.

The STB has adjustable hydro-pneumatic suspension. This allows the height of the tank to be adjusted according to the tactical situation. A schnorkel can be fitted for deep wading. Infra-red driving lights are fitted and an infra-red/white light searchlight is mounted to the left of the main gun. A Japanese-built laser rangefinder and gun stabilisation system is installed as is an NBC system.

The STB is built by Mitsubishi Heavy Industries, the 105mm gun is now built in Japan by the Japan Steel Works.

Variants
It is expected that other variants of the STB are under development including armoured recovery and bridgelayer versions. A dozer blade has been fitted for trial purposes.

Employment
In production for the Japanese Self-Defence Force.

Above: *An early model of the STB Main Battle Tank*

Type 61 Main Battle Tank　　　　　　　　　Japan

Armament: 1×90mm Type 61 gun
1×7.62mm M-1919A4 co-axial machine gun
1×12.7mm M-2 anti-aircraft machine gun
Crew: 4
Length: 8.19m (gun forward)
6.30m (hull)
Width: 2.95m
Height: 3.16m (with A/A machine gun)
2.49m (turret roof)
G/Clearance: .40m
Weight: 35,000kg (loaded)
Engine: Mitsubishi Type 12 HM, V-12, turbo-charged air-cooled diesel developing 600hp at 2100rpm
Speed: 45km/ph (road)
Range: 200km (road)
Fording: .99m
V/Obstacle: .685m
Trench: 2.489m
Gradient: 60%
Armour: 64mm
G/Pressure: .95kg.cm²

Development
Design work on the Type 61 started in 1954 and it was the first tank to be built in Japan since the end of World War II. The first prototypes were completed in March 1957 and these were called the ST-A1 and ST-A2. The ST-A1 had seven road wheels and four return rollers and the ST-A2 had six road wheels and three return rollers, both tanks were armed with a 90mm gun. After extensive trials a further series of vehicles were built,

these being called the ST-A3 and ST-A4. These were completed in 1958/1959. After trials, production commenced in 1962 by Mitsubishi Nippon Heavy Industries and the tank was named 'Type 61'. The hundredth Type·61 was completed in November 1966.
The Type 61 can be fitted with infra-red driving and fighting equipment. It does not have an NBC system and cannot be fitted with a schnorkel.

Variants
Type 67 Armoured Vehicle Launched Bridge: This is similar to the American AVLB on the M-48/M-60 chassis. Weight 35,000kg, length 7.27m, width 3.50m, height 3.50m, crew three, armament 1×7.62mm machine gun.
Type 70 Armoured Recovery Vehicle: This has a boom and a dozer blade. Weight 35,000kg, length 8.40m, width 2.95m, height 3.10m, armament 1×81mm mortar, 1×7.62mm machine gun, 1×12.7mm machine gun, crew four.
Type 67 Armoured Engineering Vehicle: Weight 35,000kg, length 7.46m, width 3.20m, height 2.23m, armament 1×7.62mm and 1×12.7mm machine guns, crew four.
Employment
Used only by the Japanese Self-Defence Force (Army).

Right: *Type 61 Main Battle Tank, this particular model is fitted with infra-red driving lights*

Type 73 Mechanised Infantry Combat Vehicle　　Japan

Armament: 1×12.7mm machine gun on roof of vehicle
1×7.62mm machine gun in bow of vehicle
Crew: 2+10
Length: 5.60m
Width: 2.80m
Height: 1.70m (w/o armament)
Weight: 14,000kg (loaded)
Engine: Mitsubishi V4, 2· cycle, air-cooled diesel, supercharged developing 300hp at 2200rpm
Speed: 60km/ph (road)
Fording: Amphibious
Gradient: 60%
Armour: Aluminium

Development/Variants
This has been designed and manufactured by Mitsubishi Heavy Industries to replace the Type SU 60 armoured personnel carriers at present used by the Japanese Self-Defence Force. The Type 73 is fully amphibious being propelled in the water by its tracks, a small

trim board is erected before the vehicle enters the water. Other features of the vehicle include a hull of aluminium armour, NBC system, infra-red driving and fighting lights. Some models have been seen with small firing ports in either side of the hull.
There are two models of the Type 73. The Model 1 (SUB 1) is armed with a bow-mounted machine gun and a simple 12.7mm machine-gun mount on the roof. At the rear of the vehicle are six smoke dischargers (three each side). The Model 11 has a turret-mounted 12.7mm machine gun with three smoke dischargers mounted either side of the turret. It also has the bow mounted machine gun. Other versions of the Type 73 are probably under development.
Employment
In production for the Japanese Self-Defence Force.

Right: *Type 73 MICV Model 11*

Type **SU 60** Armoured Personnel Carrier   Japan

Armament: 1×12.7mm M-2 machine gun, on roof
1×7.62mm M-1919A4 machine gun, bow mounted
Crew: 2+8
Length: 4.85m
Width: 2.40m
Height: 2.31m (including machine gun)
1.70m (w/o machine gun)
G/Clearance: .40m
Weight: 11,800kg (loaded)
10,600kg (empty)
Engine: Mitsubishi 8 HA-21 WT, V-8, air-cooled turbo-charged diesel developing 220hp at 2400rpm
Speed: 45km/ph
Range: 230km
Fording: .76m
V/Obstacle: .60m
Trench: 1.82m
Gradient: 60%
G/Pressure: .57kg.cm²

Development
Development of the SU armoured personnel carrier started in 1956 and prototypes were built by two companies. Komatsu built the SU-1 and Mitsubishi built the SU-2. These prototypes were completed in 1957. The trials showed that the Mitsubishi vehicle was the better and after some re-design the vehicle was placed in production at the Maruko plant of Mitsubishi Heavy Industries. The first production vehicle was completed in 1960 and production continued until 1970 by which time over 400 had been built. The SU 60 does not have any amphibious capability, nor does it have an NBC system or any infra-red driving lights.

Variants
81mm Mortar Carrier (SV): Crew five armed with an 81mm mortar in the rear of the vehicle. It retains its 12.7mm and 7.62mm machine guns. A baseplate and stand are carried on the front of the vehicle enabling the mortar to be dismounted and fired away from the vehicle.

107mm Mortar (4.2in) Carrier (SX): Crew five and has a loaded weight of 12,900kg The mortar is mounted in the rear of the vehicle and this model can easily be recognised as the rear of the hull is cut at an angle. The 12.7mm machine gun is retained. A baseplate and stand is carried on the front of the vehicle enabling the mortar to be fired away from the vehicle.

105mm Howitzer (SY): Did not progress beyond the prototype stage.

Employment
Used only by the Japanese Self-Defence Force (Army).

The 81mm Mortar Carrier version of the SU 60 APC

Type 60 Self-Propelled 106mm Recoilless Rifle Japan

Armament: 2×106mm recoilless rifles with
10 rounds of ammunition
1×12.7mm spotting machine gun
Crew: 3
Length: 4.30m
Width: 2.23m
Height: 1.38m
G/Clearance: .35m
Weight: 8020kg (loaded)
7600kg (empty)
G/Pressure: .63kg.cm²
Engine: Komatsu T120, 6 cylinder, air-cooled
diesel developing 120hp at 2400rpm
Speed: 48km/ph (road)
Range: 130km (road)
Fuel: 77 litres
Fording: .80m
V/Obstacle: .53m
Trench: 1.78m
Gradient: 67%
Armour: 15mm–30mm

Development/Variants
Design of this vehicle started in 1954 and it
was the first postwar Japanese armoured
fighting vehicle. Prototypes were built by
Komatsu (SS-1) and Mitsubishi (SS-2);
these were completed at the end of 1955.
The SS-1 had its engine at the front with its
driving sprocket at the rear, the SS-2 having
its engine at the rear and its driving sprocket
at the front. They both had different suspensions. They were both armed with 2×
105mm recoilless rifles. The vehicles were
subjected to extensive trials and the SS-2 was
found to be the better of the two vehicles.
These were followed by the SS-3 in 1956
and the SS-4 in 1959. In 1960 a production
order was placed for the Type 60. Manufacturers involved were Komatsu, Japan
Steel Works and the Howa Machinery Company. Production has been completed.
When in the lowered position the rifles have
an elevation of +10° and a depression of
−5°, traverse being 10° left and 10° right.
When raised with their mount they have an
elevation of +25° and a depression of −15°,
traverse being 30° left and 30° right. The
106mm rifles can fire HE and anti-tank
rounds, maximum range being 7700m
effective range is 1100m. Rate of fire, 6
rounds per minute. The rifles weigh 114kg,
overall length being 3.408m, barrel length
3.332m.
The Type SU 60 does not have any infra-red
driving lights nor does it have an NBC system.
Employment
Used only by the Japanese Self-Defence
Force (Army).

*Type 60 Self-Propelled 106mm Recoilless
Rifle*

YP–408 Armoured Personnel Carrier   Netherlands

Armament: 1×12.7mm machine gun, elevation +70°, depression −8°
2×3 barrelled smoke dischargers
Crew: 2+10
Length: 6.23m
Width: 2.40m
Height: 2.37m (including machine gun)
1.80m (hull top)
G/Clearance: .457m
Weight: 12,000kg (loaded)
9500kg (empty)
Track: 2.055m
Engine: DAF DS 575, 6 cylinder, in-line, water-cooled, turbo-charged diesel developing 165hp at 2400rpm
Speed: 80km/ph (road)
Range: 500km (road)
400km (cross country)
Fuel: 200 litres
Fording: 1.20m
V/Obstacle: .70m
Trench: 1.20m
Gradient: 60%
Armour: 16mm (maximum)

Development
The YP-408 was designed by Van Doorne's Automobielfabriek (DAF) NV of Eindhoven. The first mock-up was completed in 1957 and the first prototype was completed in 1958. The prototypes were followed by a pre-production batch. The first production vehicle was completed in 1964 and the last in 1968, about 750 of all versions were built. The vehicle uses many components of the YA-328 artillery tractor.
The vehicle is an 8×6, the front two and rear four being powered, steering is hydraulically assisted and is on the front four wheels. The vehicle is not amphibious, capable only of fording. It does not have an NBC system although a heater is fitted, infra-red driving and fighting lights can be fitted. There are a total of 6 roof hatches; at the rear are two doors, these being provided with a firing port each.
The basic vehicle is designated PWI-S, which means Panser Wagen Infanterie—Standard.

Variants
PWI-S (PC): This is a platoon commander's vehicle and has a crew of nine and additional radios.
PWCO: This is a company and battalion commander's vehicle and has a crew of six men. It has map tables and additional batteries and a tent can be erected at the rear if required.
PW-GWT: This is an ambulance and does not have any armament. It has a crew of three and can carry two stretcher patients and four sitting patients.
PW-V: This is a freight carrier and can carry 1500kg of freight. It has a crew of two and does not have a radio. If required it can also be used as an ambulance.
PW-MT: This is a mortar towing vehicle and tows the French Brandt 120mm mortar. A total of 50 rounds of ammunition are carried; it has a crew of seven. The rear doors are slightly different on this model.

Employment
Used only by the Netherlands Army.

The YP-408 PWCO Command Vehicle

T–62 Main Battle Tank

Soviet Union

Armament: 1×115mm smoothbore gun
(U-5TS), elevation +15°, depression −3°
1×7.62mm PKT co-axial machine gun
40 rounds of 115mm ammunition
2000 rounds of 7.62mm ammunition
Crew: 4
Length: 9.488m (including gun)
6.705m (excluding gun)
Width: 3.352m
Height: 2.40m
G/Clearance: .425m
Weight: 37,500kg
G/Pressure: .80kg.cm^2
Engine: Model V-2-62, V-12 water-cooled
diesel engine developing 700hp at 2200rpm
Speed: 55km/ph (road)
Range: 480km (road)
Fuel: 1564 litres (total)
Fording: 1.40m
3.96m (with schnorkel)
V/Obstacle: .80m
Trench: 2.80m
Gradient: 60%
Armour: 20mm–170mm

Development/Variants
The T-62 was shown to the public for the first
time in May 1965. It is believed to have
entered production in 1961/1962 and was
developed for the earlier T-54/T-55 series.
The amendments to the earlier T-54/T-55
include a longer and wider hull, a new turret
mounted slightly more to the rear, increased
track length on the ground, revised turret
hatches and no bow or anti-aircraft machine
guns.
The T-62 is armed with a 115mm gun that
fires fin-stabilised HEAT (m/v 1000 m/s) or
HVAP (1400/1600 m/s) rounds, rate of fire
is stated as five rounds a minute. The gun is
longer than that fitted to the T-54 and has a
bore evacuator. A laser rangefinder may be
under development.
The T-62 is fitted with auxiliary external fuel
tanks and can also have additional fuel tanks
at the rear of the vehicle. It can also lay its
own smoke screen from its exhaust pipes
either side of the hull. Infra-red fighting and
driving lights are fitted, as is an NBC system.
Some T-62s have recently been observed
fitted with a 12.7mm anti-aircraft machine
gun. The T-62 is probably manufactured in
Poland and Czechoslovakia, as were the
earlier T-54s and T-55s.
The T-62 is easily recognisable from the T-54
and T-55 by its longer gun and the wider
space between the road wheels.

Employment
Used by Bulgaria, Czechoslovakia, East
Germany, Egypt, Hungary, India (reported),
Poland, Rumania, Soviet Union, Syria.

Above: *T-62 Main Battle Tank*

T–54 & T–55 Main Battle Tank   Soviet Union

Armament: 1×100mm D-10T gun, elevation
+17°, depression −4°
1×7.62mm SGMT machine gun co-axial
with main armament
1×7.62mm SGMT bow machine gun (operated by driver)
1×12.7mm DShK anti-aircraft machine gun
34 rounds of 100mm ammunition
500 rounds of 12.7mm machine gun
ammunition
3000 rounds of 7.62mm machine gun
ammunition
Crew: 4
Length: 9.02m (including gun)
6.57m (excluding gun)
Width: 3.27m
Height: 2.40m
G/Clearance: .43m
Weight: 36,500kg (loaded)
G/Pressure: .80kg.cm²
Armour: 20mm–170mm
Engine: V-2-54, V-12, water-cooled diesel
developing 520hp at 2000rpm
Speed: 48km/ph (road)
Range: 630km (road)
440km (cross country)
Fuel: 1091 litres (total)
Fording: 1.50m
3.96m (with schnorkel)
V/Obstacle: .80m
Trench: 2.74m
Gradient: 60%

Note. *The range figures include external
fuel tanks.*

Development
The T-54 was developed from the earlier
T-44 (this is still used for training). The first
prototype of the T-54 appeared in 1947 and
the first production models in 1949. The first
models had a turret that was undercut at the
rear and had an external gun mantlet; some of
these have seen action in Jordan only three
years ago. The 100mm gun is the same as that
fitted to the SU-100. The T-54 and T-55 have
been manufactured in the Soviet Union,
China (under the designation T-59), Czechoslovakia and Poland. The ZSU-57-2 is based
on a modified and shortened T-54 chassis.

Variants
T-54: This is the early model with the turret
undercut at the rear.
T-54A: This has a bore evacuator, the
armament is the D-10TG. Internal modifications include the stabilisation of the main
armament in the vertical plane, electric oil
pump, bilge pump, improved air filter, infra-red
driving equipment, automatic fire extinguishers,
additional fuel capacity and power elevation
of the main armament.
T-54A(M): This is the T-54 or T-54A fitted

with night-fighting equipment, recognisable
by the horizontal bracket for the gunner's
infra-red searchlight.
T-54B: This model is recognisable by its
infra-red searchlight for the tank commander
and gunner. The commander's light is on his
cupola and the gunner's light has a vertical
bracket attached to the right front of the
turret. The T-54B can be fitted with a
schnorkel; this equipment consists of two
pipes which are carried on the rear decking
when not required. When assembled they are
placed over the loader's turret hatch, where
they are supported by wire stays. A much
wider pipe is used for training purposes.
The T-54B has the D-10T2S gun which is
stabilised in both planes.
T-54C: This is also known as the T-54(X).
The T-54C resembles the T-54B and has a
turret dome-shaped ventilator, bracket for the
gunner's infra-red searchlight is vertical as
in the T-54B. No anti-aircraft machine gun is
fitted and a simple hatch replaces the
loader's cupola.
T-55 Model 1: This is sometimes known as
the T-54C and was first shown to the public
in November 1961. It has a horizontal
bracket for the gunner's infra-red searchlight,
no turret dome ventilator, no anti-aircraft
machine gun, a simple hatch for the loader.
It has the same D-10T2S gun that is fitted to
the T-54B and this is stabilised in both
planes; the turret floor rotates. It has a V-55
diesel engine that develops 580hp as well
as an improved transmission. It has a total of
43 rounds of 100mm ammunition.
T-55 Model 2: This was first seen in May
1963. It has a raised hatch cover for the loader,
smooth metal cover at the base of the commander's cupola, no bow machine gun.
Probably has an NBC system.
Mine Clearing Tanks: Both T-54s and
T-55s have been modified for mine clearing
duties, these being known as PT-54 or
PT-55. This equipment consists of various
types of wheels mounted in front of the tank.
There are also T-54s fitted with flails for mine
clearing operations and turretless versions of
the T-54 for the same duties. There is also a
new mine-clearing T-55 with a special dozer
blade mounted on the front of the vehicle.
Mine Clearing Tanks—Czechoslovakia:
Czechoslovakia has developed two types of
mine clearing tank. One model is similar to
the PT-54 and the other is of the plough type.
In the later model there is a plough in front
of each track to clear the mines and soil and
in addition there is a rake type device between
the two ploughs to clear any anti-personnel
mines.
Bulldozer Tanks: Two basic types of bulldozer blade can be fitted. The BTU is used

for clearing topsoil and obstacles whilst the STU is used for clearing snow.

Bridgelayer Tank MTU: This is a T-54 with its turret removed. The bridge is carried on top of the vehicle and winched into position over the obstacle and then lowered down into the desired position. Performance is similar to the basic T-54; some models have been seen with a 12.7mm anti-aircraft machine gun fitted. Basic data is:

Length: 12.30m (with bridge)
Height: 2.865m (with bridge)
Width: 3.27m (with bridge)
Weight: 34,000kg (with bridge)

Bridgelayer Tank M-1967: This is similar to the above bridgelayer except that it has an additional 3.85m on the end of each end of the bridge, these fold on top of the bridge when not in use. The bridge, when opened out, is 20m long and can bridge a gap 19m. The chassis is a T-55.

Bridgelayer Tank MT-55: This has been developed by the Czechoslovakian Army, and is similar to that fitted to their T-34. The vehicle has an NBC system and can have a schnorkel. Opened out, the bridge is 18.2m long.

Amphibious Recovery Vehicle: No firm details are available of this model.

T-54 Flamethrower: Believed to exist, no details are available.

Recovery Vehicle T-54-T: This is a T-54 with its turret removed; a large spade is mounted at the rear of the vehicle; on top of the vehicle is mounted a schnorkel for deep wading. There is another model with no schnorkel and a simple box-like structure. No armament is fitted. Basic data is similar to the T-54 except:

Length: 6.475m
Height: 1.89m
Width: 3.27m
Weight: 32,000kg

Recovery Vehicle T-55-T: This is the same as the above but uses a T-55 chassis.

East German Recovery Vehicles: East Germany uses two types of recovery vehicle based on the T-54 chassis. One model is used to recover vehicles whilst the other is used to tow the recovered vehicle. Each has its turret removed, no spade at the rear, a schnorkel can be fitted, there is a push bar at the front, a boom crane can be erected if required. They can also quickly be fitted with mine-clearing rollers.

Indian T-54s and T-55s: It is reported that some Indian T-54s and T-55s have been re-armed with Russian 115mm guns and have had their machine guns replaced so that they can fire Indian ammunition.

Employment
Used by Albania, Algeria, Afghanistan, Bulgaria, China, Cuba, Cyprus, Czechoslovakia, East Germany, Finland, Egypt, Hungary, India, Israel (see section on Israel), Libya, Mongolia, Morocco, North Korea, North Vietnam, North Yemen, Pakistan (both Russian and Chinese models), Peru, Poland, Rumania, South Yemen, Soviet Union, Sudan, Syria, Yugoslavia.

T-54 of the Indian Army, note the none standard Anti-Aircraft machine gun mounting (United States type)

A T-54 MTU Bridgelayer
laying its bridge

A T-54 Armoured
Recovery Vehicle Model
T-54-T. The large tube
on the top of the vehicle
is the schnorkel

A T-54 with dozer blade
crossing a bridge, the
centre section of which
has been laid by a T-54
MTU Bridgelayer

T–34/85 Medium Tank Soviet Union

Armament: 1×85mm M1944 (ZIS-S53) gun, elevation +25°, depression −5°
1×7.62mm bow machine gun and 1×7.62mm anti-aircraft machine gun (DTs or DTMs)
56 rounds of 85mm ammunition
2394 rounds of 7.62mm ammunition
Crew: 5
Length: 8.076m (including gun)
6.096m (excluding gun)
Width: 2.997m
Height: 2.743m
G/Clearance: .38m
Weight: 31,750kg (loaded)
G/Pressure: .80kg.cm²
Engine: V-2-34, V-12 diesel, water-cooled developing 500hp at 1800rpm   OR
V-2-34m V-12 diesel, water-cooled developing 500hp at 1800rpm
Speed: 50km/ph (road)
Range: 354km (road)
Fuel: 773 litres
Fording: 1.32m
V/Obstacle: .73m
Trench: 2.50m
Gradient: 60%
Armour: 18mm–75mm

Note. *Fuel is maximum with external tanks, range includes external tanks.*

Development
The T-35/85 was developed from the earlier T-34/76 (some of which may still be found in training units) and saw widespread service with the Soviet Army in World War II and was judged by many to be the best tank of the war. The chassis is similar to that used by the SU-85 and SU-100. Postwar the T-34/85 has been in combat in Korea, Hungary, Yemen and Egypt.

Variants
T-34/85 Mineclearing Tanks: There may still be some of these in service; they are fitted with equipment similar to that fitted to the PT-54. Some T-34/85s were fitted with schnorkelling equipment.
T-34/85 Bulldozer Tanks: The vehicle can be fitted with a dozer blade.
SKP-5 Tank Recovery Vehicle: This is a T-34 with its turret removed and fitted with a crane capable of lifting about 5000kg. Additional data:
Length: 8.00m
Width: 3.00m
Height: 2.60m
Weight: 25,000kg
T-34-T Model A Recovery Vehicle: This is simply a T-34 with no turret and therefore limited to towing operations. Some models have been seen with a superstructure or cupola in place of the turret. Additional data:
Height: 1.70m
Weight: 22,000kg
T-34-T Model B Recovery Vehicle: The equipment fitted to this model includes rigging, jib crane and a platform that can be used to carry engines and transmissions to a maximum weight of 2500kg. Additional data:
Height: 2.14m
Weight: 25,000kg
T-34-T Model C Recovery Vehicle: This model has been developed by Poland and consists of a T-34 chassis with a large armoured superstructure at the front of the vehicle, a bow machine gun is fitted. Additional

A T-34/85 on display at Aberdeen Proving Ground, USA

equipment includes a spade at the rear and a schnorkel for deep wading.

T-34 with Heavy Crane: This has been developed by Czechoslovakia and is also used by Poland. It is basically a T-34 chassis with a heavy hydraulic crane mounted in place of the turret. This crane can lift a maximum of 5900kg, for example a T-54 turret.

T-34 Recovery Vehicle (East German Model): This is also known as the T-34 BG, and is similar to the T-34-T Model B but also has a push-bar on the glacis plate. It also has a winch.

T-34 Bridgelayer (Scissors Type): This is on Czechoslovakian design and it was first seen in 1960. It is a T-34 chassis with a scissors bridge that has a maximum length in position of 22.00m. Additional data is:
Length: 10.00m (with bridge)
Width: 3.20m (with bridge)

Height: 3.70m (with bridge)
Weight: 32,000kg (with bridge)
Yugoslavian T-34/85: Very few of these were built and none remain in service. They featured a cast turret with a different cupola and a different glacis plate.
Employment
The T-34/85 is still used by Afghanistan, Albania, Algeria, Bulgaria, China, Cuba, Cyprus, Czechoslovakia, East Germany, Egypt, Guinea, Hungary, Iraq, Libya, Mali, Mongolia, North Korea, North Vietnam, North and South Yemen, Poland, Rumania, Somalia, Sudan, Syria, Yugoslavia.

Below: *The T-34-T Model B Armoured Recovery Vehicle*

Bottom: *T-34/85s of the Egyptian Army on parade in Cairo*

PT–76 Amphibious Light Tank

Soviet Union

Armament: 1 × 76.2mm D-56T gun, elevation +31°, depression −3½°
1 × 7.62mm SGMT machine gun co-axial with main armament
40 rounds of 76.2mm ammunition are carried
1000 rounds of 7.62mm ammunition are carried
Crew: 3
Length: 7.625m (including gun)
6.910m (excluding gun)
Width: 3.180m
Height: 2.195m
G/Clearance: .40m
Weight: 14,000kg (loaded)
G/Pressure: .48kg.cm^2
Engine: V-6, in-line, water-cooled diesel developing 240hp at 1800rpm
Speed: 44km/ph (road)
10km/ph (water)
Range: 250km (road)
Fuel: 250 litres
Fording: Amphibious
V/Obstacle: 1.10m
Trench: 2.80m
Gradient: 70%
Armour: 10mm–15mm

Development
The PT-76 first appeared in 1952 and is a continuation of a long line of Soviet light amphibious tanks. The PT-76 is fully amphibious, being propelled in the water by two water jets at the rear of the vehicle. These are covered when not required. Before entering the water a small trim board is folded forward at the front of the vehicle. The vehicle can lay its own smoke screen if required. The PT-76 chassis, extensively modified in some cases, is used for the following vehicles: ASU-85, BTR-50, OT-62, M-1970, BMP-76BP, ZSU-23-4, Gainful missile launcher, FROG-2, 3, 4 and 5 tactical missile launchers, GSP amphibious bridging equipment, PVA tracked amphibian and the Pinguin cross country and arctic survey vehicle, in fact the Pinguin was the basis of the PT-76. Production of the PT-76 has now been completed.

Variants
Model 1: Also known as the Model B. Is armed with the D-56T gun with no bore evacuator and a long multi-slotted muzzle brake.
Model 2: Also known as the Model ·A. Is armed with the D-56TM gun with a bore evacuator and a double baffle muzzle brake. The PT-76 Model 2 fitted with a stabilised gun becomes the PT-76B.
Model 3: This has a conventional clean barrel.

Employment
The PT-76 is used by Afghanistan, Bulgaria, China (refer to Chinese section), Cuba, Czechoslovakia, East Germany, Egypt, Finland, Hungary, India, Indonesia, Iraq, Laos (Pathet Lao), North Korea, North Vietnam, Pakistan Poland. Soviet Union, Syria, Yugoslavia.

A PT-76 Model 2 leaving the water

New Soviet Light Tank

Soviet Union

On 7th November 1973 a new Soviet Light Amphibious Tank was seen for the first time. The vehicle has the provisional designation of M-1970. It has a crew of three and six infantrymen can be carried in the rear of the vehicle. The vehicle has five road wheels and four return rollers. It is fitted with a similar turret to that fitted to the BMP-76PB MICV.

A Sagger anti-tank missile is fitted over the barrel of the gun. The vehicle is fitted with a hydrojet water propulsion system.

The New Soviet Light Tank, the M-1970, was seen for the first time during the military parade held in Moscow on 7th November 1973

T–10M Heavy Tank

Soviet Union

Armament: 1 × 122mm gun, elevation + 17°, depression − 3°, 30 rounds of 122mm ammunition
1 × 14.5mm KPV machine gun, co-axial with main armament
1 × 14.5mm KPV machine gun, anti-aircraft
1000 rounds of 14.5mm ammunition are carried
Crew: 4
Length: 10.29m (including gun)
7.40m (excluding gun)
Width: 3.44m
Height: 2.26m (w/o A/A machine gun)
G/Clearance: .456m
Weight: 49,000kg
G/Pressure: 0.71kg.cm²
Engine: V-2-IS, 12 cylinder, water-cooled diesel, 690hp at 2000rpm
Speed: 35km/ph (road)
Range: 350km (road)
Fuel: 1180 litres
Fording: 1.2m
V/Obstacle: 0.9m
Trench: 3.00m
Gradient: 60%
Armour: 210mm (maximum)

Note. *The above relates to the T-10M, and fuel includes external tanks.*

T-10 Heavy Tank of the East German Army

The T-10 was developed from the earlier IS-111. The improvements over the IS-111 were a more powerful gun with a bore evacuator, larger turret, improved armour and a more powerful engine. The T-10 is externally distinguishable from the IS-111 by its seven road wheels, larger turret and cut-off corners on the rear hull plate. The T-10 has 12.7mm M1938/46 DShk machine guns.
The T-10M is a modified T-10. These modifications included the fitting of new 14.5mm machine guns, fitting of infra-red driving and fighting equipment. Some T-10Ms have had a metal stowage box welded to the rear of the turrets. It is also reported that the T-10M is fitted with stabilisation equipment for the 122mm gun and can also be fitted with a schnorkel.
The 122mm gun fires HE or APHE rounds, these rounds are of the separate loading type. This accounts for their low rate of fire which is three rounds a minute. The T-10M's barrel has a multi-baffle muzzle brake.

Employment
Bulgaria, Czechoslovakia, East Germany, Egypt, Hungary, North Vietnam, Poland Rumania, Soviet Union, Syria.

IS–111 Heavy Tank

Soviet Union

Armament: 1 × 122mm M1943 gun, elevation + 19°, depression − 2°
1 × 7.62mm DTM co-axial machine gun
1 × 12.7mm DShk anti-aircraft machine gun
28 rounds of 122mm ammunition
2000 rounds of machine gun ammunition
Crew: 4
Length: 9.98m (including gun)
6.80m (excluding gun)
Width: 3.05m
Height: 2.44m (w/o A/A machine gun)
G/Clearance: .465m
Weight: 46,500kg (loaded)
G/Pressure: .79kg.cm²
Engine: V-2 IS, V-12 diesel, water-cooled, developing 520hp at 2000rpm
Speed: 37km/ph (road)
Range: 210km (road)

Fuel: 482 litres
Fording: 1.30m
V/Obstacle: 1.00m
Trench: 2.50m
Gradient: 60%
Armour: 20mm–200mm

Development
The IS-111 was developed from the earlier IS-11, this later vehicle is still used for training in the Soviet Union. The improvements over the IS-11 include a new turret without a cupola, the armour arrangement has been improved and a more powerful engine fitted. The IS-111 entered service towards the end of 1945. The IS-IV was a postwar version of the IS-111 and had a co-axial 12.7mm machine gun, additional armour and a more

powerful engine. Very few IS-IV were built.

Variants using IS-type chassis:

ISU-122 and ISU-152 Assault Guns: See separate entry.

310mm M-1957 Self-Propelled Gun: This was first shown in November 1957, and is based on a lengthened IS chassis with eight road wheels. The weapon has a range of 22,860m. This weapon is now obsolete.

420mm M-1960 Self-Propelled Mortar: This was also shown in November 1957, and has the same chassis as the above. A modified version was shown in 1960. The weapon has a range of 18,280m. It is now obsolete.

IS-11-T and IS-111-T: Either an IS-11 or IS-111 with its turret removed and stowage boxes fitted to the front of the vehicle. Weight 35,000kg. These are only capable of towing operations.

Scamp ICBM: On IS chassis with eight road wheels.

Scrooge ICBM: On IS chassis with eight road wheels.

Scud A and Scud B: Short range missile on IS chassis, six road wheels.

Frog-1: Short range missile on IS chassis, six road wheels, now obsolete.

Employment

IS-11 is still used by China, Cuba and some Warsaw Pact Countries (for training).

IS-111 is still used by Bulgaria, Czechoslovakia East Germany, Hungary, Poland, Rumania, Soviet Union, Syria.

IS-111 Tank of the Egyptian Army on parade in Cairo in 1956

BTR–40P–2 (BTR–40PB)
Reconnaissance Vehicle

Soviet Union

Armament: 1 × 14.5mm KPVT machine gun, elevation + 30°, depression − 10°, 500 rounds of 14.5mm ammunition
1 × 7.62mm PKT machine gun, co-axial with 14.5mm machine gun
Crew: 4
Length: 5.50m
Width: 2.18m
Height: 2.15m
G/Clearance: .315m
Weight: 7000kg
Armour: 10mm
Engines: 2 × M-21, 4 cylinder, in-line, petrol engines, 70hp at 4000rpm (each)
Speed: 100km/ph (road)
10km/ph (water)
Range: 750km
Fording: Amphibious
V/Obstacle: .47m
Trench: 1.25m
Gradient: 60%

Development/Variants

The BTR-40P-2, or BRDM-2 as it is sometimes called, first appeared in 1966 and it is a replacement for the earlier BTR-40P vehicle. The primary role of the vehicle is reconnaissance.

The BTR-40P-2 is fully amphibious being propelled in the water by a hydrojet at the rear of the vehicle. A trim board is fitted under the nose of the vehicle and this is raised before the vehicle enters the water.

The engines are at the rear of the vehicle and there is a winch at the front. It has four auxiliary wheels, two each side; these are lowered by the driver when required and enable the vehicle to cross trenches. They are driven from a power take-off.

It is fitted with an NBC system and infra-red driving and fighting lights. The turret is the same as that fitted to the BTR-60PB armoured personnel carrier and the Czechoslovakian OT-64 Model 3 armoured personnel carrier. The BTR-40P-2 was called the BTR-40PB Model 1966/1 for a short time.

BTR-40PB (Sagger): This is a basic BTR-40PB with its turret removed and replaced with a launching system for 6 Sagger ATGW. The six Saggers are raised from within the vehicle complete with their overhead armour cover. Data of this model is similar to the basic vehicle except for a height of 1.90m.

BRDM-2 Sam: This was seen for the first time during the Middle East conflict of late 1973. It consists of a BRDM-2 with its turret removed and replaced by four or eight launchers for the SA-7 Strela (or Grail) low-altitude surface to air missile. It is in service with Egypt and Syria. It entered service with the Warsaw Pact Forces, including the Soviet Union in 1972/1973.

Employment

The BTR-40P-2 (BRDM-2) is used by members of the Warsaw Pact Forces including East Germany, Poland and the Soviet Union. They are also used by Egypt and Syria.

Above: BTR-40PB (BTR-40P-2) is also known as the BRDM-2

BTR–40P (BRDM) Series
Amphibious Reconnaissance Vehicle

Soviet Union

Armament: 1 × 7.62mm SGMB machine gun with 1250 rounds AND/OR
1 × 12.7mm DShK machine gun
Crew: 5
Length: 5.70m
Width: 2.25m
Height: 1.90m (w/o armament)
G/Clearance: .315m
Weight: 5600kg (loaded)
5100kg (empty)
Wheelbase: 2.80m
Engine: GAZ-40P, 6 cylinder, in-line, water-cooled petrol engine developing 90hp at 3400rpm
Speed: 80km/ph (road)
9km/ph (water)
Range: 500km
Fording: Amphibious
V/Obstacle: .47m
Trench: 1.22m
Gradient: 60%
Armour: 10mm

Note. *The data relates to the BTR-40P (BRDM) which is also known as the BRDM-1.*

Development/Variants
The BTR-40P was first shown in May 1959. It is used for a variety of roles including command, reconnaissance and radio duties. The vehicle is fully amphibious being propelled in the water by a single waterjet at the rear of the vehicle. This is covered when not required. Before entering the water the trim board is erected at the front of the vehicle, when travelling this is normally kept in the retracted position just under the nose of the vehicle. In addition to the four main wheels there are two sets of small wheels. These are powered and may be lowered as and when required. They enable the vehicle to cross ditches and climb over difficult obstacles. The tyre pressures can be adjusted to suit the ground conditions.

A further development of this vehicle is the BTR-40PB, for which there is a separate entry. Similar vehicles are the Hungarian FUG (OT-65) and the FUG-66.
BTR-40P-rkh: This is a specialised vehicle and is used to mark lane lines through chemical and radio-active contaminated areas. On the rear decking of the vehicles are two boxes, each containing 25 marker flags each. These flags are fired into the ground whilst the vehicle is moving. The crew do not have to leave the vehicle.
BTR-40Ps with anti-tank missiles:
Model A: This has three SNAPPER (AT-1) anti-tank missiles carried under light armour. When required for launching the overhead doors slide down to each side of the vehicle. The range of the missiles is about 2000m.
Model B: This has four SWATTER (AT-2) anti-tank missiles carried under light armour. When required for launching the overhead doors slide down to each side of the vehicle, as does an armoured cover at the rear. The range of these missiles is about 2400m.
Model C: This is the latest version and carries six SAGGER (AT-3) anti-tank missiles under armour. In this version the six missiles are raised complete with their overhead armour for launching. Effective range is 2400m.
Employment
The above are used by members of the Warsaw Pact Forces including Albania, Bulgaria, East Germany, Poland and the Soviet Union. They have also been used by Cuba, Egypt and Syria.

Top right: *BTR-40P (BRDM) with no armament fitted*

Right: *BTR-40P (BRDM) Model B with four Swatter ATGWs in the ready to fire position. Note that this model has different hatch covers to the Model A*

BTR-40P (BRDM) Model A with three Snapper ATGWs in the ready to fire position

BA–64 Armoured Car   Soviet Union

Armament: 1×7.62mm DTM machine gun
Crew: 2
Length: 3.44m
Width: 1.74m
Height: 1.90m
G/Clearance: .21m
Weight: 2400kg
Wheelbase: 2.13m
Engine: GAZ-MM, 4 cylinder, water-cooled, in-line, petrol engine developing 54hp at 2800rpm
Speed: 80km/ph (road)
Range: 600km
Fording: .47m

V/Obstacle: .40m
Trench: .45m
Gradient: 60%
Armour: 10mm–15mm

Development/Employment
The BA-64 armoured car was developed during World War II and it is sometimes known as the Bobby. Although it is no longer used by the Russian Army the BA-64 is still used by some satellites including Albania, East Germany and North Korea. The East German SK-1 armoured car is similar in appearance to the BA-64.

BMP–76PB
Mechanised Infantry Combat Vehicle

Soviet Union

Armament: 1×73mm gun, elevation +25°, depression −3°, 30 rounds of ammunition.
1×7.62mm PKT co-axial machine gun
1×Sagger ATGW launcher rail, with 5 missiles (internal)
Crew: 3+8
Length: 6.30m
Width: 3.05m
Height: 1.83m
G/Clearance: .40m
Weight: 12,000kg
Armour: 20mm
Engine: Modified V-6, 6 cylinder diesel, 280hp
Speed: 60km/ph (road)
6km/ph (water)
Range: 500km
Fording: Amphibious
V/Obstacle: 1.10m
Trench: 2.00m
Gradient: 60%

Development

The BMP-76PB was first shown in 1967 and for a few years was called the M-1967 Armoured Personnel Carrier in the absence of any Soviet designation. The vehicle uses some of the components of the PT-76 but basically it is a new vehicle, and could well be the basis for a whole new family of

vehicles. The new M-1970 APC does use many components of the BMP-76PB.

The engine and drive sprocket are at the front of the vehicle and the rear is taken up by the turret and fighting compartment. There are roof hatches and doors at the rear. The vehicle has a number of interesting features including: fully amphibious being propelled in the water by its tracks; the eight infantrymen can fire their small arms through the firing ports provided (although it must be very cramped). It is fitted with infra-red driving and fighting equipment and also has an NBC system.

The 73mm gun has a short recoil and a low pressure. It fires HEAT rounds and its rate of fire is 8rpm. The SAGGER ATGW has a range of about 2500m.

The above data is provisional as there have been some reports that the vehicle weighs as much as 14,500kg.

Variants

There is believed to be a command version of this vehicle. The Polish Army has a number of vehicles fitted with a smaller gun. This could possibly be a 23mm cannon.

Employment

Egypt, Poland, the Soviet Union.

The Soviet BMP-76PB Mechanised Infantry Combat Vehicle

BTR–60PK
Armoured Personnel Carrier

Soviet Union

Armament: 1 × 7.62mm SGMB machine gun with 1250 rounds of ammunition
Crew: 2+14
Length: 7.20m
Width: 2.80m
Height: 2.27m (w/o machine gun)
G/Clearance: .40m
Weight: 10,000kg (loaded)
Armour: 10mm
Engines: 2× GAZ-40P, 6 cylinder, water-cooled, in-line, petrol engines developing 90hp at 3400rpm (each)
Speed: 80km/ph (road)
10km/ph (water)
Range: 500km
Fording: Amphibious
V/Obstacle: .60m
Trench: 2.00m
Gradient: 60%

Development
The BTR-60P was first shown in November 1961. There are three basic models. details of which are given below. The BTR-60 is an 8×8 vehicle, power assisted steering is provided. The vehicle is fully amphibious, being propelled in the water by a single hydrojet at the rear of the vehicle, two smaller jets providing steering. A small trim board is erected before entering the water. The tyre pressures of all eight wheels can be adjusted from a central control to suit current ground conditions. Infra-red driving lights are fitted and later models have infra-red searchlights. Most models are fitted with winches.

Variants
BTR-60P: This was the original open-topped version. Some models have metal hoops over

the troop compartment for supporting a canvas cover. The crew are provided with small half-doors in the sides of the vehicle and there are firing ports. Armament consists of a single 12.7mm machine gun and between 1 and 3 7.62mm machine guns, for example one 7.62mm machine gun next to the 12.7mm machine gun at the front and one 7.62mm machine gun either side of the crew compartment.

BTR-60PK: This version has overhead armour and three firing ports either side. It is often called the BTR-60PA. There are at least three versions of this vehicle, each differing slightly in the arrangement of their roof hatches. Armament normally consists of a single 7.62mm or 12.7mm machine gun mounted just behind the front two hatches. There is believed to be a command version of the BTR-60PK. The BTR-60PK is fitted with an NBC system.

BTR-60PB: This is a BTR-60PK fitted with a small machine-gun turret mounting a 14.5mm and a 7.62mm machine gun. This turret has a traverse of 360°, and elevation is +30° and depression −10°. The same turret is fitted to the BTR-40P-2 (BRDM).

Employment
Used by Bulgaria, Cuba, East Germany, Egypt, Iran, Libya, Mongolia, Poland, Rumania, Soviet Union (Army and Marines), Syria, Yugoslavia.

Above: *BTR-60PBs during a parade in Moscow*

BTR–50PK
Armoured Personnel Carrier

Soviet Union

Armament: 1×7.62mm SGMB machine gun with 1250 rounds of ammunition
Crew: 2+20
Length: 6.91m
Width: 3.18m
Height: 1.97m (w/o machine gun)
G/Clearance: .40m
Weight: 14,500kg (loaded)
G/Pressure: .52kg.cm^2
Engine: Model V-6, 6 cylinder, in-line, water-cooled diesel developing 240hp at 1800rpm
Speed: 44km/ph (road)
10km/ph (water)
Range: 280km
Fording: Amphibious
V/Obstacle: 1.10m
Trench: 2.80m
Gradient: 70%
Armour: 10mm

Development
The BTR-50 was developed from the chassis of the PT-76 light amphibious tank. The vehicle was first seen in 1957. The BTR-50 series are fully amphibious being propelled in the water by two water jets at the rear of the vehicle. Later models of the vehicle are fitted with NBC equipment and infra-red lights. The Czechoslovakian version is called the OT-62, for details of this model refer to the Czechoslovakian section.
Variants
BTR-50P: This was the first model to enter

service and it has an open top. 57mm, 76mm and 85mm anti-tank guns can be carried.
BTR-50PK: This model has overhead protection and is provided with rectangular roof hatches. It has a projecting bay on the left. It has an improved vision device on the right front, and is often fitted with infra-red driving equipment and an infra-red searchlight. One radio aerial is fitted. A new model fitted with the turret of the Czech OT-64 Model 4 has recently been observed.
BTR-50PU Armoured Command Vehicle: This model has overhead protection. There are two models. Model 1 has a projecting bay on the left, Model 2 has two projecting bays. Both Model 1 and Model 2 have a hatch on the left bay, a central rotating cupola just behind the driver, two dome ventilators and two oval-shaped hatches on the roof. There are normally five radio aerials on the roof. On the Model 2 the right bay has no hatch cover and no infra-red searchlight. The Model 1 has an infra-red searchlight to the right of the driver. Both models have additional stowage boxes on the rear deck.
Employment
Used by Albania, Bulgaria, China, Czechoslovakia, East Germany, Egypt, Finland, Hungary, India, Iran, North Vietnam, Poland, Rumania, Somalia, Soviet Union, Syria Yugoslavia.

The BTR-50PK Armoured Personnel Carrier

BTR–152V1
Armoured Personnel Carrier

Soviet Union

Armament: 1 × 7.62mm SGMB machine gun with 1250 rounds (or 12.7mm)
Crew: 2+17
Length: 6.83m
Width: 2.32m
Height: 2.05m (w/o machine gun)
G/Clearance: .295m
Weight: 8950kg (loaded)
Engine: ZIL-123, 6 cylinder, in-line, petrol engine developing 110hp at 2900rpm
Speed: 75km/ph (road)
Range: 650km
Fording: .80m
V/Obstacle: .60m
Trench: .69m
Gradient: 55%
Armour: 8mm–12mm

Development/Variants
BTR-152: The first BTR-152 6×6 vehicle appeared in 1950 and was based on the ZIL-151 truck chassis. This was fitted with large single tyres and a more powerful engine. Later models of the BTR-152 used the ZIL-157 chassis. The BTR-152 can be used as an APC, load carrier, 82mm and 120mm mortar carriers, towing vehicles for heavy 160mm mortars or anti-tank guns. A more recent model has been reported with ATGW.
BTR-152V: This is based on the ZIL-157 chassis, fitted with a system enabling the tyre pressures to be regulated to suit the ground conditions. Variants of the BTR-152V are:
BTR-152V1: External air-lines and a winch. Also known as Model B.
BTR-152V2: Internal air-lines, no winch (from BTR-152). Model C.

BTR-152V3: Internal air-lines, winch, infrared driving lights. Model C.
BTR-152K: This is a BTR-152V3 with overhead armour. This increases the height of the vehicle and its loaded weight is 9200kg. There are probably earlier models of this vehicle in service, ie BTR-152V1s that have been fitted with overhead armour. The BTR-152V3 is also known as the Model D, Model 4 or Model 1961.
BTR-152U: This is a BTR-152 converted into the command role. The roof is higher (2.72m) and additional radios have been installed. Loaded weight is 9200kg, armament is not normally fitted.
BTR-152V with twin 14.5mm guns: This is a BTR-152V fitted with twin 14.5mm machine guns in a powered pount with an elevation of +80° and a depression of −5°, traverse is 360°. The machine guns are KPVs and have an effective AA range of 1400m. The vehicle weighs 9600kg, height is 2.80m and it has a crew of four.
Employment
Albania, Algeria, Bulgaria, Cambodia, China (built in China as the Type 56), Congo, Cuba, Czechoslovakia, East Germany, Egypt, Guinea, Hungary, India, Indonesia, Iran, Israel, Mongolia, North Korea, North Yemen, Palestine Liberation Army, Poland, Rumania, Somalia, Soviet Union, Sudan, Syria, Tanzania, Uganda, Yugoslavia.

Above: *BTR-152V armed with twin 14.5mm machine guns and used in the Anti-Aircraft role*

109

BTR–40 Armoured Personnel Carrier   Soviet Union

Armament: 1×7.62mm SGMB machine gun
with 1250 rounds of ammunition
Crew: 2+8
Length: 5.00m
Width: 1.90m
Height: 1.75m (w/o machine gun)
G/Clearance: .275m
Weight: 5300kg (loaded)
Wheelbase: 2.70m
Engine: GAZ-40, 6 cylinder, in-line, water-
cooled petrol engine developing 80hp at
3400rpm
Speed: 80km/ph (road)
Range: 650km (road)
Fording: .80m
V/Obstacle: .47m
Trench: .70m
Gradient: 58%
Armour: 8mm–13mm

Development
The BTR-40 was developed after the end of
World War II and entered production in 1951.
It is basically a shortened GAZ-63A 4×4
chassis with an armoured body. It is fitted
with a winch. It is still in use in small numbers
by the Soviet Army, its replacement being the
BTR-40P (BRDM) vehicle. The BTR-40 is
used as an APC and as a command and
reconnaissance vehicle.
Variants
BTR-40: This is the basic vehicle and has no
roof; it is often known as the Model A. The
data above relates to this version. The crew

can fire their personal weapons through the
firing ports in the sides and rear of the vehicle.
It has side and rear doors.
BTR-40K: This model has overhead armour.
This consists of two sets of hinged doors and
in some vehicles these overhead doors have
been provided with firing ports. The BTR-40K
is also known as the Model B and is fitted
with tyre pressure regulation system. Weight
is 5700kg.
**BTR-40 with twin 14.5mm heavy machine
guns:** This is the basic BTR-40 fitted with
twin 14.5mm KPV heavy machine guns in a
power operated mount with a traverse of 360°,
elevation between −5° and +80°. The guns
have an effective AA range of 1400m and can
also be used against ground targets. The
vehicle weighs 6000kg, has a crew of four,
and a height of 2.50m
BTR-40kh: This mode is fitted with equipment enabling it to dispense marking pennants
in nuclear contaminated areas.
Employment
Used by Albania, Bulgaria, Czechoslovakia,
China (also built there as the Type 55 APC),
Cuba, East Germany, Egypt, Guinea, Hungary,
Iran, Laos (Pathet Lao), Mali, North Korea,
North Vietnam, North Yemen, Poland,
Somalia, Soviet Union, Sudan, Syria, Tanzania,
Uganda, Yugoslavia and rebels in Mozambique
and the Middle East.

Above: *BTR-40K Armoured Personnel Carrier*

M–1970
Multi-Purpose Tracked Vehicle

Soviet Union

Armament: 1 × 7.62mm machine gun
Crew: 3 + 10
Length: 6.35m
Width: 2.80m
Height: 2.25m
G/Clearance: .35m
Weight: 10,000kg
Engine: Modified V-6, 6 cylinder, in-line, diesel, 280hp
Speed: 55km/ph (road)
5km/ph (water)
Range: 400km
Fording: Amphibious
V/Obstacle: 1.10m
Trench: 2.00m
Gradient: 60%

Development/Variants
The M-1970 Multi-Purpose Tracked Vehicle was first seen in 1970 and entered troop service in 1971/1972. The above data is provisional information.

The vehicle is believed to be based on the BMP-76PB, the requirement being for a much cheaper vehicle than the BMP-76PB. The M-1970 is used for a wide range of roles including towing anti-tank guns, towing mortars and field artillery, armoured personnel carrier, command vehicle, artillery fire control vehicle and cargo carrier.
The driver is on the left side of the vehicle and on the right side is a cupola mounted 7.62mm machine gun. There are twin doors at the rear of the vehicle and these are provided with firing ports; in addition there are hatches in the roof of the vehicle. The vehicle is amphibious and is believed to be propelled in the water by its tracks.
Employment
Used by the Soviet Union.

The M-1970 Multi-Purpose Tracked Vehicle

ISU–122 and ISU–152 Assault Guns   Soviet Union

Armament: 1 × 122mm M1931/44(A-19S) gun, elevation +19°, depression −4°, total traverse 11°. 30 rounds of 122mm ammunition 1 × 12.7mm M1938 DShK anti-aircraft machine gun
Crew: 5
Length: 9.80m (including gun)
6.80m (excluding gun)
Width: 3.12m
Height: 2.50m (w/o A/A machine gun)
G/Clearance: .46m
Weight: 46,000kg (loaded)
G/Pressure: .78kg.cm²

Engine: Model V-2 IS, V-12 diesel, water-cooled, developing 520hp at 2000rpm
Speed: 37km/ph (road)
Range: 250km (road)
Fuel: 500 litres
Fording: 1.30m
V/Obstacle: 1.00m
Trench: 2.50m
Gradient: 60%
Armour: 30mm–200mm

Note. *The data above relates to the ISU-122 with 122mm gun A-19S.*

Development/Variants

ISU-122: This was developed in 1943/1944 and was based on a modified IS-11 chassis. The first models were fitted with the D-25S (M1944) gun but later vehicles were armed with the A-19S (M1931/44) gun. The D-25S gun had the higher rate of fire, six rounds a minute, as it had a wedge type breach block. The A-19S has a screw type breech block. The D-25S gun has an elevation of +16° and a depression of −3°, total traverse is 14°. The ISU-122 (D-25S) and the ISU-122 (A-19S) can be distinguished as the D-25S has a double baffle muzzle brake and a thinner barrel, the A-19S has no muzzle brake, a projecting gun tube and a thicker barrel.

ISU-152: This has a similar hull to the ISU-122. It is armed with a 152mm assault gun M1937/44 (ML-20S) which has an elevation of +20°, a depression of −3°, total traverse being 10°. Only 20 rounds of 152mm ammunition are carried. The gun is shorter than those fitted to the ISU-122, total length including gun being 9.01m.

Recovery Vehicles based on ISU chassis
There are five basic models, and all have their guns removed and plated over.

Model A: This is used for the towing role and weighs 41,500kg.

Model B: This is similar to Model A but has a cargo platform and a jib crane. Some models have a spade at the rear and are fitted with a schnorkel for deep wading. Loaded weight is 44,000kg and height 3.00m.

Model C: This is similar to Model B but has a spade. Weight 45,000kg, length 7.825m.

Model D: This is similar to Model C and is capable of being fitted with a schnorkel. There are two bars at the front of the vehicle for pushing damaged tanks. Weight 45,500kg, length 8.325m.

Model E: This is a modified Model C. It has an 'A' frame and a jib crane, loaded weight is 45,500kg. Jordan has a few of these.

Employment

Used by Warsaw Pact Forces including:

ISU-122: Algeria, Bulgaria, China, Czechoslovakia, North Vietnam, Poland, Rumania.

ISU-152: Algeria, China, Czechoslovakia, Egypt, Finland, Poland, Syria.

ARVs: These are used by most Warsaw Pact Forces and countries that have received Soviet aid.

ISU-152 Assault Gun

SU–100 Assault Gun   Soviet Union

Armament: 1×100mm M-1944 (D-10S) gun, elevation +17°. depression −2° (post-war SU-100s have a depression of −4°), traverse 17° (total)
34 rounds of 100mm ammunition are carried
Crew: 4
Length: 9.96m (including gun)
6.22m (excluding gun)
Width: 3.00m
Height: 2.45m
G/Clearance: .35m
Weight: 31,611kg (loaded)
G/Pressure: .82kg.cm²

Engine: V-2-34M, 12 cylinder diesel, developing 500hp at 1800rpm OR
V-2-3411, 12 cylinder diesel, developing 520hp at 2100rpm
Speed: 55km/ph (road)
Range: 320km
Fuel: 614 litres*
Fording: .89m
V/Obstacle: .685m
Trench: 2.51m
Gradient: 60%
Armour: 20mm–110mm
* *Including four external tanks.*

Development/Variants

The SU-100 was developed from the earlier SU-85. The SU-100 is recognisable from the SU-85 as the latter has a shorter 85mm gun and no commander's cupola on the right of the superstructure. Another wartime vehicle was the SU-122, none of which remain in service. Most SU-85s were converted into SU-100s or ARVs, or used for training.

The 100mm gun of the SU-100 is the same as that fitted to the T-54 MBT and fires the same ammunition as a number of Soviet field and anti-aircraft guns. Many postwar SU-100s have been fitted with an additional stowage box on the right side of the superstructure.

The SU-85 recovery vehicle is designated SU-85-T and is simply a SU-85 with the gun removed and plated over. The SU-100 recovery vehicle is similar to the SU-85-T and is designated SU-100-T. The SU-85-T is the more common of the two models, both models may be seen with or without winches fitted. There is also a command model of the SU-100. This is similar to the SU-100-T.

There is also a SU-85 with the gun removed and plated over and a hydraulically operated dozer blade mounted on the front.

Employment

Used by Albania, Algeria, Bulgaria, Communist China, Cuba, Czechoslovakia, East Germany, Egypt, Mongolia, Morocco, North Korea, North Yemen, Rumania, Soviet Union, Syria Yugoslavia.

SU-100 Assault Gun captured by French forces in Egypt in 1956

ASU–85 Self-Propelled Anti-Tank Gun   Soviet Union

Armament: 1×85mm gun, elevation +15°, depression −4°, total traverse 12°. 40 rounds of ammunition
1×7.62mm PKT machine gun, co-axial with 85mm gun
Crew: 4
Length: 8.54m (including gun)
6.10m (excluding gun)
Width: 2.80m
Height: 2.10m
G/Clearance: .40m
Weight: 15,000kg (loaded)
G/Pressure: .48kg.cm²
Engine: Model V-6, 6 cylinder, in-line, diesel, developing 240hp at 1800rpm
Speed: 44km/ph (road)
Range: 260km (road)
Fuel: 250 litres
Fording: 1.10m
V/Obstacle: 1.10m
Trench: 2.80m
Gradient: 70%
Armour: 10mm–40mm

Development
The ASU-85 was first shown in May 1962, and uses many components of the PT-76 tank. The ASU-85 is not amphibious. The primary role of the vehicle is anti-tank and it is used by the airborne regiments. Each Soviet airborne regiment has a battery of ASU-85s. This battery has three platoons each with three ASU-85s.
The barrel of the 85mm gun has a fume extractor fitted two-thirds of the way along the barrel, and it is also fitted with a double baffle muzzle brake. This gun fires HE, APHE and HVAP rounds, and its rate of fire is about 3–4 rounds per minute.
The ASU-85 is fitted with infra-red driving and fighting equipment, and recent reports indicate that it may be fitted with more advanced aids for night fighting.
Employment
Used by members of the Warsaw Pact including the Soviet Union, East Germany and Poland.

ASU-85

SU–76 Self-Propelled Gun   Soviet Union

Armament: 1×76.2mm M1942/43 gun, elevation +20°, depression −5° traverse 20° left and 12° right
60 rounds of 76.2mm ammunition carried
1×7.62mm Degtyarev machine gun
Crew: 4
Length: 4.88m
Width: 2.73m
Height: 2.17m
G/Clearance: .32m
Weight: 11,176kg (loaded)
G/Pressure: .57kg.cm²

Armour: 10mm–25mm
Engines: 2×GAZ-202, 6 cylinder, in-line, water-cooled petrol engines developing 70hp at 3400rpm (each)
Speed: 45km/ph (road)
Range: 450km (road)
Fuel: 447 litres
Fording: .89m
V/Obstacle: .66m
Trench: 1.98m
Gradient: 47%

Development/Variants

The SU-76 was developed during World War II as a tank destroyer and was based on a lengthened T-70 light tank chassis. The SU-76 was however quickly relegated to the infantry support role as its armour was very thin and the better SU-85 was entering service.

There were a number of slightly different versions of the SU-76: model with the gun in the centre of the vehicle; model with the gun to the left (data above relates to this model). This model could also be seen with a slightly different armour arrangement at the rear, and a model with a fully enclosed turret. Some SU-76s were fitted with two GAZ-203 engines of 85hp, these being designated SU-76M. An anti-aircraft version was designated the SU-37. It is now obsolete. The East Germans have modified a number of SU-76s into armoured workshop and recovery vehicles. These modifications include the fitting of a new EM-6 six cylinder diesel developing 120hp at 2000rpm. armament deleted, external stowage boxes added and internal equipment including a lathe, forge and welding equipment.

Employment

Used by Albania, Communist China, East Germany, North Korea, North Vietnam, Yugoslavia.

SU-76 on display at Aberdeen proving ground, Maryland, USA

ASU–57 Self-Propelled Anti-Tank Gun   Soviet Union

Armament: 1 × 57mm gun, elevation +12°, depression −5°, total traverse 16° (lightweight model)

1 × 57mm gun, elevation +15°, depression −4°, total traverse 12° (standard model)

Both carry a 7.62mm machine gun and about 40 rounds of 57mm ammunition

Crew: 3–5

Length: 6.10m (5.79m) (including gun) 3.73m (3.48m) (excluding gun)

Width: 2.21m (2.086m)

Height: 1.46m (cover up)

1.18m (shield down)

G/Clearance: .30m

Weight: 5400kg (3350)kg (loaded)

G/Pressure: .35kg.cm² (lightweight)

Engine: *Standard* – ZIL-123, 6 cylinder, water-cooled, in-line, petrol engine developing 110hp at 2900rpm

Lightweight – M-20E, 4 cylinder water-

Note. *The data in brackets relates to the light-weight version.*

cooled, in-line, petrol engine developing 55hp at 3600rpm
Speed: 64 (45)km/ph (road)
Range: 320 (250) km
Fording: .70m
V/Obstacle: .50m
Trench: 1.40m
Gradient: 60%
Armour: 6mm

Development/Variants
The ASU-57 was first shown during the May Day Parade in 1957. It is designed for use by the airborne forces and is therefore readily transportable by aircraft and helicopter. It can be air-dropped. The top side and front armour folds down for transport.
There are two basic models of the ASU-57. One is made of standard metal materials and the other is slightly smaller; extensive use of aluminium is made in the latter version.

There are two types of gun used on the ASU-57. Model A has a long thin multi-slotted muzzle brake and uses the Ch-51 gun. Model B has a double baffle muzzle brake and has the Ch-51M gun. The gun fires HE, APHE and HVAP rounds, maximum rate of fire is 6–10rpm.
If required the ASU-57 can carry three infantrymen. The ASU-57 is developed at battalion level, whilst the ASU-85 is at regimental level.
Employment
The ASU-57 is used by members of the Warsaw Pact Forces including East Germany, Poland and the Soviet Union. It is also used by Yugoslavia.

ASU-57s moving at speed

ZSU–23–4   Soviet Union
Self-Propelled Anti-Aircraft Gun System

Armament: 4×23mm automatic cannons, elevation +80°, depression −7°, traverse 360° 1000 rounds of 23mm ammunition carried
Crew: 4
Length: 6.30m
Width: 2.95m
Height: 2.25m (w/o radar)
G/Clearance: .40m
Weight: 14,000kg (loaded)
G/Pressure: .48kg.cm²

Engine: V-6, 6 cylinder, in-line, water-cooled diesel developing 240hp at 1800rpm
Speed: 44km/ph (road)
Range: 260km
Fording: 1.07m
V/Obstacle: 1.10m
Trench: 2.80m
Gradient: 70%
Armour: 10mm-15mm

Development/Variants

The ZSU-23-4 anti-aircraft gun system was first seen by the public at the parade held in Moscow on 7th November 1965. The vehicle incorporates many components of the PT-76 tank.

When travelling the large radar scanner folds down behind the rear of the turret. The radar provides the necessary information to fire the guns, and the high rate of fire make this an effective weapon.

Each gun has a cyclic rate of fire of 800 to 1000 rounds per minute, per barrel, although the normal figure is 200 rounds per minute, per barrel. The guns can fire either HEI or API rounds. In the anti-aircraft role the guns have an effective slant range of 2000m. They can also be used against ground targets and would be effective against armoured personnel carriers and soft-skinned vehicles. The ZSU-23-4 is also known as the SHILKA.

A similar chassis to that of the ZSU-23-4 is used for the GAINFUL (NATO designation) anti-aircraft missile carrier. This carries a total of three missiles. The GAINFUL is also known as the SA-6 or SAM-6.

Employment

Warsaw Pact Forces including East Germany, Poland and the Soviet Union. Other countries that use the system include Egypt, North Vietnam and Syria; it is on order for Iran.

ZSU-23-4 with its radar up

ZSU–57–2
Self-Propelled Anti-Aircraft Gun

Soviet Union

Armament: 2×57mm anti-aircraft guns
Crew: 6
Length: 8.53m (including guns)
6.22m (excluding guns)
Width: 3.27m
Height: 2.75m
G/Clearance: .425m
Weight: 28,100kg (loaded)
G/Pressure: .63kg.cm^2
Engine: Model V-54, V-12, water-cooled diesel, developing 520hp at 2000rpm
Speed: 48km/ph (road)
Range: 400km (road)
Fording: 1.40m
V/Obstacle: .80m
Trench: 2.70m
Gradient: 60%
Armour: 20mm–100mm

The guns can be used against both air and ground targets, against aircraft the practical range is 4000m. An optical fire control system is fitted, although there have been reports that there is a radar equipped model in service. The vehicle is fitted with infra-red driving equipment and has no capacity for deep wading.
Employment
Used by Bulgaria, Czechoslovakia, East Germany, Egypt, Finland, Hungary, Iran, North Korea, North Vietnam, Poland, Rumania, Soviet Union, Syria, Yugoslavia.

Development/Variants
The ZSU-57-2 first appeared in 1957. It consists of a shortened and modified T-54 tank chassis with four road wheels, and is fitted with a turret mounting twin S-68 anti-aircraft guns. The turret has a traverse of 360° and the guns can be elevated from −5° to +85°. The guns are traversed and elevated hydraulically, with hand controls for use in an emergency.
A total of 316 rounds of ammunition are carried of which 264 rounds are ready for immediate use, the ammunition is in clips of four rounds. The empty cartridge cases are ejected into the wire cage on the rear of the turret. The ammunition used is both HE and AP, and are the same rounds as used in the 57mm S-60 anti-aircraft gun. The guns have a maximum rate of fire of 105/120rpm per barrel (cyclic), but practical rate of fire is 70rpm per barrel.

Right: ZSU-57-2 of the Finnish Army

Below right: The SA-6 (SAM-6) Gainful Surface-to-Air Missile on its mobile tracked launcher, this is based on PT-76 components. This system was widely employed by Syrian and Egyptian Forces during the Middle East War of 1973

Below: The SA-4 (SAM-4) Ganef Surface-to-Air Missile on its mobile tracked launcher. The new Soviet Armoured Tracked Minelayer is believed to use a similar chassis to that used for the SA-4

12

AT–P Armoured Tracked Artillery Tractor   Soviet Union

Armament: 1 × 7.62mm SGMT machine gun
Crew: 3 + 6
Length: 4.054m
Width: 2.335m
Height: 1.707m
G/Clearance: .30m
Weight: 6300kg (loaded)
G/Pressure: .56kg.cm²
Engine: ZIL-123 6 cylinder, in-line, water-cooled petrol engine developing 110hp at 2900rpm
Speed: 60km/ph
Range: 300km
Fording: .90m
V/Obstacle: .60m
Trench: 1.22m
Gradient: 60%
Armour: 12mm (maximum)

Development/Variants

The AT-P's primary role is one of towing artillery including 85mm and 100mm anti-tank guns, 122mm Howitzer D-30 and anti-aircraft guns. The crew of three consists of a commander, driver and a gunner for the machine gun which is on the right of the front superstructure. The rest of the men are in the rear of the vehicle. The vehicle can also be used as a personnel carrier or cargo carrier.

Early models of the vehicle have the rear compartment with no overhead protection, although a canvas cover could be erected in bad weather. Later models have overhead armour protection and a rear compartment that is the full width of the vehicle. Some of these later models have firing/vision ports in the rear doors. It has been reported that some vehicles have had the limited traverse machine gun replaced by a small cupola with all round traverse.

There is a command model called AT-P (Command). This model has overhead protection and a higher cupola for the commander. It is also fitted with fender stowage boxes and the exhaust pipe has been moved from the side to the top of the vehicle.

Employment

Used only by members of the Warsaw Pact Forces.

The AT-P Artillery Tractor

The Vickers ABBOT
105mm Self-Propelled
Gun   /Vickers Limited

Above: *Panhard M-3 with 20mm Turret
/Panhard*

Below: *French Panhard AML Armoured Car
with a turret mounting SS-11 Anti-Tank
Missiles /Panhard and Levassor*

Above: *The new Scorpion, Combat Vehicle Reconnaissance (tracked)* /Alvis Limited

Below: *The Vickers ABBOT 105mm Self-Propelled Gun* /Vickers Limited

ENTP PZ 65 Armoured Recovery Vehicle
of the Swiss Army

Above: *The Type 60 Armoured Personnel Carrier of the Japanese Self-Defence Force /Japanese Self-Defence Force*

Below: *A V-150 Commando being put through its paces /Cadillac Gage Company*

Above: *The Jagdpanzer Kanone (JPZ 4-5) of the German Army* /*Rheinstahl*

Below: *The UR-416 Armoured Personnel Carrier* /*Rheinstahl*

A V-150 Commando climbing a steep gradient /Cadillac Gage Company

Stridsvagn 103B Main Battle Tank　　Sweden

Armament: 1×105mm automatic gun with 50 rounds
1×7.62mm machine gun on commander's cupola
2×7.62mm machine guns on left hull front
2750 rounds of 7.62mm ammunition are carried
2×4 barrelled smoke dischargers and 24 smoke grenades
Crew: 3
Length: 9.80m (including gun)
8.40m (excluding gun)
Width: 3.60m
Height: 2.50m (including machine gun)
2.14m (commander's cupola)
G/Clearance: .50m (maximum)
Weight: 39,000kg (loaded)
Engines: One Rolls-Royce K.60 multi-fuel engine developing 240hp at 3650rpm. One Boeing 553 turbine developing 490shp at 38,000rpm
Speed: 50km/ph (road)
Range: 390km
Fuel: 960 litres
Fording: 1.50m
V/Obstacle: .90m
Trench: 2.30m
Gradient: 60%
G/Pressure: .90kg.cm²

Development
The STRV.103 (known as the 'S' tank), was first proposed in 1956; feasibility trials were carried out using a Sherman and Ikv.103 chassis. In mid-1958 a contract was awarded to the Bofors company to develop the tank while Volvo developed the power-pack and Landsverk the running gear.

The prototype was completed in 1960. This had no return rollers. After extensive trials a production order was given to Bofors and the first production tank was completed in 1966. The first vehicles built were called the Strv 103A and did not have a flotation screen, other differences included a less powerful turbine. Later models were the Strv 103B. These have the more powerful engine and are fitted with a flotation screen. All Strv 103As have been rebuilt to Strv 103B standards.

The gun is fixed, and aimed in elevation by lowering and raising the road wheels, as the tank has hydro-pneumatic suspension. This gives the gun an elevation of +12° and a depression of −10°. The 105mm gun, which is 11 calibres longer than the British 105mm L7A1 gun, is automatically loaded and can fire APDS, HE or smoke rounds, rate of fire is 10–15 rounds per minute.

Prototypes had a ranging machine gun but this was discarded and it now has an optical rangefinder. A laser rangefinder is however under development.

The tank has a flotation screen permanently mounted under armour. When raised it enables the vehicle to swim at 6km/ph with the aid of its tracks. A bulldozer blade is fitted at the front.

Variants
There are no variants of the Strv 103B although components of the tank are incorporated in the 155mm SPG and the now defunct VEAK 2×40mm anti-aircraft gun system.

Strv 103B, note the dozer blade under the hull front, the flotation screen around the hull, and the infra-red driving lights

Ikv 91 Light Tank/Infantry Support Vehicle   Sweden

Armament: 1×90mm Bofors gun, elevation +15°, depression −10°
1×7.62mm machine gun, co-axial with main armament
1×7.62mm anti-aircraft machine gun on loader's cupola
2×6 barrelled smoke dischargers at rear of turret
59 rounds of 90mm ammunition
4500 rounds of 7.62mm ammunition
Crew: 4
Length: 8.83m (including gun)
6.41m (hull only)
Width: 3.00m
Height: 2.36m (overall)
G/Clearance: .40m
Weight: 15,500kg (loaded)
G/Pressure: .45kg.cm²
Engine: Volvo TD 120, 6 cylinder, turbo-charged diesel developing 295bhp at 2200rpm
Speed: 69km/ph (road)
7 km/ph (water)
Range: 550km (road)
Fuel: 405 litres
Fording: Amphibious
V/Obstacle: .80m
Trench: 2.80m
Gradient: 60%

Development/Variants
The contract to develop the IKV 91 (Infanterik-anonvagn 91) was awarded to Hägglund and Söner in April 1968. The first of three prototypes was completed and assigned to manufacturer's tests in December 1969, and was delivered to the Army in January 1971. The other two prototypes were completed in 1970. After extensive trials a production order was awarded to Hägglund and Söner in March 1972, with production of the vehicle commencing in 1974. The vehicle will replace the Strv 74, Ikv 102 and Ikv 103 vehicles in the Swedish Infantry Brigades and Norrland Brigades.

The vehicle is fully amphibious being propelled in the water by its tracks. A trim vane is erected at the front of the vehicle before entering the water. The hull is of welded construction and the sides of the hull are of the double-plate type. The vehicle is fitted with an NBC system. The vehicle has a speed of 69km/ph at 2200rpm and a maximum speed of 71km/ph at 2450rpm.

The 90mm Bofors low-pressure gun fires fin stabilised HE and HEAT (m/v 825 m/s) rounds, the turret has electro-hydraulic traverse and elevation. The gun is not stabilised in traverse or elevation although provision has been made for this to be installed. Comprehensive sighting and vision equipment which includes a laser rangefinder and a computer is fitted.

Employment
In production for the Swedish Army.

The Ikv 91 Light Tank Infantry/Support Vehicle, note the smoke dischargers on the rear of the turret and the 7.62mm machine gun on the loader's cupola

Stridsvagn 74H and 74V Light Tank   Sweden

Armament: 1×75mm gun, elevation +15°, depression −15°
1×7.62mm machine gun, co-axial with main armament
1×7.62mm anti-aircraft machine gun on commander's cupola
2×6 barrelled smoke dischargers
Strv 74H has 45 rounds of 75mm ammunition and the Strv 74V has 40 rounds of 75mm ammunition
Crew: 4
Length: 7.93m (gun forward)
6.08m (hull only)
Width: 2.43m
Height: 3.30m (including machine gun)
3.00m (commander's cupola)
G/Clearance: .40m
Weight: 26,200kg (loaded)
G/Pressure: .80kg.cm²
Engines: Two Scania-Vabis Type 607 petrol engines developing 170hp at 2300rpm (each)
Speed: 45km/ph (road)
Range: 125km
Fuel: 350 litres
Fording: 1.00m
V/Obstacle: .86m
Trench: 2.40m
Gradient: 60%
Armour: 40mm

Development/Variants
The Stridsvagn 74 is a rebuild of the older m/42 vehicle. They were rebuilt between 1956 amd 1958. These modifications included a new turret mounting a 75mm gun with a

sighting system similar to that fitted to the Centurion tank; the turret is balanced by the large bulge on the rear. This contains the auxiliary Volkswagen engine. The turrets were built by Landsverk and Hägglunds and Söner. The Strv 74H and Strv 74V differ in the amount of ammunition that they carry and that the Strv 74H has an hydraulic gearbox and the Strv 74V has a manual gearbox. There are no other variants of the tank in service.
Employment
In service with the Swedish Army, to be replaced from 1974 by the IKV 91.

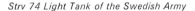

Strv 74 Light Tank of the Swedish Army

Pbv 302 Armoured Personnel Carrier   Sweden

Armament: 1×20mm cannon, elevation +50°, depression −10°
2×5 smoke grenade launchers
505 rounds of 20mm ammunition
Crew: 2+10
Length: 5.35m
Width: 2.86m
Height: 2.50m (including turret)
2.06m (without turret)
G/Clearance: .40m
Weight: 13,500kg (loaded)
G/Pressure: .60kg.cm²
Engine: Volvo THD 100B, 6 cylinder, in-line, turbo-charged diesel developing 280hp at 2200rpm
Speed: 66km/ph (road)
8km/ph (water)
Range: 300km (road)
Fuel: 285 litres
Fording: Amphibious
V/Obstacle: .61m
Trench: 1.80m
Gradient: 60%

Development

In October 1961 a contract was awarded to AB Hägglund and Söner to develop the Pbv 302 (Pansarbandvagn 302). The first two prototypes were completed in January 1963. After extensive trials a production order was awarded to Hägglund and Söner and the first production vehicle was completed in February 1966. Production of the vehicle was completed in December 1971. Components of the Pbv 302 are used in the Ikv 91, Bgbv 82 and Brobv 941.

The hull is of welded construction and the vehicle is not fitted with an NBC system. The Pbv 302 is fully amphibious being propelled in the water by its tracks. Before entering the water the bilge pumps are switched on and the trim vane erected at the front of the vehicle. The driver, commander and gunner are provided with separate hatches. The crew are provided with two large doors at the rear of the vehicle in addition to roof hatches; the latter are hydraulically operated and allow the crew to fire their weapons. The gun can be used against both ground and air targets.

Variants

The basic vehicle can be used as an ambulance (carrying 4–8 stretchers), load carrier or armoured recovery vehicle (fitted with a winch in the rear compartment). Other variants are:

Stripbv 3021: Armoured Command Vehicle, has four radios, map boards, tables.

Epbv 3022: Armoured Observation Post Vehicle. This has a driver, gunner, fire control officer and operators. The commander's hatch has been replaced with a large cupola fitted with a combined binocular and rangefinder.

Bplpbv 3023: Armoured Fire Direction Post Vehicle. Battery commanders vehicle, has additional radios and fire direction computer.

Product Improved Pbv 302

This the basic vehicle modified with the following:
(a) 25mm Oerlikon cannon replacing the 20mm cannon.
(b) Fitting an automatic Allison HT 740 gearbox (trials have taken place with this modification).
(c) Fitting the hydrostatic steering system that has been fitted to the Bgbv 82 and Brobv 941 vehicles.
(d) Fitting the later Volvo THD 100C engine developing 310hp.
(e) Sloping the sides of the vehicle and fitting firing ports and vision blocks so that the crew can aim and fire their weapons from within the vehicle. About eight men would be carried instead of ten.

Employment

In service only with the Swedish Army.

The Pbv 302 Armoured Personnel Carrier

155mm Bandkanon 1A Self-Propelled Gun   Sweden

Armament: 1×155mm fully automatic gun L/50 with one magazine of 14 rounds. Elevation from −3° to +40°, traverse 15° left and 15° right
1×7.62mm anti-aircraft machine gun
Crew: 5
Length: 11.00m (including gun)
6.55m (excluding gun)
Width: 3.37m
Height: 3.85m (including machine gun)
3.35m (w/o machine gun)
G/Clearance: .42m (maximum)
Weight: 53,000kg (loaded)
G/Pressure: .85kg.cm²
Engines: One Rolls-Royce K.60 multi-fuel engine developing 240hp at 3750rpm. One Boeing 502/10MA gas turbine developing 300shp at 38,000rpm
Speed: 28km/ph (road)
Range: 230km (road)
Fuel: 1445litres
Fording: 1.00m
V/Obstacle: .95m
Trench: 2.00m
Gradient: 60%
Armour: 10mm–20mm

Development/Variants
The prototype of this vehicle was built in 1960. This differed from the production vehicles in a number of ways, the most noticeable being that it had three return rollers. The first production vehicle was completed in 1966 and production has now been completed. Production was undertaken by Bofors in association with Volvo and Landsverk.
The vehicle incorporates components of the 'S' tank including the power pack, steering system and hydro-pneumatic suspension.
The gun is fully automatic and has a maximum range of 25,600m and is capable of firing 14 rounds a minute. The magazine holds 14 rounds in two layers of seven. When the ammunition is expended a lorry is brought up with a new magazine. It takes only two minutes to load a new magazine.
The weapon is not fitted with a spade at the rear as its suspension can be locked out when firing, thus providing a very stable firing platform. No variants have been announced, although when the vehicle was first introduced into service it did not have an anti-aircraft machine gun.
Employment
Used only by the Swedish Army.

Above: 155mm Bandkanon 1A with gun elevated to fire

Bgbv 82 Armoured Recovery Vehicle   Sweden

Armament: 1×20mm cannon, elevation +50°, depression −10°
8 smoke dischargers mounted either side of turret
Crew: 4
Length: 7.23m
Width: 3.25m
Height: 2.63m (including spades)
2.45m (including turret)
G/Clearance: .40m
Weight: 26,500kg (loaded)
G/Pressure: .82kg.cm²
Engine: Volvo THD 100C, 6 cylinder, in-line, diesel, turbo-charged developing 310hp at 2200rpm
Speed: 56km/ph (road)
8km/ph (water)
Range: 400km (cruising)
Fuel: 550 litres
Fording: Amphibious
V/Obstacle: .60m
Trench: 2.50m
Gradient: 60%

Development/Variants

The Bgbv 82 (Bärgningsbandvagn 82) has been developed and produced by Hägglund and Söner. The prototype was built in 1968 and a total of 24 were built between April and December 1973. The vehicle has a similar chassis to that of the Brobv 941 Bridgelaying Vehicle. The later Ikv 91 uses components of these two vehicles.

The vehicle can be used as a recovery vehicle, towing vehicle (for example it can tow a disabled S tank), replacement of tank components (the loaded weight of 26,500kg includes a spare S tank engine pack), grading and levelling operations and the transportation of equipment.

The Bgbv 82 has a hull of all-welded construction; its side plates are of double-plate type. The front of the vehicle can withstand attack from 20mm ammunition. It is fully amphibious being propelled in the water by its tracks; a flotation screen is erected, trim vane erected and bilge pumps switched on before the vehicle enters the water.

The main winch has a capacity of 20,000kg and has two ranges. The crane has a lifting capacity of 9000kg. There are two anchor spades at the rear of the vehicle and these are hydraulically operated. A hydraulically operated bulldozer blade is fitted at the front of the vehicle and this can be used for both dozing operations and to stabilise the vehicle when the crane or winch is being used.

The vehicle is fitted with infra-red driving lights and there is provision for the fitting of an NBC pack.

Employment

In service with the Swedish Army.

The Bgbv 82 Armoured Recovery Vehicle in travelling order

Brobv 941 Bridgelaying Vehicle   Sweden

Armament: 2 × 7.62mm machine guns
2 × 6 barrelled smoke dischargers
Crew: 4
Length: 17.00m (with bridge)
6.71m (vehicle only)
Width: 4.00m (with bridge)
3.25m (vehicle only)
Height: 3.50m (with bridge)
2.75m (vehicle only)
G/Clearance: .40m
Weight: 29,400kg (with bridge)
22,400kg (without bridge)
G/Pressure: .91kg.cm² (loaded)
Engine: Volvo THD 100C, 6 cylinder, in-line,
turbo-charged diesel developing 310hp at
2200rpm
Speed: 56km/ph (road)
8km/ph (water)
Range: 400km
Fuel: 550 litres
Fording: Amphibious
V/Obstacle: .60m
Trench: 2.50m
Gradient: 60%

Development/Variants
The Brobv 941 (Brobandvagn 941) has been
designed and manufactured by Hägglund and
Söner. It uses the same basic chassis as the
Bgbv 82 Armoured Recovery Vehicle. The
first prototype Brobv 941 was built in 1968
and production vehicles were delivered to the
Swedish Army in 1973.

The basic role of the vehicle is that of laying
a bridge although it can also transport
bridging equipment and can be used for
grading operations.
The vehicle is fully amphibious being propelled in the water by its tracks. The only
preparation required is to switch on the bilge
pumps and lower the trim vane at the front
of the vehicle. The bridge is towed behind the
vehicle when the vehicle is in the water.
A 15m bridge that weighs 7000kg is carried;
this takes less than five minutes to place in
position and can be taken up for the other end.
The bridge is hydraulically operated. A dozer
blade is mounted at the front of the vehicle,
which is used to stabilise the vehicle when
the bridge is being put into position. It can
also be used to clear river banks so that the
bridge can be correctly positioned.
The bridge has a capacity of 50,000kg. The
bridgelaying mechanism is journalled in the
chassis with two supporting legs and two
hydraulic cylinders. The bridge is laid and
picked up by a telescopic beam that can be
extended to the far pickup point of the bridge.
The Brobv 941 is fitted with infra-red driving
lights and can be fitted with an NBC pack.
Employment
In service with the Swedish Army.

*The Brobv 941 Bridgelaying Vehicle in
travelling order*

Other Swedish Armoured Fighting Vehicles

An SKP APC with no armament fitted. Note the winch on the side of the vehicle

SKP and VKP m/42 Armoured Personnel Carriers

The m/42 SKP and VKP APCs were introduced into the Swedish Army in 1944 and for many years were the only Swedish APCs. The SKP has a chassis and engine made by Scania-Vabis and the VKP a chassis and engine by Volvo; their armoured bodies were manufactured by Bröderna Hedlund of Stockholm. These vehicles have seen overseas service with the Swedish Army (as part of United Nations Forces) in the Congo, Cyprus and Egypt. Brief data is as follows:

Armament: 2×8mm machine guns
Crew: 2+16
Length: 6.80m
Width: 2.30m
Height: 2.20m
Weight: 8500kg
Speed: 73km/ph (road)
Fording: .74m
Armour: 5mm–10mm

Strv.40 Light Tank

No longer in service with the Swedish Army but some may still be in service with the Dominican Army. Armament is a 37mm gun and two 8mm machine guns.

VEAK 40 x 60 Self-Propelled Anti-Aircraft Gun System

Development of this weapon by Bofors has now been stopped.

Pbv.301 Armoured Personnel Carrier

Phased out of service in 1971. Replaced by the Pbv 302.

Ikv.102, Ikv.103 and m/43

These self-propelled guns/infantry support weapons are being replaced by the Ikv 91 from early 1974.

Landsverk 180 Armoured Car

Some of these six-wheeled amoured cars are still used by Eire. Their armament consists of a turret-mounted 20mm cannon and a co-axial 7.62mm machine gun; in addition there is a 7.62mm machine gun next to the driver. Loaded weight is about 6170kg and it has a crew of four or five.

PZ.61 and PZ.68 Main Battle Tank   Switzerland

	PZ.61	PZ.68
Crew:	4	4
Length Gun Forward:	9.43m	9.43m
Length Hull:	6.78m	6.78m
Width:	3.06m	3.14m
Height Cupola:	2.72m	2.74m
G/Clearance	.42m	.40m
Weight Loaded:	38,000kg	39,000kg
Weight Empty:	37,000kg	38,000kg
G/Pressure:	.85kg.cm^2	.86kg.cm^2
Speed Road:	50km/ph	60km/ph
Range:	300km	300km
Fuel:	760 litres	760 litres
Fording:	1.10m	1.10m
V/Obstacle	.75m	.80m
Trench:	2.60m	2.60m
Gradient:	70%	70%
Main Armament Calibre:	105mm	105mm
Sec. Armament Calibre:	20mm	7.5mm
A/A Armament Calibre:	7.5mm	7.5mm
Main Armament Elev./Dep.:	$+21°$ $-10°$	$+21°$ $-10°$
Smoke Dischargers:	6	6
Ammunition 105mm:	52	52
Ammunition 20mm:	240	—
Ammunition 7.5mm:	3000	4600
Engine:	MB-837 V-8 diesel	MB-837 V-8 diesel
Bhp/rpm:	630/2200	660/2200
Armour:	60mm (maximum)	60mm (maximum)

Development

The design of the Pz 61 dates to the early 1950s. Prototypes were constructed in 1958 and 1959 and these were armed with a 90mm gun or a 83.4mm gun (as used in the Centurion at that time). These prototypes were followed by 10 pre-production tanks known as the Pz 58. After extensive trials a development of the Pz 58 was ordered into production. The production model was known as the Pz 61 and was armed with the British 105mm gun as used in late Centurions, Leopard, M-60 and so on. Production started in 1964 and 150 were built at Thun before production was completed in 1966.

In 1968 a further development of the Pz 61 was announced, this being called the Pz 68. After trials a production order for 170 was given and the vehicle entered production at Thun; the first production vehicle was completed in 1971. The improvements of the Pz 68 over the earlier Pz 61 included: 20mm cannon has been replaced by a 7.5mm machine gun, the turret has been modified, the engine develops more power which has increased the road speed, the gun is stabilised so that it has a better chance of hitting an enemy tank when it is firing on the move, it has new tracks with rubber pads. A laser rangefinder is under development.

Variants

155m Self-Propelled Howitzer: Under development is the Panzer-Kanone 68. This is based on a Pz 68 hull with a turret mounting a Swiss 155m howitzer with a traverse of 360°, range of weapon is at least 30,000m. Loaded weight is 47,000kg and road speed 55km/ph. It is also armed with a 7.5mm AA machine gun and six smoke dischargers. It was first shown in 1972.

Bridgelayer: A number of types of bridge have been tested both on the Pz 61 and Pz 68 chassis. The vehicle is called the Brücken-panzer, or Bru. Pz 68 for short.

Armoured Recovery Vehicle: This was developed in 1965 and production vehicles are based on the Pz 68 chassis. It is called the Entpannungspanzer 65. It is designed to recover disabled vehicles, carry out repairs and do minor engineer work. A dozer blade is mounted at the front of the vehicle, 'A' frame can lift 15,000kg, main winch has a capacity of 25,000kg, also has an auxiliary winch and tow bars, tools, etc. Basic data is given below:

Armament: 1×7.5mm machine gun and 6 smoke dischargers
Overall Length: 7.60m
Overall Height: 3.25m
Width: 3.15m (including spade)
Width: 3.06m

Weight: 39,000kg (loaded)
Speed: 56km/ph
Crew: 3–5
G/Clearance: .45m
Gradient: 60%
V/Obstacle: .80m
Fording: 1.10m
Trench: 2.50m

Anti-Aircraft Vehicle: This is reported to be under development.
Employment
In service only with the Swiss Army.

Pz 61 Main Battle Tank of the Swiss Army

Above: *Pz 68 Main Battle Tank of the Swiss Army*

The Entpannungspanzer 65 Armoured Recovery Vehicle

Mowag
Armoured Fighting Vehicles

Switzerland

The Mowag Company of Kreuzlingen has for many years been engaged in the design and construction of both tracked and wheeled armoured fighting vehicles. In addition they have built numerous military trucks. Listed below are some of the more recent products of the Mowag Company.

Mowag MR 8-01 Armoured Personnel Carrier

Crew: 3–5
Length: 5.31m
Width: 2.20m
Height: 2.22m
G/Clearance: .50m
Weight: 8200kg
Speed: 80km/ph (road)
Wheelbase: 2.60m
Track: 1.95m
Engine: Chrysler R319, 161hp

In 1959 Mowag sold 20 of these vehicles to Germany. Subsequently production of these was undertaken in Germany for the Federal German Border Police. They have two models SW1 (Geschützer Sonderwagen 1) Kfz-91; this has a crew of seven and no armament; some models have been fitted with a shield at the front for clearing obstacles. SW11 (Geschützer Sonderwagen 11) Kfz-91; this has a crew of four and is armed with a turret-mounted 20mm cannon. Other models developed by Mowag included: MR 8-09 with 20mm gun, MR 8-23 with 90mm gun, MR 8-30 with twin 80mm rocket launchers and the MR 9-32 armed with a 120mm mortar. Crew of four.

Mowag Pirate Armoured Personnel Carrier

Armament: 1×20mm cannon, elevation +70°, depression −10° traverse 360°
Crew: 12
Length: 6.20m
Width: 2.90m
Height: 2.07m (turret)
Weight: 18,600kg (loaded)
Engine: Mowag 10 cylinder diesel, 430hp
Speed: 70km/ph (road)
Range: 500km
G/Pressure: .66kg.cm^2
Trench: 2m
Armour: 8mm–30mm

The Mowag Pirate is a development of an earlier Mowag APC. The Pirate has been further developed into the new Tornado. This has a turret-mounted 20mm cannon, a retractable launcher for Bantam ATGW to the right of the 20mm turret, at the rear are two mountings for 7.62mm machine guns. These can be fired by remote control from within the vehicle. The Tornado has a crew of 12; the crew can fire their weapons through firing ports; there is also a large ramp at the rear of the vehicle. Mowag are also building some components for the German Marder vehicle.

Mowag Puma Armoured Personnel Carrier

Crew: 1+10
Length: 6.50m
Width: 2.60m
Height: 2.98m (turret)
Weight: 15,100kg (loaded)
Engine: Mowag 8 cylinder diesel developing 320hp at 2200rpm
Speed: 80km/ph (road)
12km/ph (water)
Range: 500km
V/Obstacle: .48m

This vehicle has not entered service. It is fully amphibious being propelled in the water by two propellers at the rear of the vehicle. Various models have been built including the

The SW1 as used by the Federal German Border Police

following: armed with 2 machine guns in open mountings, armed with a mortar and a single 7.62mm machine gun, armed with a turret-mounted 20mm cannon (two types of turret) and another with 80mm rocket launchers. It is fitted with an NBC system. The crew are provided with overhead hatches and there are doors at the rear of the vehicle, these doors are fitted with special ball mountings enabling the crew to fire their weapons from within the vehicle. Other 4×4 (11,000kg) and 8×8 (20,000kg) vehicles have been projected, but not so far built.

Mowag Roland Armoured Personnel Carrier

Mowag built prototypes of this vehicle some years ago and production has now reported to have been undertaken in Argentina or Chile.

Mowag Amphibious Armoured Personnel Carrier

Crew: 2+10
Length: 5.75m
Width: 2.50m
Height: 2.225m (w/o turret)
Engine: Mowag Model M4DU, 4 cylinders, 170hp
Speed: 80km/ph (road)
13km/ph (water)
Range: 800km
Weight: 10,000kg
This vehicle is fully amphibious being propelled in the water by two propellers at the rear of the vehicle. Various types of armament can be fitted including 7.62mm and 12.7mm machine guns and 20mm cannon. Production of this vehicle may be underway in South America.

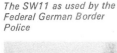

The Mowag Puma armed with a turret mounted 20mm cannon

The SW11 as used by the Federal German Border Police

MBT–70 Main Battle Tank   Germany/United States

Armament: 1×152mm XM-150 Shillelagh gun/missile launcher **OR**
1×120mm gun (projected for German MBT-70)
1×7.62mm machine gun, co-axial with main armament
1×20mm Rheinmetall Cannon for A/A or ground use
4 smoke dischargers mounted either side of turret
Crew: 3
Length: 9.10m (gun forward)
6.99m (hull only)
Width: 3.51m
Height: 2.59m (maximum)
2.29m (normal)
1.99m (minimum)
G/Clearance: .74m (maximum)
.44m (normal)
.14m (minimum)
Weight: 46,000kg (loaded)
Engine: Continental AVCR, 12 cylinder, multi-fuel, air-cooled engine developing 1475hp at 2800rpm **OR**
Daimler-Benz 12 cylinder, multi-fuel, water-cooled engine developing 1500hp at 2600rpm
Speed: 70km/ph (road)
Range: 650km
Fuel: 1514 litres (estimate)
Fording: 2.55m
5.50m (with schnorkel)
V/Obstacle: 1.10m
Trench: 2.80m
Gradient: 70%
G/Pressure: .78kg.cm²

Development/Variants
On 1st August 1963, the American and German Governments signed an agreement to develop a Main Battle Tank for the 1970s. This was to be in production by 1970. The prime contractors were the Allison Division of the General Motors Corporation (USA) and Deutsche Entwicklungs Gesellschaft MBH (a consortium) in Germany. Each country was to build eight prototypes using its own engine, transmission and so on. The first American prototype was handed over to the US Army on 17th July 1967. America and Germany each showed prototypes in their own countries to the press on 9th October 1967. The MBT-70 had a number of advanced features including a crew of only three men, an automatic loader, adjustable suspension, passive night fighting and night driving equipment, NBC pack, fire control computers. The most interesting feature was its 152mm gun/missile launcher which could fire Shillelagh missiles or conventional ammunition. During development the cost of the vehicle rose considerably; there were also troubles with equipment including the automatic loader and the fire control system.
In January 1970 the United States and Germany agreed to stop working together on the tank. The United States then modified the MBT-70 as the XM-803, the so-called 'austere' MBT-70. However costs of this began to rise sharply and this too, was cancelled. In 1973 development contracts were awarded to Chrysler (who make the M-60A1) and the Allison Division of GMC (who built the MBT-70) to build prototypes of a new MBT, designated XM-1. These will be tested together in 1976. Other vehicles will not doubt be based on the XM-1 chassis. Variants of the MBT-70 were to have included the XM-742 ARV, XM-743 AVLB and the XM-745 CEV. Germany is developing the Leopard 2 and a more advanced MBT.

Employment
MBT-70 prototypes are still being used for trials purposes in the United States and Germany. Switzerland had one for trials purposes in 1972/1973.

Above: One of the American prototypes of the MBT-70

M-60 Series Main Battle Tank — United States

	M-60	M-60A1	M-60A2
Crew:	4	4	4
Length Gun Forward:	9.309m	9.436m	7.315m
Length Hull Only:	6.946m	6.946m	6.946m
Width:	3.631m	3.631m	3.631m
Height Overall:	3.213m	3.257m	3.20m
G/Clearance:	.463m	.463m	.463m
Weight Loaded:	46,266kg	48,081kg	44,000kg
Weight Empty:	42,184kg	43,999kg	40,000kg
G/Pressure:	.78kg.cm^2	.79kg.cm^2	.76kg.cm^2
Speed Road:	48km/ph	48km/ph	51km/ph
Range Road:	500km	500km	535km
Fuel:	1457 litres	1420 litres	1136 litres
Fording Without Kit:	1.219m	1.219m	1.219m
Fording With Kit:	2.743m	2.743m	2.743m
V/Obstacle:	.914m	.914m	.914m
Trench:	2.59m	2.59m	2.59m
Gradient:	60%	60%	60%
Main Armament Calibre:	105mm	105mm	152mm
Co-Axial MG Calibre:	7.62mm	7.62mm	7.62mm
A/A Armament Calibre:	12.7mm	12.7mm	12.7mm
Ammunition 105mm:	57	63	—
Ammunition 7.62mm:	5950	5950	5950
Ammunition 12.7mm:	900	900	900
Engine:	see below	see below	see below
Armour:	25mm–110mm	25mm–110mm	25mm–110mm

Development

The M-60 was based on the M-48A2 tank and was developed by the Chrysler Corporation. The vehicle entered production at the end of 1959 and entered service in 1960. The vehicle has the 105mm gun as used on the late model Centurion, Leopard, Vickers MBT and Swiss Pz 61 and Pz 68. The first M-60A1 was completed in May 1961, the development designation was M-60E1. The first production M-60A1 was completed in October 1962 and the vehicle is still in production at the Detroit Tank Arsenal which is operated by the Chrysler Corporation.
Both the M-60 and the M-60A1 have a full range of night fighting and night driving aids and have the American type NBC system, a dozer blade can be mounted on the front of the vehicle if required. A kit is available which enables the vehicle to deep ford to a depth of 4.11m. This kit consists of a telescopic tube that fits over the loader's hatch, various parts of the tank are sealed with rubber seals. When not in use the equipment is stowed on the rear of the turret.

Variants

M-60: This is the basic model and has the same turret as the M-48A2. It is powered by a Continental AVDS-1790-2 12 cylinder, air-cooled diesel developing 750hp at 2400rpm. It has three return rollers and no idler tension wheel or fender dust shields. It is armed with the 105mm M-68 in mount M-116, this has an elevation of $+19°$ and a depression of $-10°$, a 7.62mm co-axial machine gun M-73 and a 12.7mm anti-aircraft machine gun M-85.
M-60A1: This has a new turret which has more room as well as giving greater ballistic protection. On the rear of the turret is a stowage basket that extends completely around the rear of the turret, the lower portion of the turret is screened. It has no fender dust shields, nor rear idler tension wheels and three return rollers. It is powered by an AVDS-1790-2A which develops 750hp at 2400rpm. It has the same armament as the M-60 except that its 105mm gun is in mount M-140. It also has a more recent fire control system. A laser rangefinder is under development.
M-60A2: This is an M-60A1 hull fitted with a new turret mounting the Shillelagh weapons system. The prototypes were designated M-60A1E1 or M-60A1E2 depending on the vehicle used. Development started in April 1964 and the first prototype was completed in September 1965, although trials were unsuccessful production was ordered in September 1966. The first order was for 300 tanks. By 1971 they had still not entered service.
By the end of 1971 the problems had been solved and on 29th November 1971, a contract was signed for retrofit production of 526 M-60A2 tanks along with continued production of the M-60A1. The 152mm tube can fire either the Shillelagh missiles or con-

ventional type rounds. It has an elevation of $+20°$ and a depression of $-10°$, a total of 46 rounds of ammunition are carried of which 13 can be Shillelagh missiles. The type of ammunition carried does, of course, depend on the tactical situation. Also fitted is a co-axial 7.62mm machine gun, a 12.7mm anti-aircraft gun and smoke dischargers.

M-60A3: This is under development and has three phases:

Phase 1: This covers an add-on stabilisation system, a top-loading air cleaner and an improved steel track with replaceable track shoes. The new track has twice the life of the old track.

Phase 2: This includes a laser rangefinder, a solid state computer, a tube-over-bar suspension system, a more reliable engine and a new electrical system

Phase 3: This includes an engine of 900hp, a new transmission, new final drives and an advanced night vision system. This vehicle will have increased performance.

Chrysler 'K' Tank: This was a private venture by the Chrysler Corporation and consists of an M-60A1 with a new turret mounting a long-barrelled 152mm Shillelagh gun. It was a project only.

M-60 AVLB: This is similar to the M-48 AVLB except that it uses an M-60 chassis. The bridge can take a load of 60 tons and can span a gap of 18.288m. The bridge takes less than two minutes to lay; the vehicle has a crew of two. Performance is similar to the M-60A1; additional data is:
Length: 11.048m (with bridge)
Width: 4.012m (with bridge)
Height: 4.038m (with bridge)
Weight: 55,230kg (with bridge)
Weight: 41,330kg (vehicle only)
Weight: 13,900kg (bridge only)

M-728 Combat Engineer Vehicle (CEV): This vehicle is based on the M-60A1 chassis and turret; its development designation was T-118E1. The vehicle entered production in 1965 and was issued to the 1st Armoured Division in 1968. The vehicle is designed to destroy enemy positions and fortifications, clear roadblocks and obstacles. Armament consists of a 165mm demolition gun, a 7.62mm co-axial machine gun and a 12.7mm anti-aircraft machine gun. Ammunition carried is 30 rounds of 165mm, 2000 rounds of 7.62mm and 600 rounds of 12.7mm ammunition. An 'A' frame is mounted on the front of the vehicle for lifting operations, a winch with a capacity of 11,340kg is provided. A hydraulically operated dozer blade is also provided. Kits for fording and night operations are available. Performance is similar to the M-60A1; additional data is as follows:
Length: 9.30m (boom erected)
Length: 7.88m (with blade)
Width: 3.70m (with blade)
Height: 3.20m
Weight: 52,163kg (loaded)
Weight: 48,500kg (empty)
Ground Pressure: .86kg.cm^2
Employment
The M-60 and M-60A1 are in service with Austria (M-60A1), Iran, Israel (M-60A1), Italy (200 built in Italy by Oto Melara), Jordan, South Korea, Spain (M-60 AVLB only), Turkey, United States. The Australians have also tested an M-60A1 as a possible replacement for their Centurions.

An early M-60 Tank of the United States Army

Above left: *M-60A1 of the Austrian Army. The difference between the M-60 and the M-60A1 can be clearly seen*

Left: *The M-60 Armoured Vehicle Launched Bridge, this particular vehicle is used by the Spanish Army*

Above: *The M-728 Combat Engineer Vehicle is based on the M-60A1*

Right: *The M-60A1E1 later became the M-60A2*

Right: *M-60A1 Tank with Xenon searchlight over the gun barrel*

M–48 Series Main Battle Tank   United States

	M-48	M-48A1	M-48A2	M-48A3	M-48A4
Crew:	4	4	4	4	4
Length Gun Forward:	8.444m	8.729m	8.686m	8.686m	9.296m
Length Hull:	6.705m	6.870m	6.870m	6.882m	6.870m
Width:	3.758m	3.631m	3.631m	3.631m	3.631m
Height Overall:	3.241m	3.130m	3.089m	3.124m	3.130m
G/Clearance:	.393m	.393m	.387m	.406m	.406m
Weight Loaded:	44,906kg	47,173kg	47,173kg	47.173kg	47,173kg
Weight Empty:	42,240kg	43,999kg	43,999kg	44,452kg	43,317kg
G/Pressure:	.78kg.cm²	.83kg.cm²	.83kg.cm²	.83kg.cm²	.83kg.cm²
Speed Road:	42km/ph	42km/ph	48km/ph	48km/ph	48km/ph
Range Road:	112km	112km	260km	470km	390km
Fuel:	757 litres	757 litres	1268 litres	1420 litres	1401 litres
Fording W/O Kit:	1.219m	1.219m	1.219m	1.219m	1.219m
Fording With Kit:	2.438m	2.438m	2.438m	2.438m	2.438m
V/Obstacle:	.915m	.915m	.915m	.915m	.915m
Trench:	2.59m	2.59m	2.59m	2.59m	2.59m
Gradient:	60%	60%	60%	60%	60% .
Main Armament Calibre:	90mm	90mm	90mm	90mm	105mm
Co-Axial MG:	7.62mm	7.62mm	7.62mm	7.62mm	7.62mm
Anti-Aircraft MG:	12.7mm	12.7mm	12.7mm	12.7mm	12.7mm
Ammunition Main:	60	60	64	62	57
Ammunition Sec.:	5900	5900	5590	6000	5000
Ammunition A/A:	180	500	1365	630	1040
Engine:	See below for details				
Armour:	25mm–110mm for all models				

Development

The M-48 was developed from the earlier M-47. Design work started in 1950 by the Chrysler Corporation and the first pilot model was completed in December 1951 this being designated T-48. Early M-48s used the same engine and transmission as the M-47. In March 1951 additional production lines were established by the Ford Motor Company (they built 900 tanks at Livonia), and the Fisher Body Division of the General Motors Corporation. Production commenced in 1952 and was completed in 1956. The cost of the M-48 and M-48A1 programme was some 1,249 million dollars. Components of the M-48 are also used in the M-53 and M-55 self-propelled guns and the M-88 ARV. The M-48 was further developed into the M-60 series.

Variants

M-48 and M-48C: This was the first production model and has a small driver's hatch; the commander has a machine gun in an open mount, five return rollers and no idler. The M-48C is similar except that it has a hull of mild steel and is not suitable for combat. The gun has an elevation of $+19°$ and a depression of $-9°$, this being the same as all M-48 series. The vehicle is powered by a Continental AV-1790-5B, -7, -7B or -7C, 12 cylinder, air-cooled engine developing 810hp at 2800rpm. It has no fender dust shields and either a 'T' or cylindrical blast deflector on the barrel.

M-48A1: This has a large driver's hatch, a commander's cupola complete with machine gun, fender dust shields, rear track idler wheel and five support rollers, and a 'T' type blast deflector. It is powered by a Continental AV-1790-7C engine developing 810hp at 2800rpm.

M-48A2 and M-48A2C: Development of the M-48A2 started in 1954 and it was designated T-48E2, the prototype was completed in 1955. The improvements over the earlier vehicle included an engine with a fuel-injection system, improved engine deck, constant pressure turret control system, improved fire control system. It could also be fitted with additional fuel tanks which give it a range of 400km. The first production order went to Alco Products of Schenectady, New York, in 1956. A later contract was awarded to Chrysler Delaware Defense Plant (Lenape Ordnance Modification Centre) Newark, Delaware. The main difference between the M-48A2 and the M-48A2C is in vision and fire control equipment, the only visual difference between them is the absence of the track tension idler wheels on the M-48A2C. Both are powered by a Continental AVL-1790-8, 12 cylinder, air-cooled petrol engine developing 825bhp at 2800rpm. Other distinguishing features are three return rollers, raised rear engine covers, stowage basket on the turret rear and a 'T' blast deflector.

M-48A3: Development designation M-

48A1E2, this has only three support rollers (although some may be seen with five), no track idler wheel, 'T' blast deflector, fender dust shields. It is powered by a Continental AVDS-1790-2A, 12 cylinder, air-cooled diesel engine developing 750bhp at 2400rpm. It is fitted with infra-red driving and fighting equipment, including a XENON searchlight. Some M-48A3s in Vietnam had revised armament and an improved cupola. Also has improved fire control system and can be fitted with a schnorkel.

M-48A4: Development designation M-48A1E1. In 1959 a project was started to update the M-48A1 with M-60 components, the first of six pilots was delivered in February 1960. The basic idea was to fit turrets from M-60A1s as the latter were fitted with new turrets armed with the Shillelagh gun/missile system. The present status of the M-48A4 is still uncertain.

M-67: The M-67 was standardised in 1955, development designation was T-67 and a total of 74 were built for the USMC. It is a modified M-48A1. The 90mm gun has been replaced by an M7-6 flamethrower gun. This has a slightly shorter tube and is slightly larger in diameter than the standard 90mm tube. The headlamps are slightly lower as the flame-thrower has an elevation of $+45°$ and a depression of $-12°$.

M-67A1: This is an M-48A2 modified for use by the United States Army. It is similar to the above except that it has an M7A1-6 flame gun.

M-67A2: This is an M-48A3 for use by the USMC. It has the M7A1-6 flame gun with a range of 100–250m depending on the weather conditions.

Note *At the time of writing none of the flamethrower tanks were in service, they are however held in reserve. They saw extensive service in Vietnam. Basic data of the flame-thrower tanks is given below, other data being similar to the basic M-48 tank:*

	M-67	M-67A1	M-67A2
Crew:	3	3	3
Length Gun Forward:	8.23m	8.13m	8.15m
Length Hull:	6.97m	6.87m	6.87m
Width:	3.63m	3.63m	3.63m
Height:	3.13m	3.13m	3.12m
G/Clearance:	.39m	.39m	.39m
Weight Loaded:	47,530kg	47,990kg	48,990kg
Weight Empty:	45,350kg	45,810kg	46.800kg
G/Pressure:	.84kg.cm²	.84kg.cm²	.86kg.cm²
Speed Road:	51km/ph	51km/ph	48km/ph
Range:	160km	260km	470km
Fuel:	763 litres	1268 litres	1420 litres

M-48 AVLB: The M-48 AVLB (Armoured Vehicle Launched Bridge) is based on the hull of the M-48A2. A scissors bridge is fitted. Early M-48 AVLBs were fitted with two machine gun turrets each fitted with a 12.7mm machine gun. Most of these have been removed The bridge is laid hydraulically and can cross ditches up to 18.29m in width.

Additional data is:
Crew: 2
Length: 11.15m
Width: 4.01m
Height: 3.99m
Weight: 58.29 tonnes

M-48A1 of the Spanish Army

Bulldozer: An hydraulic bulldozer blade can be fitted to the M-48 series. The width of the blade is 3.71m and two types of blade are available:

M-8 for the M-48, M-48C and M-48A1; this has a weight of 3.98 tonnes.

M-8A1 for the M-48A2 and other members of the family, weight 3.81 tonnes.

Note *The M-48 tanks have been updated a number of times in their lives and it is very difficult to distinguish between models.*

Employment

It is in service with Germany (and AVLB), Greece, Israel, Jordan, Norway, Pakistan, South Korea, South Vietnam, Spain, Taiwan, Turkey, Thailand, United States (Army and Marine Corps).

Right: *M-48 Armoured Vehicle Launched Bridge of the German Army*

Centre right: *M-48A1, note the 5 return rollers and the small tension idler below the drive sprocket*

Bottom right: *M-48A3 of the United States Marine Corps in Vietnam*

Below: *M-48A2 of the German Army*

Bottom: *M-48 Tank of the Pakistani Army knocked out by the Indian Army in 1971*

M–47 Medium Tank

United States

Armament: 1×90mm gun M-36, elevation
+19°, depression −5°
1×7.62mm co-axial machine gun model
M-1919A4E1
1×7.62mm bow machine gun model
M-1919A4E1
1×12.7mm anti-aircraft machine gun model
M-2
71 rounds of 90mm ammunition
4125 rounds of 7.62mm ammunition
440 rounds of 12.7mm ammunition
Crew: 5
Length: 8.508m (including gun)
6.362m (hull only)
Width: 3.51m
Height: 3.35m (inc. A/A machine gun)
2.95m (w/o A/A machine gun)
G/Clearance: .469m
Weight: 46,170kg (loaded)
42,130kg (empty)
G/Pressure: .935kg.cm²
Engine: Continental AV-1790-5B, 7 or 7B,
12 cylinder, air-cooled petrol engine develop-
ing 810bhp at 2800rpm
Speed: 58km/ph (road)
Range: 130km
Fuel: 875 litres
Fording: 1.219m
V/Obstacle: .914m
Trench: 2.59m
Gradient: 60%
Armour: 25mm–115mm

Development
The M-47 was developed during the Korean
War. It is basically a modified M-46 chassis
with a T-42 turret mounting a T-119 gun.
The M-46 chassis was given a better cooling
system, improved hull armour and different
electrical equipment. M-47s were built by the
Detroit Tank Arsenal and the American
Locomotive Company. M-47s may be seen
with two types of blast deflector, one has a
'T' type and the other a cylindrical type.

Variants
M-102 Combat Engineer Vehicle with
165mm gun; none remain in service.
T-66 Flame Thrower Tank: Trials only.
French M-47 with 105mm gun: The
French DTAT have fitted an M-47 with the
complete gun of the AMX-30 MBT. This
would be for export only.
Italian M-47 with 105mm gun: Oto
Melara have re-built an M-47 with the
105mm gun of the M-60 as well as fitting the
vehicle with the engine, transmission and
electrical system of the M-60. This would be
for export as the Italian Army has ordered 800
Leopards.
M-47 with Swingfire ATGW: This was
shown at the Farnborough Air Display in 1966
and was a proposal only.
M-47 with bridge: The Italian Company of
Astra SpA of Piacenza have built a bridgelayer on an M-47 chassis. At the end of each
end of the bridge is a ramp that can be used
as a pile, thus allowing two bridges to be
used.
Korean ARV: The Korean Army have adopted
a number of M-47s so that they can be used
as ARVs. The gun has been removed and an
'A' frame fitted on the glacis plate with the
winch inside of the turret, the rope being taken
out through the mantlet where the main gun
was fitted.
Spanish M-47 with new engine: It was
reported in 1973 that Spain was testing an
M-47 with a new engine.
Employment
Used by Austria, Belgium (Reserve), Brazil,
France, Greece, Iran, Italy, Jordan, Pakistan,
Portugal, Saudi-Arabia, South Korea, Spain,
Taiwan, Turkey, Yugoslavia. Japan had some
for trials. M-47s are no longer used by the
United States or Germany. M-26s are reported
to be used by Greece and Turkey.

M-47s of the Spanish Army

Italian M-47 with 105mm gun

M-47 of the Austrian Army

French M-47 with the 105mm gun of the AMX-30

Sherman Medium Tank United States

	M-4A1(WET)	M-4A2(WET)	M-4A3(WET)	M-4A3E8
Crew:	5	5	5	5
Length:	7.39m	7.39m	6.273m	7.518m
Width:	2.717m	2.653m	2.667m	2.667m
Height:	3.425m	3.425m	3.374m	3.425m
G/Clearance:	.43m	.43m	.43m	.43m
Weight Loaded:	32,044kg	33,320kg	31,574kg	32,284kg
G/Pressure:	1.02kg.cm^2	1.05kg.cm^2	1.00kg.cm^2	.72kg.cm^2 (wide tracks)
Speed Road:	39km/ph	45km/ph	42km/ph	48m/ph
Range Cruising:	160km	160km	160km	160km
Fuel:	651 litres	560 litres	636 litres	636 litres
Fording:	1.066m	1.016m	.914m	.914m
V/Obstacle:	.609m	.609m	.609m	.609m
Trench:	2.286m	2.286m	2.286m	2.286m
Gradient:	60%	60%	60%	60%
Main Armament Cal.:	76mm	76mm	75mm	76mm
Sec. Armament Cal.:	7.62mm	7.62mm	7.62mm	7.62mm
Bow. Armament Cal.:	7.62mm	7.62mm	7.62mm	7.62mm
A/A Armament Cal.:	12.7mm	12.7mm	12.7mm	12.7mm
Ammunition Main:	71	71	104	71
Ammunition 7.62mm:	6250	6250	6250	6250
Ammunition 12.7mm:	600	600	600	600
Elevation:	All have an elevation of $+25°$ and depression $-10°$			
Engine Type:	R-975-C4	GMC 6046D	Ford GAA	Ford GAA
Bhp/rpm:	400/2400	375/2100	450/2600	460/2600
Armour:	12mm–75mm	12mm–75mm	12mm–75mm	12mm–75mm

Development

The Sherman was developed in the early part of World War II and was built in very large numbers. The above listing is a cross section of typical Shermans that are still in service. The Sherman chassis was used as a basis for a number of other vehicles including the M-7, M-10 and M-36; these have their own pages in the book. For details of the Israeli Shermans refer to the Israeli section. Other variants in service include:

Recovery Vehicle, Fully Tracked M-32 and M-32A1: Based on a variety of chassis including the M-4, M-4A1, M-4A2 and M-4A3. It has an 'A' frame, winch with a capacity of 27.22 tonnes, tools, blocks and so on. The later M-32 has wider tracks (.584m). Basic data is as follows:

Crew: 5
Length Overall: 5.93m
Height: 2.736m (excluding machine gun)
Width: 2.616m
Engine: Continental R-975-C1, 350bhp at 2400rpm
Armament: 1×81mm mortar, 1×7.62mm

Argentina still uses the famous Sherman Firefly

bow machine gun, 1×12.7mm A/A machine gun
Fuel: 651 litres
Weight: 28,123kg (loaded)
Speed: 41.8km/ph
Range: 165km
Recovery Vehicle, Full Tracked, Medium M-74: This is a postwar development and is a rebuild based on M-4A3 chassis. Equipment fitted includes a blade at the front, 'A' frame, winch tools, blocks and so on. Basic data is:
Crew: 4
Length Overall: 7.95m
Height: 3.11m (excluding machine gun)
Width: 3.09m
Weight: 42,525kg (loaded)
Engine: Ford GAA, 8 cylinder petrol, 525hp at 2800rpm
Armament: 1×3.5in rocket launcher, 1×7.62mm bow machine gun and 1×12.7mm anti-aircraft machine gun
Fuel: 636 litres

Gradient: 60%
Fording: .91m
V/Obstacle: .61m
Speed: 34km/ph
Sherman Firefly: This was a British modification. A powerful 76.2mm gun replaced the standard gun. No bow machine gun.
Sherman Bridgelayer: Japan has some Shermans with a scissors bridge fitted.
Employment
Shermans are still used by Argentina, Brazil, Chile, Colombia, Cuba, Egypt, Guatemala, India, Iran, Israel, Japan, Mexico, Pakistan, Paraguay, Peru, Portugal, Philippines, South Africa, South Korea, Uganda (from Israel), Yugoslavia.
M-32s are still used by Austria, Brazil, Japan, Israel.
M-74s are still used by Belgium, Spain, Turkey.
Sherman Firefly is still used by Argentina, Lebanon, Yugoslavia.

Rear view of the M-74 Armoured Recovery Vehicle

The M-32 Armoured Recovery Vehicle

M–551 General Sheridan
Light Tank/Reconnaissance Vehicle

United States

Armament: 1×152mm launcher M-81, elevation +19.5°, depression −8°
1×7.62mm M-73 co-axial machine gun
1×12.7mm M-2 machine gun, commander's cupola
8 grenade launchers, 4 either side of turret
20 conventional rounds, 10 Shillelagh missiles
3000 rounds of 7.62mm ammunition
1000 rounds of 12.7mm ammunition
Crew: 4
Length: 6.299m (overall)
Width: 2.819m
Height: 2.946m (including machine gun)
G/Clearance: .48m
Weight: 15,830kg (loaded)
13,589kg (empty)
G/Pressure: .49kg.cm^2
Engine: Detroit Diesel 6V53T, 300hp at 2800rpm
Speed: 70km/ph (road)
5.8km/ph (water)
Range: 600km (road)
Fuel: 598 litres
Fording: Amphibious
V/Obstacle: .838m
Trench: 2.54m
Gradient: 60%

Development
The development of the Sheridan dates back to 1959 and the first prototype, the XM-551, was completed in 1962. Production was undertaken by the Allison Division of the General Motors Corporation at the Cleveland Tank-Automotive Plant. The first production vehicle was completed in June 1966. Production has now been completed, about 1700 having been produced for the American Army.
The M-551 or to give its full title, M-551, Armoured Reconnaissance/Airborne Assault Vehicle, was developed to replace the M-41 light tank and M-56 SP anti-tank gun, which it has done.
The Sheridan has a number of interesting features including a hull of welded aluminium armour, turret of steel; it is fully amphibious, although a small flexible barrier system is erected around the vehicle before entering the water.
The most interesting part of the Sheridan is its weapons system; this consists of a launcher that can fire Shillelagh missiles, which have a range of some 3000m or a variety of conventional rounds including HEAT and cannister. The Sheridan was deployed to Vietnam where a number of faults showed up. Since then most of the faults have been corrected and the vehicle has now been deployed to Germany. The M-551 has a full range of night driving and fighting aids. In 1971 an 8.3 million dollar contract was awarded to Hughes for the production of a laser rangefinder for the M-551.

Variants
Numerous variants of the M-551 were projected including missile armed anti-aircraft vehicles, mortar carriers and flamethrower vehicles. A prototype with a scissors bridge is under construction. Trials versions include one with a 76mm gun M-41 and another with a 105mm gun.

Employment
In service with the United States Army in the USA and Germany, some reported to be in service with South Vietnamese Army.

M-551 Sheridan, note the ammunition boxes on the sides of the turret

M–41 Light Tank   United States

Armament: 1×76mm gun M-32, elevation +20°, depression −10°
1×7.62mm M-1919A4E1 machine gun, co-axial with 76mm gun
1×12.7mm M-2 anti-aircraft machine gun
65 rounds of 76mm ammunition
5000 rounds of 7.62mm ammunition
2175 rounds of 12.7mm ammunition
Crew: 4
Length: 8.212m (including gun)
5.819m (excluding gun)
Width: 3.198m
Height: 3.075m (with machine gun)
2.726m (w/o machine gun)
G/Clearance: .45m
Weight: 23,495kg (loaded)
G/Pressure: .72kg.cm²
Engine: M-41 and M-41A1, Continental or Lycoming AOS-895-3 M-41A2 and M-41A3, Continental or Lycoming AOS1-895-5, 6 cylinder, air-cooled petrol engine, super-charged, developing 500hp at 2800rpm
Speed: 72km/ph (road)
Range: 161km
Fuel: 530 litres
Fording: 1.06m (without kit)
2.44m (with kit)
V/Obstacle: .711m
Trench: 1.828m
Gradient: 60%
Armour: 12mm–40mm

Development/Variants
The M-41 (development designation T-41 and T-41E1) was a development from the T-37 experimental light tank. The M-41 was manufactured by the Cadillac Division of the General Motors Corporation at Cleveland. The first production M-41 was completed in mid-1951. The M-41 is often called the 'Walker Bulldog'.

The M-41 and M-41A1 are the same except that the M-41A1 has late traversing and elevating mechanism. This gives the tank commander control of both the turret and the guns; in the M-41 the commander has only power control of the turret. The M-41A2 and M-41A3 have the later traversing and elevating mechanism and also the fuel injection engine. Many components of the M-41 are used in the M-42, M-44 and M-52. There were also a number of experimental vehicles on the M-41 chassis, including one with a Sheridan development turret.
The M-41A1s used by Denmark are fitted with an AEG infra-red searchlight type B30A and infra-red sighting device B8V (ELTRO).
Employment
The M-41 has been replaced in the United States Army by the M-551 but it is still used by Argentina, Austria, Belgium, Bolivia, Brazil, Chile, Denmark, Ecuador, Ethiopia, Greece, Japan, Lebanon, Nationalist China, New Zealand, Pakistan, Philippines, Portugal, Saudi Arabia, South Vietnam, Spain, Thailand, Tunisia, Turkey.

M-41 Light Tank of the Austrian Army. This vehicle is not fitted with its Anti-Aircraft machine gun, note that it does have infra-red driving lights fitted

M–24 Chaffee Light Tank

United States

Armament: 1×75mm gun M-6, elevation +15°, depression −10°
1×12.7mm M-2 anti-aircraft machine gun
1×7.62mm machine gun, co-axial with main armament
1×7.62mm machine gun mounted in bow
Ammunition 48 rounds of 75mm, 440 rounds of 12.7mm and 3750 rounds of 7.62mm
Crew: 4/5
Length: 5.486m (including gun)
5.028m (excluding gun)
Width: 2.95m
Height: 2.77m (including machine gun)
2.46m (commander's cupola)
G/Clearance: .457m
Weight: 18,370kg (loaded)
16,440kg (empty)
G/Pressure: .78kg.cm²
Engines: 2× Cadillac Model 44T24 petrol, V-8, water-cooled, developing 110hp at 3400rpm (each)
Speed: 55km/ph (road)
Range: 178km (cruising)
Fuel: 416 litres
Fording: 1.02m
V/Obstacle: .91m
Trench: 2.44m
Gradient: 60%
Armour: 10mm–38mm

Development
Development of the M-24 was authorised in March 1943 as the T-24, this became the T-24E1. The first production M-24 was completed in April 1944, production being undertaken by Cadillac and Massey-Harris. The M-24 was the replacement for the M-5

Light Tank and saw action in the last few months of the war in Europe and the Far East. Postwar it has seen extensive action in the Far East with French (Indochina), Cambodian and American (Korea) forces. It was replaced in American service by the M-41.

Variants
The following were built using the M-24 chassis. None of them are known to be in service:
M-19 self-propelled anti-aircraft gun
M-37 self-propelled 105mm gun (howitzer)
M-41 self-propelled 155mm gun (howitzer)
In addition there were numerous trials vehicles, both during and after World War II.
M-24 with 90mm Gun: The French DTAT in association with Thune-Eureka A/S (Norway) have carried out the following modifications to the Chaffee: new French 90mm gun, 12.7 AA and co-axial machine gun, no bow machine gun, General Motors 6V-53T diesel engine, Allison MT 650 gearbox, four smoke dischargers each side of the turret, new tracks and shock absorbers, night fighting devices and so on. This gives the vehicle a much more powerful armament, all weather fighting capability and a higher road range (400km). It is at present under test.

Employment
Austria, Cambodia, Ethiopia, France, Greece, Iran, Iraq, Japan, Laos, Nationalist China, North Vietnam, Pakistan, Philippines, Saudi Arabia, South Vietnam, Spain, Thailand Turkey, Uruguay.

Above: *A Pakistani M-24 Chaffe captured by the Indian Army in 1971*

Light Tank M-3A1 and M-5A1
Self Propelled Howitzer M—8

United States

	M-3A1	M-5A1	M-8
Crew:	4	4	4
Length:	4.53m	4.84m	4.97m
Width:	2.24m	2.25m	2.32m
Height:	2.30m	2.40m	2.30m
G/Clearance:	.42m	.35m	.35m
Weight Loaded:	12,927kg	15,397kg	15,680kg
G/Pressure:	.74kg.cm²	.88kg.cm²	.88kg.cm²
Speed Road:	56km/ph	58km/ph	58km/ph
Range Cruising:	120/145km	160km	160km
Fuel:	212 litres	310 litres	310 litres
Fording:	.91m	.91m	.91m
V/Obstacle:	.61m	.46m	.46m
Trench:	1.83m	1.62m	1.62m
Gradient:	60%	60%	60%
Main Armament:	37mm	37mm	75mm
Co-Axial Armament:	7.62mm	7.62mm	—
Bow Armament:	7.62mm	7.62mm	—
Anti-Aircraft Armament:	7.62mm	7.62mm	12.7mm
Ammunition Main:	108	147	46
Ammunition 7.62mm:	6890	6500	—
Ammunition 12.7mm:	—	—	400
Engine:	see below	see below	see below
Armour:	10mm–44mm	10mm–54mm	10mm–54mm

Development/Variants

M-3s: The M-3 was developed from the earlier M-2 and saw service with the British Army from 1941. The above data relates to the M-3A1. This was powered either by a Continental W670-9A, 7 cylinder petrol engine developing 250hp at 2400rpm. This gives the tank a range of 120km. Or a Guiberson Model T1020-4, 9 cylinder diesel engine, developing 220hp at 2200rpm. This gives it a range of 145km. In addition to the fuel carried internally an additional 151 litres of fuel could be carried in external jettisonable tanks. The 37mm gun has an elevation of $+20°$ and a depression of $-10°$. The later M-3A3 had an all-welded hull, increased fuel capacity (386 litres), additional stowage box at the rear, sand shields, additional ammunition stowage. This was made possible as the glacis plate was extended forward and the sponsons lengthened to the rear of the vehicle.

M-5s: Developed from the M-3, the M-5 was originally designated M-3 but this was changed to avoid confusion. It was powered by two V-8 Cadillac Series 42 petrol engines developing 110hp at 3200rpm. The later M-5A1 had an improved turret with a radio bulge at the rear and the anti-aircraft gun repositioned on the right side of the turret.

M-8: This is an M-5 chassis and hull fitted with a new turret mounting a 75mm howitzer with an elevation of $+40°$ and a depression of $-20°$. The range of the gun was about 8800m. The same turret was fitted to the LVT(A)4.

Employment

M-3s are still used by Bolivia, Brazil, Chile, Dominican Republic, Ecuador, Guatemala, Haiti, Honduras, Indonesia, India, Mexico, South Korea, Taiwan, Uruguay, Venezuela.

M-5s are still used by Mexico.

M-8s are still used by Mexico.

M-8s on parade in Mexico a few years ago

XM–800
Armoured Reconnaissance Scout Vehicle (ARSV)

United States

	Lockheed ARSV	FMC ARSV
Crew:	3	3
Length:	4.914m	4.521m
Width:	2,438m	2.438m
Height:	2.489m	2.48m
G/Clearance:	.406m	.406m
Weight Loaded:	7697kg	8250kg
G/Pressure:	.42kg.cm^2	.31kg.cm^2
Speed Road:	104km/ph	84km/ph
Speed Water:	8km/ph	7km/ph
Range:	725km	725km
Fuel:	341 litres	462 litres
Fording:	Amphibious	Amphibious
V/Obstacle:	.914m	.762m
Gradient:	60%	60%

Development/Variants/Employment
On 23rd May 1972, the United States Army awarded two contracts to the FMC Corporation and Lockheed Missiles and Space Company to build prototypes of the ARSV. This vehicle will replace the M-114 vehicles at present used for this purpose. Each company is to build four prototypes and deliver three of them to the United States Army for testing by the end of 1974. The remaining vehicle will remain with the parent company for trials. After extensive testing, a decision will be taken on which vehicle will be built in quantity.
Lockheed Vehicle: This is a 6×6 vehicle powered by a Detroit Diesel Model GM6V53T developing 300hp at 2800rpm. The vehicle is fully amphibious being propelled in the water by waterjets. It is armed with a M-139 20mm cannon and a 7.62mm M-60D machine gun. Elevation is +65° and depression −20°. 500

rounds of 20mm and 2000 rounds of 7.62mm ammunition are carried.
FMC Vehicle: This is a full-tracked vehicle and is powered by a Detroit Diesel Model GM6V53AT engine developing 280hp at 2800rpm. It has the same armament as the Lockheed vehicle. It is propelled in the water by its tracks.
Each vehicle will have a comprehensive range of day and night vision devices, laser range-finder, stabilised weapons system, surveillance radar and other sensors. In the late 1970s the 20mm weapon will be replaced by a new 20mm–30mm weapon called the Bushmaster which is at present under development.

The Lockheed Missile and Space Companies Scout prototype under test. Note the smoke dischargers fitted to the turret

XR311 High Mobility Wheeled Vehicle   United States

Armament: Various machine guns and anti-tank weapons, depending on mission requirements
Crew: 1+2
Length: 4.34m
Width: 1.93m
Height: 1.60m
G/Clearance: .28m (minimum)
Weight: 2767kg (loaded)
2177kg (empty, including fuel)
590kg (maximum payload)
G/Pressure: .49kg.cm²
Engine: Chrysler V-8 petrol 5.2 litres, developing 190hp at 4000rpm
Speed: 130km/ph (road)
90km/ph (10% slope)
10km/ph (60% slope)
Range: 480km (cruising)
Fuel: 106 litres
Fording: .76m
V/Obstacle: .51m
Trench: not applicable
Gradient: 60%+

Development
The primary role of this 4×4 vehicle is to provide high-performance combat mobility, both on and off the road. To carry out this role, the vehicle is fitted with power steering, full-time automatic four-wheel drive, four-wheel independent torsion-bar suspension, disc brakes on all wheels, three-speed automatic transmission, centre-mounted transfer gear case with interaxle differential and limited-slip clutch, limited-slip clutches in front and rear differentials, heavy duty shock absorbers, low-pressure tyres and a 5000kg winch at the front of the vehicle.
FMC began proprietary development of the XR311 in 1969, and completed the first of two prototypes in 1970. The vehicle was demonstrated to the US Army, which resulted

in considerable interest. In 1971, the US Army purchased ten second-generation XR 311 prototypes for military potential tests. These vehicles were four anti-armour with the TOW missile system, three reconnaissance vehicles with 12.7mm machine guns and three escort/security vehicles with 7.62mm machine guns and crew armour kits.
The military potential tests were completed in the spring of 1972. Test reports indicated that the XR311 offered unique high-speed cross-country mobility characteristics and was particularly suitable for the prescribed missions. Since then FMC has modified the vehicle design.
Because of the highly favourable reactions to date from all test agencies and many officers in the US Army and several other countries, it is anticipated that the XR311 will be adopted world-wide for a variety of roles.
Variants
The vehicle can be quickly fitted out for a variety of roles by installation of special purpose kits:
Anti-Tank: Fitted with the TOW missile launcher system and eight TOW missiles.
Radio: Fitted with ground-to-ground and ground-to-air communications equipment.
Reconnaissance: Armed with a 12.7mm machine gun on a ring mount.
Security: Armed with a variety of weapons including 7.62mm machine guns, 40mm grenade launchers, 6.56mm or 7.62mm miniguns.
Other roles could include ambulance, mortar, military police and riot control. A crew compartment armour kit is available, consisting of (1) high-hardness steel doors, side body panels, toe panel, and firewall; and (2) bullet proof windshield and door glass.
Employment
This vehicle has been tested by the United States Army.

Lockheed Twister, XM–808
High Mobility Reconnaissance Vehicle
United States

Armament: 1 × 20mm M-139 Hispano-Suiza cannon
Crew: 3
Length: 5.587m
Width: 2.667m
Height: 2.463m
G/Clearance: .457m
Weight: 9276kg (loaded)
Engines: 2 × Chrysler 440, 8 cylinder petrol engines developing 580hp (total)
Speed: 104.6km/ph (road)
Fuel: 115 litres
Fording: 1.066m
V/Obstacle: .914m
Gradient: 60%
G/Pressure: .42kg.cm²

Development/Variants

Development of the Lockheed Twister was started as a private venture by the Lockheed Missiles and Space Company in December 1964. The first prototype, designated Lockheed Twister Testbed was completed in October 1965. This vehicle was given extensive trials over snow, mud, deserts, mountains and rice-paddies. The vehicle performed very well during these trials.

In January 1968, the United States Tank-Automative Command awarded Lockheed a 3.3 million dollar contract for three Twister vehicles. These consisted of one XM-808, one O6 Testbed and one O6 Testbed (with amphibious capability).

The XM-808 is armed and the crew compart-ment is fitted with aluminium armour. The O6 Testbed has no armour or armament and has a weight of 7560kg, height of 2.08m and a ground pressure of .35kg.cm², other data being similar to the basic XM-808. The O6 Testbed (Amphibious) is fitted with waterjets which give it a speed of 9.6km/ph in the water. By 1972 the Twisters had been built and tested by the United States Army. A total of 29,000km of testing was carried out at Fort Knox, Aberdeen Proving Grounds and Lockheed's own facilities at Sunnyvale, California. The results of these tests are being evaluated. The eight wheels of the Twister are all powered. The vehicle consists of two bodies, each body has its own engine and the bodies are connected by a pivoted yoke providing three degrees of freedom in pitch, roll and yaw. Lockheed have plans for two weight classes of Twister. A light weight series of 7710/8160kg and a medium class of 13,600/14,500kg. Variants would include infantry fighting vehicles, anti-tank, assault and air defence vehicles.

Lockheed are also building prototypes of the ARSV (see separate entry) and have built a larger version of the Twister called the Dragon Wagon. This could be used for heavy construction work.

Employment

Trials completed by the United States Army.

The Lockheed XM-808 Twister being put through its paces

Carrier, C & R, M–114
Command and Reconnaissance Vehicle

United States

Armament: 1 × 12.7mm M-2 machine gun with 1000 rounds of ammunition
1/2 × 7.62mm M-60 machine guns with 3000 rounds of ammunition
Crew: 3/4
Length: 4.46m
Width: 2.33m
Height: 2.31m
G/Clearance: .36m
Weight: 6846kg (loaded)
5852kg (empty)
G/Pressure: .35kg.cm²
Engine: Chevrolet Model 283, V-8, OHV, liquid petrol engine developing 160hp at 4650rpm
Speed: 58km/ph (road)
5.4km/ph (water)
Range: 480km (cruising)
Fuel: 416 litres
Fording: Amphibious
V/Obstacle: .51m
Trench: 1.52m
Gradient: 60%

Development/Variants
Development of the M-114 started in 1956. The prototype was the T-114 and this was fitted with a turret-mounted machine gun. The T-114 was classified as limited production in 1961, and Standard A in May 1963.
The production vehicles were designated M-114 and these did not have a machine gun turret. Production was undertaken by the Cadillac Division of the General Motors Corporation. The first order was for 1215 vehicles and the first 615 of these were built to M-114 standard, the remainder of the batch were built to M-114A1 standard, as was the second batch of 1295 and the third batch of 1200. The M-114A1 (development designation T-114E1) has a commander's cupola with a single hatch (the M-114 has a two-piece commander's hatch) and electrical firing gear for the 12.7mm machine gun, the machine gun on the M-114A1 can be fired from within the vehicle. Data of the M-114A1 is similar to the M-114 except for a weight of 6928kg and a height of 2.33m.
The M-114 is constructed of welded aluminium armour and has torsion bar suspension. It is fully amphibious in the water being propelled by its tracks. Infra-red driving equipment is fitted as is a crew NBC system. Various other weapons have been fitted including the M-139 (20mm Hispano-Suiza HS-820), 90mm turret as fitted to the AML-90 and the TRW 25mm cannon. Early replacement of the M-114 is intended when numerous shortcomings were found when the vehicle was deployed to Vietnam. Replacement vehicle will be the XM-800 ARSV, now under development.
Employment
United States and South Vietnam.

The M-114A1E1 armed with a 7.62mm machine gun and a 20mm canon

Lynx
Command and Reconnaissance Carrier

United States

Armament: 1×12.7mm machine gun with 1150 rounds of ammunition
1×7.62mm machine gun with 2000 rounds of ammunition
2×3 smoke grenade launchers
Crew: 3
Length: 4.597m
Width: 2.413m
Height: 2.171m (including cupola)
1.652m (hull top)
G/Clearance: .406m
Weight: 8775kg (loaded)
7725kg (air-drop)
G/Pressure: .48kg.cm²
Engine: GMC 6V53 diesel, 215hp
Speed: 70.8km/ph (road)
5.6km/ph (water)
Range: 523km
Fuel: 303 litres
Fording: Amphibious
V/Obstacle: 0.61m
Trench: 1.52m
Gradient: 60%
Armour: 38mm (maximum)

Development

The initial vehicle, developed by FMC Corporation as a private venture was called the Command and Reconnaissance Vehicle, C & R. This vehicle is often called the M-113½. The principal suspension and power-train components are the same as the M-113A1 (diesel). The prototype was built in 1963.
The C & R has the commander and driver located side by side. This model was ordered by the Netherlands and the first production vehicle was completed in September 1966.
When Canada purchased the vehicle, they requested certain changes, such as the commander and driver placed in tandem. They named their vehicle Armoured, Full-Tracked, Command and Reconnaissance Carrier, Lynx, the first production vehicle for Canada was completed in May 1968.
Both configurations have only four dual road wheels per side, with a hull lower than the M-113, and the engine at the rear. The vehicle is fully amphibious being propelled in the water by its tracks. It has infra-red night driving lights but no NBC system.

Variants

1. Fitted with twin 7.62mm M73 or 7.62mm M37 machine guns in a single cupola.
2. Fitted with a cupola-mounted 20mm cannon, a 7.62mm machine gun being mounted on the front right hatch.
3. At various times it has been proposed to fit small ATGWs in launcher boxes on the roof of the vehicle.
4. A 106mm recoilless rifle mounting is reported to be under development.
5. For trials purposes Rheinmetall have fitted a Netherlands C & R with a turret mounting the Rh 202 20mm cannon.
6. For trials purposes Oerlikon have fitted a Netherlands C & R with a new turret mounting a 25mm cannon.
7. Other weapon stations can be incorporated at the time of construction at the discretion of the buyer.

Employment

Lynx used by Canada.
C & R used by the Netherlands.

The FMC Command and Reconnaissance Carrier

M-8 and T-17E1 Armoured Cars
M-20 Utility Vehicle

United States

	M-8	M-20	T-17E1
Crew:	4	2–6	5
Length:	5.00m	5.00m	5.49m
Width:	2.54m	2.54m	2.69m
Height:	2.25m	2.31m	2.37m
G/Clearance:	.29m	.29m	.38m
Weight Loaded:	7892kg	7937kg	13,925kg
Speed Road:	90km/ph	90km/ph	90km/ph
Range Road:	560km	560km	724km
Fuel:	212 litres	212 litres	519 litres
Fording:	.61m	.61m	.81m
V/Obstacle:	.30m	.30m	.53m
Gradient:	60%	60%	57%
Main Armament:	37mm	—	37mm
Co-Axial Armament:	7.62mm	—	7.62mm
A/A Armament:	12.7mm	12.7mm	7.62mm
Bow Armament:	—	—	7.62mm
Ammunition 37mm:	80	—	103
Ammunition 12.7mm:	400	1000	—
Ammunition 7.62mm:	1500	—	5250
Engine:	Hercules JXD	Hercules JXD	GMC 270(2)
Bhp/rpm:	110/3000	110/3000	97/3000(each)
Armour:	3mm–20mm	3mm–20mm	7mm–45mm
Track:	1.93m	1.93m	2.26m

Development/Variants

M-8 and M-20: The M-8 was developed in 1942 by the Ford Motor Company. Ford subsequently undertook the production of the vehicle. More M-8s were built than any other American armoured car. The vehicle entered service in 1943 and a small quantity were supplied to the British, who called them Greyhounds. The only other model to enter service was the M-20. This was the chassis and hull of the M-8 but with its turret removed and replaced by a superstructure, over this was mounted a ring mount for a 12.7mm machine gun. France has recently fitted an M-20 Utility Car with the complete turret of the AML-90 armoured car. This has a 90mm gun and a 7.62mm co-axial machine gun. At the time of writing none had been produced in quantity. Brazil has some M-8s fitted with rocket launchers.

The M-8 Armoured Car, this particular vehicle does not have its 12.7mm Anti-Aircraft gun fitted

Employment

Brazil, Cambodia (and M-20), Cameroon, Colombia, Congo, Dahomey, Ethiopia, Greece (and M-20), Iran (and M-20), Laos, Malagasy, Mexico, Morocco, Niger (and M-20), Norway, Peru, Saudi Arabia, Senegal, South Korea, South Vietnam, Taiwan, Thailand, Tunisia, Turkey, Venezuela, Yugoslavia.

T-17E1 Staghound

The Staghound (American designation T-17E1) was manufactured by Chevrolet between 1942 and 1943. All production Staghounds were sent to the British. The T-17E2 was an anti-aircraft version and was called Staghound AA by the British. Most were stripped of their armament and used in the command role. The T-17E3 was a close support version and used the turret of the M-8 self-propelled howitzer. This did not enter production. The British developed two models of the Staghound. The Staghound 11 had a 76.2mm howitzer and the Staghound 111 had the gun and turret of the Crusader tank.

Employment

Still reported to be used by Cuba, Honduras, Lebanon, Rhodesia, Saudi Arabia, and South Africa.

M-20 Armoured Utility Vehicle modified by fitting the turret of the AML 90 Armoured Car

Staghound Armoured Car (World War II Photograph)

Chrysler MAC–1 Armoured Car — United States

Armament: 1×20mm turret-mounted cannon, traverse 360°
Crew: 4
Length: 5.26m
Width: 2.44m
Height: 2.11m (including turret)
G/Clearance: .46m (maximum)
Weight: 6710kg (loaded)
Speed: 104km/ph (road)
Range: 480km
Fording: .76m
V/Obstacle: .30m
Gradient: 50%
Engine: Chrysler 361

Development/Variants/Employment
The Chrysler MAC was developed as a private venture by the Chrysler Corporation and a small number were delivered to Mexico in 1963. The vehicle uses a number of standard truck components and is powered by the same engine as the M-113 armoured personnel carrier. It is not amphibious and is capable only of fording. Other Chrysler projects that have not reached prototype stage include a 4×4 light armoured car and the 8×8 SWAT vehicle.

Commando Multi-Mission Vehicle — United States

	V-100	V-150	V-200
Crew (according to role):	12	12	12
Length:	5.689m	5.689m	6.12m
Width:	2.26m	2.26m	2.438m
Height (over hull):	1.93m	1.95m	1.981m
G/Clearance (axles):	.406m	.381m	.431m
Weight Loaded:	7370kg	9550kg	12,730kg
Weight Empty (basic vehicle curb):	5910kg	6820kg	9298kg
Speed Road:	100km/ph	89km/ph	94km/ph
Speed Water:	4.8km/ph	4.8km/ph	4.8km/ph
Range Road:	965km	965km	500km
Fuel:	303 litres	303 litres	379 litres
Fording:	Amphibious	Amphibious	Amphibious
V/Obstacle:	.609m	.609m	.609m
Gradient:	50%	60%	60%
Engine:	Petrol (200hp)	Petrol (210hp)*	Petrol (275hp)
Track:	1.866m	1.95m	2.038/2.076m
Wheelbase:	2.667m	2.667m	3.263m

Note. *The crew, weight loaded and weight empty depends on the role and type of armament that is fitted. (* or a 155hp diesel engine.)*

Development
The V-100 Commando was developed as a private venture by the Cadillac Gage Company of Warren, Michigan. The first prototype was built in March 1963, and the first production vehicle was built in January 1964. The V-100 was designated XM-706 by the US Army; later this became the M-706. All members of the family are fully amphibious being propelled in the water by their wheels. They are fitted with front mounted winches. All have all-welded hulls, firing ports and vision blocks enabling the crew to fire their weapons from within the vehicle. A wide range of armament systems can be installed, some of which are described below.

Variants
V-100: The following models are available:

(a) Fitted with a turret mounting twin 7.62mm machine guns with 1000 ready rounds and 9000 rounds in reserve, and 12 smoke dischargers.
(b) Fitted with turret-mounted 7.62mm and 12.7mm machine gun, and 12 smoke dischargers.
(c) Fitted with a pod for use in the command/armoured personnel carrier role.
(d) Open topped model on which can be fitted turret, pod, or single 7.62mm machine gun.
(e) Police, rescue, riot control or fire fighting vehicle.
(f) Fitted with TOW missile launcher.
(g) Fitted with turret-mounted 7.62mm minigun.
(h) Fitted with Dragon anti-tank weapons.
V-150: This was first shown during 1971 and is designed to fill the gap between the V-100 and the larger V-200. There are four basic versions:
1. Has a crew of two and can carry 10 infantry.

Armed with twin 7.62mm machine guns or 1×7.62mm and 1×12.7mm machine guns, and 12 smoke dischargers.

2. Mortar carrier with a crew of five, armed with an 81mm mortar with 60–80 rounds of ammunition, 7.62mm machine guns and 12 smoke dischargers. 2000 rounds of machine gun ammunition are carried.

3. Armed with a turret-mounted 20mm Oerlikon cannon, a 7.62mm co-axial machine gun and a 7.62mm anti-aircraft machine gun and 12 smoke dischargers. The 20mm gun has an elevation of +60° and a depression of −8°. 400 rounds of 20mm and 3000 rounds of 7.62mm ammunition are carried. It has a crew of eight.

4. Armed with a 90mm Mecar gun, a 7.62mm co-axial machine gun, a 7.62mm anti-aircraft machine gun and 12 smoke dischargers. 40 rounds of 90mm and 3000 rounds of 7.62mm ammunition are carried. Crew of four men. Recovery, command and TOW missile versions are also available.

V-200: This was first shown in 1969 and has been produced in the following roles:

(a) Personnel carrier seating 12 men, armed with 7.62mm machine guns.

(b) Armed with 90mm gun, 7.62mm co-axial machine gun, 7.62mm anti-aircraft machine gun and 12 smoke dischargers.

(c) Armed with a turret-mounted 20mm gun, 7.62mm co-axial machine gun, 7.62mm anti-aircraft machine gun, 12 smoke dischargers. Crew of 11.

(d) Mortar vehicle with 81mm mortar, 7.62mm machine guns and a crew of five.

(e) 120mm mortar carrier, crew of seven and 7.62mm machine guns.

(f) Recovery vehicle, crew of eight, armed with 7.62mm machine guns. Also fitted with an 'A' frame.

Employment

Commandos are used by 21 countries including: Bolivia, Lebanon, Muscat and Oman, Portugal, Somalia, South Vietnam, Sudan, United States (Army and Air Force).

Commando with turret mounted twin 7.62mm machine guns

Commando armed with a turret mounted 20mm cannon, co-axial 7.62mm machine gun and 7.62mm Anti-Aircraft machine gun

XM-701
Mechanised Infantry Combat Vehicle

United States

Armament: 1 × 20mm cannon
1 × 7.62mm M-73 machine gun
Crew: 3 + 9
Length: 6.22m
Width: 3.15m
Height: 2.84m
G/Clearance: .46m
Engine: GMC 8V71T, 8 cylinder diesel engine
developing 425hp
Weight: 23,587kg
Speed: 59km/ph (road)
Range: 640km
Fording: Amphibious
G/Pressure: .79kg.cm²

Development/Variants/Employment
The XM-701 MICV was developed by the Pacific Car and Foundry Company of Renton, Washington. The first of five prototypes was handed over to the US Army on 15th May 1965. The vehicle is based on the chassis of the M-107/M-110 SPGs. The vehicle is fully amphibious being propelled in the water by its tracks, intra-red driving lights are fitted and there are firing ports in the hull. No production order was given for the XM-701, although the vehicle is being used in the development of the XM-723, for example testing certain components.

Above: *The XM-701 MICV. Note the firing ports towards the rear of the vehicle*

XM-723
Mechanised Infantry Combat Vehicle

United States

Late in 1972 FMC Corporation, who build the M-113 APC, were awarded a 29.2 million dollar contract to start development of the XM-723 Mechanised Infantry Combat Vehicle. The vehicle will be fully amphibious and will be armed with a turret-mounted M-139 20mm cannon and a 7.62mm M-219 machine gun, stabilised control for these weapons will be fitted. It will carry a total of 12 men, including the crew. There will be firing ports and vision blocs in the sides and rear of the vehicle. The commander, gunner and driver will be provided with passive day and night vision equipment.

Rams Vehicles

In the 1960s a study was undertaken by the United States Army to find vehicles suitable for operation in a Vietnam-type environment. This study was called RAMS—Remote Area Mobility Study. Two of these vehicles are described below:

XM-729 Assault Vehicle: This was based on the M-116 amphibious tracked cargo vehicle built by the Pacific Car and Foundry Company of Renton. The XM-729 is fully amphibious and has a crew of two. It is armed with a 7.62mm M-60 machine gun and a 40mm grenade launcher, mounted in a single turret.

XM-733 Assault Vehicle: This has the same chassis as the above. In 1967 the Pacific Car and Foundry Company were awarded a contract to build 93 of these vehicles for trials, but no large scale deployment has taken place.

Some are being used to develop vehicle components. The XM-733 is armed with a 40mm grenade launcher and one or two 7.62mm M-60 machine guns. A later model was the XM-733E1. This had a simple cupola for the machine gun. Both the XM-729 and XM-733 are powered by a Chevrolet V-8 petrol engine developing 160bhp at 4600rpm. It has a road speed of 60km/ph and a water speed of 5km/ph, road range is 480km, Loaded weight of the XM-733 is 4760kg, gradient 60%, vertical obstacle .46m and trench 1.47m.

An XM-733 vehicle under test by the United States Marine Corps in 1970. This particular vehicle is armed with a 40mm grenade launcher, two 7.62mm machine guns and a single 12.7mm machine gun

Armoured Infantry Fighting Vehicle (AIFV)

Armament: 1 × 20mm gun, elevation + 60°. depression −10° OR
1 × 25mm cannon OR
1 × 12.7mm machine gun
1 × 7.62mm co-axial machine gun
600 rounds of 20mm ammunition **or**
415 rounds of 25mm ammunition
Crew: 3+7
Length: 5.359m
Width: 2.845m
Height: 2.667m (including turret)
2.007m (hull top)
G/Clearance: .432m
Weight: 12,698kg (loaded)
11,349kg (empty)
G/Pressure: .62kg.cm² (loaded)
Engine: Detroit Diesel 6V53T 2-stroke turbo-

charged, liquid-cooled diesel engine developing 260hp at 2800rpm
Speed: 61.6km/ph (road)
5.5km/ph (water)
Range: 490km
Fuel: 416 litres
Fording: Amphibious
V/Obstacle: .64m
Trench: 1.68m
Gradient: 60%
Armour: Aluminium and steel

Development/Variants
In 1967, FMC Corporation built two XM-765s for the United States Army. These vehicles used a number of M-113 components and were tested in the USA and Korea. FMC

160

developed this vehicle further as a private venture, with the end result being the AIFV, the prototype of which was completed in 1970. The vehicle has been changed and improved in many ways, including additional steel armour attached to the hull (with a gap between it and the aluminium armour), a power-operated weapon station (turret) with a 20mm or 25mm automatic cannon and a co-axial 7.62mm machine gun (currently being designed), five firing ports for individual weapons (two each side and one at the rear), an engine turbo-charger that increases the hp from 215 to 260, and new high-capacity shock absorbers. The vehicle is equipped with the M34 day sight, the M36 day/night sight, or the Philip day/night sight. The vehicle uses the improved T130E1 track recently adapted for use on the M-113A1. A unique torsion bar and tube suspension system results in superior cross-country performance.

The AIFV is fully amphibious, being propelled in the water by its tracks. It is fitted with infra-red lights for night driving. No NBC system is fitted at present.

Employment

The AIFV has been widely tested in Europe, and prototypes will be tested by the Royal Netherlands Army in the spring of 1974.

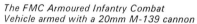
The FMC Armoured Infantry Combat Vehicle armed with a 20mm M-139 cannon

M–113 Series   United States

Development

The M-113 was developed from 1956 by the FMC Corporation who built the earlier M-59 APC. The prototypes were built in 1958 and these were designated T-113E1 and T-113E2. In 1959 a production order was awarded to FMC and by 1960 production was underway. The M-113 is fully amphibious being propelled in the water by its tracks. It is built of welded aluminium armour. The driver is provided with an infra-red periscope for night driving. The vehicle does not have an NBC system. The M-113 was succeeded in production by the M-113A1; this has a diesel engine. The installation of a diesel engine gave a slight increase in speed, but most important of all, a substantial increase in the operating range of the vehicle. By 1973 over 44,000 M-113s and variants had been built

in the USA and over 3000 M-113s had been built in Italy by Oto Melara. The M-113A1 has been further developed into the AIFV, for which there is a separate entry. Listed below are the more important variants of the M-113, in addition there are many local variants.

Variants

Mortar Carrier M-106 and M-106A1: The M-106 has a petrol engine and the M-106A1 a diesel engine. It is armed with a 107mm (4.2in) mortar which has a traverse of 90° and fires through a three part circular hatch in the roof. A mortar base and stand are carried externally on the left side of the vehicle enabling the mortar to be fired away from the vehicle. The M-106 carried 93 rounds and the M-106A1 carries 88 rounds of 107mm mortar ammunition.

Armoured Personnel Carrier M-113 and

	M-106	M-106A1	M-113	M-113A1	M-125A1	M-132A1	M-577A1
Crew:	6	6	1+12	1+12	6	2	5
Length:	4.93m	4.93m	4.87m	4.87m	4.87m	4.87m	4.87m
Width:	2.86m	2.86m	2.69m	2.69m	2.69m	2.69m	2.69m
Width Reduced:	2.54m	2.54m	2.54m	2.54m	2.54m	2.54m	2.54m
Height Overall:	2.50m	2.50m	2.50m	2.50m	2.50m	2.43m	2.68m
Height Reduced:	2.02m	2.02m	2.02m	2.02m	2.02m	2.29m	2.57m
G/Clearance:	.41m	.41m	.41m	.41m	.41m	.41m	.41m
Weight Loaded kg:	11,650	11,865	10,670	10,930	11,140	10,840	11,000
Weight Empty kg:	8790	9010	9210	9470	9035	9475	9940
G/Pressure kg.cm²:	.57	.57	.52	.54	.55	.54	.54
Speed Road km/ph:	64.4	66.8	64.4	68.4	68.4	68.4	68.4
Speed Water km/ph:	5.6	5.6	5.6	5.8	5.8	5.8	5.8
Range km:	298	475	322	500	483	490	495
Fuel litres:	322	360	322	360	360	360	454
Fording:	AMP	AMP	AMP	AMP	AMP	AMP	AMP
V/Obstacle:	.61m	.61m	.61m	.61m	.61m	.61m	.61m
Trench:	1.68m	1.68m	1.68m	1.68m	1.68m	1.68m	1.68m
Gradient:	60%	60%	60%	60%	60%	60%	60%
Armament MG:	12.7mm	12.7mm	12.7mm	12.7mm	12.7mm	7.62mm	—
Ammunition MG:	2000	2000	2000	2000	2000	2000	—
Engine:	CHRY	GMC	CHRY	GMC	GMC	GMC	GMC

Note. *The Chrysler engine is a Model 75M petrol engine developing 209hp and the GMC engine is a Model 6V53 diesel developing 215hp. Maximum armour is 38mm.*

M-113A1: This is the basic vehicle. In its normal role it carries 12 infantrymen. A wide range of kits are available to adapt it for various roles, these include ambulance, cargo, dozer vehicle, fitters' vehicle, recovery vehicles. It can be fitted with HOT, TOW, ENTAC anti-tank missile systems. Other models in service include the M-113 bridge-payer. This was developed for use in Vietnam and has a bridge that spans a gap up to 10m in width and can carry vehicles of 15,000kg. The ACAV (Armoured Cavalry Assault Vehicle) which is armed with a 12.7mm and two 7.62mm machine guns. Each of these machine guns is protected by an armoured shield. The German and Danish Armies have M-113s modified to carry the British Green Archer mortar locating radar system. The American and Vietnamese Army have some M-113s with two 7.62mm machine guns and a 40mm grenade launcher. The Australians have M-113s with the complete Saladin armoured car turret fitted on the roof of the vehicle. They also have some M-113s with turrets from Commando armoured cars; this turret mounts a 12.7mm and a 7.62mm machine gun. This version is called the M-113A1 Carrier Personnel/Reconnaissance, the Saladin model is known as the M-113A1 (FS) Fire Support Vehicle. The German Army has a number of M-113s with 120mm mortars.

Mortar Carrier M-125 and M-125A1: This is armed with an 81mm mortar mounted on a baseplate giving the mortar a traverse of 360°. It fires through the three part circular hatch in the roof, baseplate and stand are carried externally enabling the mortar to be fired away from the vehicle. 114 rounds of 81mm mortar ammunition are carried. First production vehicles were delivered in 1966.

Self-Propelled Flamethrower M-132A1: Prototypes used the M-113 chassis, but production vehicles used the M-113A1 chassis. It is armed with a turret mounting a 7.62mm M-73 machine gun and a M10-8 flame gun; the turret has a traverse of 360°, elevation being +55° and depression −5° The flame thrower has a maximum firing range of 180m and a sustained duration of 32 seconds. Deliveries commenced in 1965, the installation of the turret was carried out by CONDEC of Schenectady, New York. Production was completed in 1967. The vehicle is supported in action by the M-45 (a modified M-548) vehicle. This carries additional fuel for the flame gun.

M-163 Vulcan Air Defence System: This is a Vulcan 20mm cannon mounted on a M-113A1 chassis, the chassis in this case is designated M-741. The Vulcan gun has six barrels and has two rates of fire, 1000 or 3000 rounds per minute, thus allowing it to be used against both ground and air targets. The turret has a traverse of 360°, elevation being +80° and depression −5°. A crew of four is carried. First models were delivered to the Army in August 1968.

Command Post M-577 and M-577A1: Both petrol- and diesel-engined models. This is basically an M-113 or an M-113A1 with a higher hull. The vehicle is fitted with additional radios, mapboards, tables and so on; it is also fitted with an NBC system. A tent can be erected at the rear of the vehicle to give additional working space. No armament is fitted. The first production M-577 was completed in 1962.

XM-734 Mechanised Infantry Combat Vehicle: This was basically an M-113 with firing ports in the sides of the vehicle. Trials only.

XM-765 Mechanised Infantry Combat Vehicle: Two of these were built for the US Army in 1967 by FMC. It had firing ports, additional armour and a turret-mounted gun. It was further developed by FMC into the AIFV.

M-548 Cargo Carrier: Development commenced in May 1963 and the vehicle was in production between 1967 and 1970. It uses the engine and suspension of the M-113A1 APC. Its role is to carry cargo and ammunition in the battle zone. It is fully amphibious and is armed with a 7.62mm or 12.7mm machine gun. A recovery vehicle was designated XM-696 but this did not enter service.

CHAPARRAL missile carrier: This is an M-548 with four Chaparral surface to air missiles mounted on the rear of the vehicle. It is deployed with the 20mm Vulcan Air Defence System. It entered service in 1968/1969.

HAWK missile carrier: This carries three HAWK surface to air missiles on the rear of the vehicle. These are fired from the vehicle. It is designated M-727.

LANCE system: The Lance missile is carried and fired by the M-752. The chassis was developed from M-113A1 components and is the M-667. Spare missiles are carried by the loader-transporter, the M-688.

Lynx C & R Vehicle: This was developed using components of the M-113. For this vehicle there is a separate entry.

Employment

Argentina, Australia (and M-125A1, M-577A1, M-548), Bolivia, Brazil, Cambodia, Canada (and M-577A1, Lynx, M-548), Chile, Denmark, Ecuador, Germany, Greece, Iran, Israel (and M-577A1 and M-548), Italy (and M-577), Laos, Lebanon, Libya (from Italy), Netherlands (M-577A1, M-106A1, Lynx), New Zealand, Norway (and M-577), Pakistan, Philippines, South Korea, South Vietnam, Spain (and M-577A1, M-125A1, M-548), Switzerland (and M-106, her M-113s are known as Spz-63s), Thailand, Turkey (from Italy), United States, Uruguay.

M-113A1 Carrier Personnel/Reconnaissance of the Australian Army

Top left: *M-113A1 Armoured Personnel Carrier of the Netherlands Army*

Above left: *M-113A1 APC being used in the ambulance role, this particular vehicle belongs to the Netherlands Army*

Left: *M-113 Fitters Vehicle, as used by the Australian Army*

Right: *An Australian M-125A1 Mortar Carrier, this photograph clearly shows the 81mm mortar*

Left: *M-577 Command Vehicle built by Oto Melara for the Italian Army*

Below Left: *The XM-548E1 with four Chaparral Anti-Aircraft missiles, this system is now known as the M-730*

Below: *M-132A1 Flamethrower Vehicle*

M–59 Armoured Personnel Carrier   United States

Armament: 1 × 12.7mm M-2 machine gun
2000 rounds of 12.7mm ammunition
Crew: 2+10
Length: 5.613m
Width: 3.263m
3.149m (minimum)
Height: 2.387m (including cupola)
2.235m (hull top)
G/Clearance: .457m
Weight: 19,323kg (loaded)
17,916kg (empty)
G/Pressure: .50kg.cm²
Engines: 2 × GMC Model 302, 6 cylinder,
water-cooled, in-line, petrol engines develop-
ing 127hp at 3350rpm (each)
Speed: 51.50km/ph (road)
5.5km/ph (water)
Range: 193km (road)
Fuel: 518 litres
Fording: Amphibious
V/Obstacle: .46m
Trench: 1.676m
Gradient: 60%
Armour: 16mm

Development

The M-59 was designed and manufactured
by FMC. The prototypes were designated
T-59 (Cadillac powered) and T-59E1 (GMC
powered). The vehicle was in production
from February 1954 until March 1959. The
whole M-59 programme ran from December

1952 until February 1960 and cost a total of
202 million dollars.
The M-59 is fully amphibious being propelled
in the water by its tracks, infra-red driving
lights are fitted. There are hatches in the roof
and a single ramp at the rear of the vehicle.

Variants

The basic vehicle was armed with a pintle-
mounted 12.7mm machine gun; some models
were fitted with a cupola mounted 12.7mm
machine gun and these vehicles were known
as M-59A1s.
Experimental models of the M-59 included a
missile carrier, recoilless rifle carrier and the
LVTP-6 amphibious vehicle for the United
States Marines.
The basic M-59 could also be used as a load
carrier, command vehicle or ambulance.
The M-84 was armed with a 4.2in mortar and
had a cupola-mounted 12.7mm machine gun
and a crew of six men. The contract for the
M-84 ran from May 1956 until May 1958 and
a total of 21.7 million dollars was spent on the
programme.

Employment

The M-59 has been replaced in the United
States Army by the M-113. The vehicle is
still in service with Brazil, Greece, Lebanon,
South Vietnam and Turkey.

M-59 Armoured Personnel Carrier

M–75 Armoured Personnel Carrier   United States

Armament: 1×12.7mm M-2 machine gun
1800 rounds of 12.7mm ammunition
Crew: 2+10
Length: 5.193m
Width: 2.84m
Height: 3.041, (with machine gun)
2.755m (including cupola)
G/Clearance: .457m
Weight: 18,828kg (loaded)
16,632kg (empty)
G/Pressure: .57kg.cm²
Engine: Continental AO-895-4, 6 cylinder,
air-cooled petrol, developing 295hp at
2660rpm
Speed: 71km/ph (road)
Range: 185km
Fuel: 568 litres
Fording: 1.129m
2.082m (with kit)
V/Obstacle: .457m
Trench: 1.67m
Gradient: 60%
Armour: 16mm (maximum)

Development
The M-75 was designed in 1950 by the
International Harvester Company. The development designations were T-18, T-18E1 and
T-18E2. The vehicle used many components
of the M-41 light tank, including the engine
and transmission.
The first production M-75 was completed in
March 1952 and the last one was built in
February 1954. A total of 1729 were built by
the International Harvester Company and
FMC.
The M-75 was not amphibious which was a
drawback, and it was a very expensive
vehicle to build. The vehicle is fitted with
infra-red driving lights. The crew were
provided with roof hatches and there were
two doors at the rear of the vehicle. The M-75
can be recognised from the M-59 and M-113
as the M-75 is much higher.

Variants
There were few minor differences between
production batches. Experimental vehicles
included the T-64 mortar carrier (with a
4.2in mortar) and the T-73 Infantry Vehicle.

Employment
The M-75 is no longer used by the United
States Army although it is used by the
Belgian Army.

*The M-75 Armoured Personnel Carrier, no
machine gun is mounted on this particular
vehicle*

Armoured Half-Track Vehicles   United States

	M-2	M-3	M-3A1	M-4A1	M-9A1	M-16
Crew:	10	13	13	6	10	5
Length Overall:	6.146m	6.34m	6.337m	6.194m	6.32m	6.514m
Width:	2.196m	2.22m	2.22m	2.22m	2.19m	2.159m
Height:	2.26m	2.501m	2.692m	2.26m	2.31m	2.616m
G/Clearance:	.28m	.28m	.28m	.28m	.28m	.28m
Weight Loaded:	8980kg	9072kg	9298kg	9135kg	9348kg	9810kg
Weight Empty:	6940kg	7030kg	6940kg	7144kg	7756kg	8450kg
Speed Road:	73km/ph	73km/ph	73km/ph	73km/ph	73km/ph	64km/ph
Range Road:	242km	321km	321km	321km	321km	250km
Fuel:	227 litres	227 litres	227 litres	227 litres	227 litres	227 litres
Fording:	.812m	.812m	.812m	.812m	.812m	.812m
Gradient:	60%	60%	60%	60%	60%	60%
Armament:	12.7mm	—	12.7mm	—	12.7mm	12.7mm(4)
	7.62mm	7.62mm	7.62mm	7.62mm	7.62mm	—
Mortar:	—	—	—	81mm	—	—
Engine:	White	White	White	White	I.H.C.	White
Bhp/rpm:	147/3000	147/3000	147/3000	142/3000	124/2600	142/3000
Armour:	7-13mm	7-13mm	7-13mm	7-13mm	7-13mm	7-13mm

Full designations and manufacturers are as follows:
Car, Half Track, M-2 (Autocar Company, White Motor Company);
Carrier, Personnel, Half Track, M-3 and M-3A1 (Autocar Company, Diamond T Motor Company, White Motor Company);
Carrier, 81mm Mortar, Half Track, M-4A1 (White Motor Company);
Carrier, Half Track, M-9A1 (International Harvester Company);
Carriage, Motor, Multiple Gun, M-16 (White Motor Company).

Development/Variants
The United States developed half track vehicles in the 1930s and they were produced in large numbers by various manufacturers during World War II. The above listing is only a selection of those that may be found in service. The dimensions vary on whether the vehicle has a winch or roller mounted at the front, whether a 12.7mm machine gun is fitted and whether racks are fitted on the sides of the vehicle. Many local modifications are in service, refer also to the section on Israel.

Employment
Half Tracks are still used by Argentina, Austria (including M-3 and M-21 (81mm mortar)), Belgium, Brazil, Colombia, Cuba, Dominican Republic, Greece, Israel, Guatemala, Italy, Japan (M-15 and M-16), Mexico, Morocco, Portugal, Philippines, South Vietnam, Spain (including M-16), Taiwan, Thailand (including M-16), Turkey, Uruguay, Venezuela (M-2 and M-9), Yugoslavia.

M-16 Anti-Aircraft Half-Tracks of the Spanish Army, these particular vehicles have front mounted winches

CAR, Scout, 4 x 4, M–3A1   United States

This was manufactured by the White Motor Company. It is a 4×4 vehicle and was used as a radio vehicle, command vehicle, troop carrier and reconnaissance vehicle. Its basic data is as follows:

Length: 5.625m
Width: 2.032m
Height: 1.993m
Weight: 5920kg (loaded)
Armament: 1×12.7mm and 1×7.62mm machine guns
Engine: Hercules JXD developing 87hp at 2400rpm
Speed: 90km/ph (road)

Range: 410km
Fording: .71m
Gradient: 60%
Employment
Still in service with Brazil, Cambodia, Chile, Congo, Greece, Laos, Liberia, Mexico, Nicaragua, Peru, South Vietnam, Spain, Thailand, Turkey.

LVTP–7 Amphibious Assault Vehicle   United States

The Prototype LVTPX-12

Armament: 1×12.7mm M-85 machine gun elevation + 60°, depression − 15°
1000 rounds of ammunition
Crew: 3+25
Length: 7.94m
Width: 3.27m
Height: 3.26m (O/A)
3.12m (turret)
G/Clearance: .406m
Weight: 23,655kg (loaded)
18,257kg (empty)
G/Pressure: .576kg.cm²
Engine: Detroit diesel model 8V53T, 8 cylinder, developing 400hp at 2800rpm
Speed: 64.37km/ph (road)
13.5km/ph (water)
Range: 482km (land)
Fuel: 681 litres
Fording: Amphibious
V/Obstacle: .914m
Trench: 2.438m
Gradient: 70%
Armour: 10mm–45mm

Development
The first prototype was completed in October 1967 and was known as the LVTPX-12. A total of 15 prototypes were built by July 1968. These vehicles were armed with a 20mm cannon. Development and production of the vehicle was undertaken by FMC under the supervision of the Naval Ships Systems Command. A production order for the LVTP-7

was given to FMC in June 1970 and the first vehicle was delivered to the USMC on 26th August 1971; production is scheduled to continue until September 1974. The LVTP-7 is fully amphibious being propelled in the water by two waterjets. It is constructed of welded aluminium armour. It has torsion bar and tube suspension and is fitted with infrared driving lights.

Variants
LVTC-7: Landing Vehicle Tracked, Command Model 7. Prototype built in 1968 as LVTCX-2. It is a command vehicle and has a crew of 13. It carries additional radios and has an auxiliary power unit. A shelter can be erected if required.
LVTR-7: Landing Vehicle Tracked, Recovery Model 7. Prototype built in 1968 as the LVTRX-2. It has a winch, crane, welding equipment, pump, compressor, tools, etc.
LVTE-7: Landing Vehicle Tracked, Mine Clearing Model 7. Prototype built in 1970 as the LVTRX-3. Developed to clear paths through minefields. Not placed in production and no further development.
LVTHX-5: This was to have been a gun support vehicle, but did not enter production.
Employment
The LVTP-7 has replaced the LVTP-5 series in the United States Marine Corps and is also in service with the Spanish Marines, and on order for Italy.

LVT–4 Amphibious Assault Vehicle   United States

Armament: 2×12.7mm machine guns
2×7.62mm machine guns
5000 rounds of 12.7mm ammunition
4000 rounds of 7.62mm ammunition
Crew: 6
Length: 7.974m
Width: 3.251m
Height: 3.073m (w/o machine guns)
G/Clearance: .457m (hard ground)
.387m (soft ground)
Weight: 16,510kg (loaded)
12,428kg (empty)
G/Pressure: .59kg.cm² (hard ground)
Engine: Continental W670-9A, 7 cylinder
radial developing 250hp at 2400rpm
Speed: 24km/ph (road)
11km/ph (water)
Range: 240km (land)
160km (water)
Fuel: 617 litres
Fording: Amphibious
V/Obstacle: .914m
Trench: 1.524m
Gradient: 60%

Development/Variants
Development of the LVT can be traced back
to the 1930s. The first vehicles for the
United States Marine Corps were the un-
armoured LVT-1; these entered service in
1941. Later vehicles included the following
the (A) indicating that it was armoured:

LVT(A)1, LVT2, LVT(A)2, LVT3, LVT4,
LVT(A)4, LVT(A)5. The LVT(A)4 had a turret
mounting a 75mm howitzer. This was from
the M-8 self-propelled howitzer. Manu-
facturers of LVTs included the Food Machinery
Corporation, Borg-Warner Corporation, St
Louis Car Company and Graham-Paige
Motor Corporation. Since World War II
LVTs have seen service with the Americans in
Korea, French in Vietnam and with the
British at Suez.
In recent years the French Army has been
using an LVT to test equipment, including an
earth moving shovel, that is to be fitted to the
ENFRAC support vehicle.
Employment
The LVT is still in service with Italy (to be
replaced by LVTP-7), Spanish Marines (to be
replaced by LVTP-7), Taiwan and Thailand.

Above: *LVT-4 being used for tests by the
French Army in 1968*

M–107 and M–110 Self-Propelled Guns   United States

	M-107	M-110
Crew:	5	5
Length in Travelling Order:	11.256m	7.43m
Length Hull W/O Spade:	5.72m	5.72m
Width:	3.149m	3.149m
Height (Top of Mount):	2.809m	2.809m
Height (Top of Barrel-Travelling):	3.679m	2.93m
G/Clearance:	.466m	.466m
Weight Loaded:	28,168kg	26,534kg
Weight Empty:	25,945kg	24,312kg
G/Pressure:	.81kg.cm²	.76kg.cm²
Speed Road:	56km/ph	56km/ph
Range Cruising:	725km	725km
Fuel:	1137 litres	1137 litres
Fording:	1.066m	1.066m
V/Obstacle:	1.016m	1.016m
Trench:	2.362m	2.362m
Gradient:	60%	60%
Main Armament Calibre:	175mm	203mm
Main Armament Designation:	M-113	M-2A1
Mount Designation:	M-158	M-158
A/A Armament:	—	—
Ammunition Carried:	2	2
Engine:	see below	see below

Development

Both of these weapons use a standard chassis designed by the Pacific Car and Foundry Company. The chassis is used for the M-107, M-110 and the M-578 ARV. This chassis was also used for the now discontinued T-119 and T-121 ARVs, 155mm T-245 SPG; parts were also used in the MICV-70 (XM-701). The M-107 and M-110 each have a total crew of 13 men, five are carried on the gun (driver in the front and two men either side of the gun), and the other eight in an M-548 support vehicle. This vehicle also carries the ammunition. The British Army uses the 6×6 Stalwart for this role. The M-107 and M-110 use the same engine, transmission and final drive as the M-108 and M-109. The vehicles do not have anti-aircraft guns and the driver is the only member of the crew under cover. The British and American Armies have experimented with various covers to provide the crew with some protection against the weather and NBC warfare.

Variants

M-107: Design dates from 1957 and first prototype completed in February 1958 as the T-235; this became the T-235E1. The first production M-107 was completed in August 1962, the first unit was equipped at Fort Sill, Oklahoma, in January 1963. Manufacturers of the chassis have included FMC, Bowen-McLaughlin-York and Pacific Car and Foundry. The gun, which is made by Watervliet Arsenal, New York, has a traverse of 30° left and 30° right, elevation being +65° and depression −2°. It is powered by a General Motors 8V71T eight cylinder, liquid-cooled diesel developing 405hp at

M-107 of the British Army at the Royal School of Artillery, Larkhill

2300rpm. The gun has a maximum range of 32,600m and fires an HE or chemical round.

M-110: Prototype was designated T-236 and later T-236E1, production dates, manufacturers and engine data is similar to the M-107. The 203mm (8in) howitzer has an elevation of $+65°$ and a depression of $-2°$, traverse being 30° left and 30° right. Maximum range is 16,800m and it can fire nuclear or conventional shells.

M-110E2: Development started in December 1969 and this weapon is scheduled to replace both the M-107 and M-110 in a few years time. It has a longer barrel than the standard M-110 and fires HE, incendiary, nuclear, improved conventional munitions and dual purpose rounds. Range of the weapon has not been released. The loaded weight of the gun is 28,350kg.

Employment

M-107: Germany, Great Britain, Greece, Iran, Israel, Italy, Netherlands, South Vietnam, Spain, United States (Army and Marines).

M-110: Belgium, Germany, Great Britain, Iran Israel, Netherlands, South Korea, United States.

An M-110 Eight inch Howitzer of the German Army being prepared for firing

M-107 175mm gun of 'A Battery, 2nd Battalion, 94th Artillery, firing in support of Marine Units in the As Hua Valley, Vietnam

M–108 & M–109
Self-Propelled Howitzers
United States

	M-108	M-109
Crew:	7	6
Length Gun Forward:	6.114m	6.612m
Length Vehicle Only:	6.114m	6.114m
Width Overall:	3.295m	3.295m
Width Reducable to:	3.149m	3.149m
Height Inc. Machine Gun:	3.28m	3.28m
Height W/O Machine Gun:	3.048m	3.048m
G/Clearance:	.451m	.477m
Weight Loaded:	22,452kg	23,786kg
Weight Empty:	18,436kg	19,730kg
G/Pressure:	.71 kg.cm^2	.766kg.cm^2
Speed Road:	56km/ph	56km/ph
Speed Water:	6.43km/ph	6.43km/ph
Range Cruising:	360km	360km
Fuel:	511 litres	511 litres
Fording:	1.828m	1.828m
V/Obstacle:	.53m	.53m
Trench:	1.828m	1.828m
Gradient:	60%	60%
Main Armament Calibre:	105mm	155mm
Main Armament Designation:	M-103	M-126
Anti-Aircraft Gun:	12.7mm	12.7mm
Ammunition (Main) Rounds:	87	28
Ammunition (A/A) Rounds:	500	500
Engine:	Both are powered by a Detroit Diesel Model 8V71T turbo-charged engine developing 405hp at 2300rpm	

Development/Variants
M-108: Development of the 110mm T-195 self-propelled howitzer commenced in 1953 and in 1956 it was decided to mount a 105mm weapon in place of the 110m weapon. In 1959 designation was changed from T-195 to T-195E1, which became the M-108 in 1961. Production started in October 1962 and finished in September 1963, being produced by the GMC. Its 105mm gun can be elevated from −4° to +74°, turret traverse being 360°. Amphibious capabilities are the same as those of the M-109.

M-109: Development designations were T-196 and later T-196E1. The first prototype was built in 1961 followed by the first production vehicle in November 1962. The vehicle is built by the Allison Division of the General Motors Corporation at the Cleveland

The T-195E1 which became the M-108 Light Self-Propelled Howitzer

Tank-Automotive Plant. By 1970 2000 M-109s had been built. The turret has a traverse of 360°, elevation being +75° and depression −3°. The 155mm gun has a range of 14,700m and can fire three rounds a minute; it has a nuclear capability. Full designation is Howitzer, Medium, Self-Propelled M-109. The flotation equipment consists of nine air bags which are positioned four each side and one at the front of the vehicle, they are inflated in less than two minutes. The tracks propel the vehicle whilst in the water.

M-109A1: Development designation M-109E1. This version has a barrel 1.549m longer than that fitted to the M-109. This gives the weapon a range of 18,000m. Development started in 1967 and conversion of M-109s started in 1972 at depot maintenance level. All M-109s will be converted.

M-109G: This is a German model of the M-109. Its differences are that it has a horizontal sliding breech-block by Rheinmetall (American M-109s have an interrupted screw breech-block), German aiming equipment. Range is 18,500m.

M-109U: This is the designation given to the model used by the Swiss Army. It has a semi-automatic loader of Swiss design. Rate of fire is 6 rounds a minute.

M-109 (Italy): The M-109s used by Italy have their armament built by Oto Melara. They have also developed and tested a model of the M-109 that has a new long barrel and fires rounds designed for the SP70. This has a range of 22,000m or 24,000m with SP70 shells.

Employment

M-108: Belgium, Brazil, Spain, United States.

M-109: Austria, Belgium, Canada, Denmark, Germany, Great Britain. Iran, Israel, Italy, Libya (from Italy), Netherlands (they also have some without turrets used for driver training), Norway, Spain, Switzerland, United States.

XM-179: 155mm Self-Propelled Howitzer is under development by the General Motors Corporation.

Below: An Italian M-109 with armament built in Italy by Oto Melara

Bottom: An M-109 of the British Army, note that spades are in position and that no Anti-Aircraft machine gun is fitted

M–53 and M–55 Self-Propelled Guns United States

	M-53	M-55
Crew:	6	6
Length Overall (Incl Spade):	10.21m	7.908m
Length Hull:	6.908m	7.149m
Width:	3.555m	3.58m
Height W/O A/A MG:	3.555m	3.469m
G/Clearance:	.469m	.469m
Weight Loaded:	43,545kg	44,452kg
Weight Empty:	39,916kg	40,823kg
G/Pressure:	.78kg.cm²	.78kg.cm²
Speed Road:	48km/ph	48km/ph
Range Cruising:	257km	257km
Fuel:	1438 litres	1438 litres
Fording:	1.219m	1.219m
V/Obstacle:	1.016m	1.016m
Trench:	2.26m	2.26m
Gradient:	60%	60%
Main Armament Calibre:	155mm	203mm
A/A Armament Calibre:	12.7mm	12.7mm
Ammunition (Main) Rounds:	20	10
Ammunition (A/A) Rounds:	900	900
Armour:	13mm–26mm	13mm–26mm
Engine:	see below	see below

Development/Variants

The M-53 and M-55 use the same engine, transmission and auxiliary engine and other components of the M-48 tank. The engine, transmission and drive sprocket are at the front of the vehicle, the rear part of the vehicle has the turret which carries all of the crew including the driver. At the rear of the vehicle is a spade which is let down when the vehicle is in its firing position.

M-53: Development designation was T-97 and the prototype was built by the Pacific Car and Foundry Company in 1950, design work having been started in 1948. It is armed with a 155mm gun M-46 in mount M-86. This has an elevation of +65° and a depression of −5°. The turret can traverse 30° left and 30° right. The full designation is: Field Artillery, Self-Propelled, 155mm, M-53. The M-53 is distinguishable from the M-55 by its longer and thinner barrel.

M-55: Development designation was T-108. It is armed with a 203mm (8in) howitzer M-47 in mount M-86. This has an elevation of +65° and a depression of −5°. The turret can traverse 30° left and 30° right. The M-55 can fire either an HE round or a nuclear round. Its full designation is Howitzer, Heavy, Self-Propelled: Full Tracked, 8in M-55. A later vehicle, the M-55E1, had improved engine cooling and other improvements, but it did not enter service.

Employment

The M-55 is now used by the Belgium and Italian Armies. Both the M-53 and M-55 may be found in reserve units of the United States Army, as well as in other countries.

M-55 203mm (8in) Howitzer on display at Aberdeen Proving Ground

Above: A T-97 155mm
Self-Propelled Gun at
Aberdeen Proving
Ground, Maryland, USA

Right: An M-53 of the
United States Marine
Corps 11th Artillery
Regiment. 1st Marine
Division, in Vietnam

Below: A T-108/M-55
on display at Aberdeen
Proving Ground,
Maryland, USA

M–44 & M–52 United States
Self-Propelled Howitzers

	M-52	M-44	M-44A1
Crew:	5	5	5
Length Overall:	5.80m	6.159,	6.159m
Width:	3.149m	3.238m	3.238m
Height Inc. A/A MG:	3.31m	—	—
Height W/O A/A MG:	3.067m	—	—
Height with Canvas Cover:	—	3.11m	3.11m
G/Clearance:	.49m	.48m	.48m
Weight Loaded:	24,040kg	28,349kg	29,030kg
Weight Empty:	22,588kg	26,308kg	26,980kg
G/Pressure:	.60kg.cm²	.66kg.cm²	.67kg.cm²
Speed Road:	56km/ph	56km/ph	56km/ph
Range Cruising:	160km	122km	122km
Fuel:	678 litres	568 litres	568 litres
Fording:	1.219m	1.066m	1.066m
V/Obstacle:	.914m	.762m	.762m
Trench:	1.828m	1.828m	1.828m
Gradient:	60%	60%	60%
Main Armament Calibre:	105mm	155mm	155mm
A/A Armament Calibre:	12.7mm	12.7mm	12.7mm
Ammunition (Main) Rounds:	105	24	24
Ammunition (A/A) Rounds:	900	900	900
Armour:	20mm (max)	20mm (max)	20mm (max)
Engine:	see below	see below	see below

Development/Variants

General: Both the M-44 and M-52 use many components of the M-41 light tank, including the engine, transmission and auxiliary engine. The M-44 and M-52 have similar chassis. Both have their engine and transmission at the front and the turret or the fighting compartment at the rear. All of the crew are in the rear of the vehicle.

M-44: Development started in 1947 as the T-99 and the first prototypes were built in 1950 at Detroit Arsenal. The next model was the T-99E1; in 1952 this was redesignated T-194. In 1953 it was standardised as the M-44. The M-44 is armed with a 155mm M-45 howitzer in a mount M-80, traverse being 30° left and 30° right, elevation being +65° and depression −10°. The vehicle is powered by a Continental AOS-895-3 petrol

engine developing 500hp at 2800rpm. The M-44A1 is similar to the M-44 but is powered by a Continental AOS1-895-5 petrol engine with a fuel injection system. There is no overhead armour protection for the crew of the M-44. A canvas cover can be erected over the fighting compartment if required. When in the firing position a spade is let down at the rear of the vehicle and the back of the fighting compartment folds down to provide a platform for the crew to operate the gun.

M-52: The first pilot model was designated the T-98 and armed with a 155mm howitzer. It was built at Detroit Arsenal in 1950. This was followed by the T-98E1 which was armed

M-44 of the Spanish Army

with a 105mm howitzer. This became the
M-52. The M-52 is armed with an M-49
105mm howitzer in a mount M-85. The turret
has a traverse of 60° left and 60° right.
Elevation is +65° and depression is −10°.
The M-52 is powered by a six cylinder air-
cooled petrol engine; this is a Continental
AOS-895-3 developing 500hp at 2800rpm.
The M-52A1 is powered by a Continental
AOS1-895-5 with a fuel injection system
fitted. This gives the vehicle a maximum
speed of 68km/ph.

Employment
M-44: Greece, Italy, Japan, Spain, Turkey.
M-52: Belgium (reserve), Greece, Japan,
Jordan.

Below: *M-52 of the Japanese Self-Defence
Force*

Bottom: *M-44 on display at the Museum at
Aberdeen Proving Ground, Maryland, USA.
The struts over the rear of the vehicle
support the canvas cover*

M–7 and M–7B1
Self-Propelled Howitzer

United States

Armament: 1 × 105mm howitzer, elevation +35°, depression —5°, traverse 30° left and 15° right of centre line
69 rounds of 105mm ammunition carried
1 × 12.7mm anti-aircraft machine gun and 300 rounds of ammunition
Crew: 7
Length: 6.02m (6.18m) (overall)
Width: 2.88m (2.93m)
Height: 2.946m (including machine gun)
G/Clearance: .43m (.44m)
Weight: 22,970kg (25,610kg) (loaded)
G/Pressure: .73kg.cm²
Engine: See below
Speed: 39km/ph (32km/ph)
Range: 137km (200km)
Fuel: 677 (636) litres
Fording: 1.22m (.91m)
V/Obstacle: .61m
Trench: 2.23m
Gradient: 60%
Armour: 12mm–62mm

Note. *The data in brackets relates to the M-7B1. Deep fording equipment could be fitted.*

Development
Development commenced in June 1941 as the T-32, pilots were built by the American

Locomotive Company and it was standardised as the M-7 in February 1942. Production commenced in 1942. The vehicle saw extensive service with Allied Forces from the battle of El Alamein onwards. It was given the name 'Priest'. The 105mm howitzer had a range of 11,160m.

Variants
M-7: This was based on the M-4 chassis and manufactured by the American Locomotive Company. Powered by a Continental Model R-975-C1, 9 cylinder, radial petrol engine developing 350hp at 2400rpm.
M-7B1: This was based on the M-4A3 chassis and built by Pressed Steel Company. Powered by a Ford GAA V8 engine developing 450hp at 2600rpm. It was standardised in September 1942.
M-7B2: Very few of these were built by Federal Machine and Welder Company.

Employment
Used by Austria, Belgium, Brazil, Israel, Italy, Jordan, Pakistan, Turkey, Yugoslavia.

An M-7 in post-war service with the French Army this photograph was taken in the 1950s. It is no longer in service in France

M–56 Scorpion
Self-Propelled Anti-Tank Gun

United States

Armament: 1×90mm gun M-54 in mount M-88 with 29 rounds of ammunition
Crew: 4
Length: 5.841m (including gun)
4.555m (excluding gun)
Width: 2.577m
Height: 2.057m
G/Clearance: .38m
Weight: 7030kg (loaded)
5783kg (empty)
G/Pressure: .316kg.cm²
Engine: Continental AO1-403-5, 6 cylinder, air-cooled, fuel injection petrol engine developing 200bhp at 2750rpm
Speed: 45km/ph (road)
Range: 225km (cruising)
Fuel: 280 litres
Fording: 1.066m (without kit)
1.524m (with kit)
V/Obstacle: .762m
Trench: 1.524m
Gradient: 60%
Armour: See below

Development
The M-56 uses many components of the M-76 amphibious carrier OTTER. The development designation of the M-56 was the T-101 and later T-101E1. The production contract was signed in 1950. The weapon was troop tested with the 101st Airborne Division in 1953. The M-56 was in service by 1957 and the last vehicle was completed in May 1959.
The Scorpion is armed with a 90mm gun that fires similar ammunition to the M-48 tank. The gun has a vertical sliding breech-block and has an elevation of +15° and a depression of −10°, traverse being 30° left and 30° right.

The chassis of the M-56 is unarmoured and fabricated from sheeting and rolled sections of aluminium and is riveted and welded together. The only armour on the vehicle is the shield.
The vehicle has been replaced in the United States Army by the M-551 Sheridan. The M-56 was too light for the gun fitted and when the main armament was fired the vehicle moved several feet.

Variants
There are no variants in service although many versions were projected or built as prototypes including: missile carrier, anti-aircraft vehicle with 4×12.7mm machine guns, 81mm and 107mm mortar carriers, 106mm recoilless rifle carriers, amphibious armoured personnel carrier. One was also fitted with a gas turbine engine.

Employment
Used by Morocco and the Spanish Marines.

The M-56 Scorpion Self-Propelled Anti-Tank Weapon

M–10 and M–36
Self-Propelled Anti-Tank Gun

United States

	M-10	M-10A1	M-36	M-36B1	M-36B2
Crew:	5	5	5	5	5
Length:	5.97m	5.97m	5.97m	6.27m	5.97m
Width:	3.05m	3.05m	3.05m	2.55m	3.05m
Height:	2.47m	2.47m	3.19m	2.66m	3.15m
G/Clearance:	.43m	.43m	.44m	.43m	.46m
Weight Loaded:	29,940kg	29.030kg	27,670kg	30,840kg	29,940kg
G/Pressure:	.86kg.cm^2	.86kg.cm^2	.95kg.cm^2	.94kg.cm^2	.67kg.cm^2
Speed Road:	48km/ph	48km/ph	42km/ph	42km/ph	40km/ph
Range Cruising:	320km	260km	180km	160km	180km
Fuel:	621 litres	727 litres	727 litres	636 litres	625 litres
Fording:	.91m	.91m	.91m	.91m	1.07m
V/Obstacle:	.61m	.61m	.46m	.61m	.48m
Trench:	2.29m	2.29m	2.29m	2.29m	2.29m
Gradient:	60%	60%	60%	60%	60%
Main Armament:	76.2mm	76.2mm	90mm	90mm	90mm
Bow Armament:	—	—	—	7.62mm	—
A/A Armament:	12.7mm	12.7mm	12.7mm	12.7mm	12.7mm
Ammun. Main:	54	54	47	47	47
Ammun. 7.62mm:	—	—	—	450	—
Ammun. 12.7mm:	300	300	1000	1000	1000
Engine:	GM(2)	Ford GAA	Ford GAA	Ford GAA	GMC(2)
Bhp/rpm:	375/2100	450/2600	450/2600	450/2600	375/2100
Armour:	12mm-50mm	12mm-50mm	12mm-50mm	12mm-50mm	12mm-50mm

Development/Variants
The above tank destroyers were developed during World War II and saw service in Europe from 1943 onwards. The M-10, M-10A1, M-36 and M-36B2 all incorporate a Sherman chassis with a new hull and turret. The M-36B1 retains the chassis and hull (and its bow machine gun) of the M-4A3, and is fitted with a new turret and gun. The M-36 uses an M-10A1 chassis and the M-36B2 the M-10 chassis. A prime mover version of the M-10 was called the M-35.

The British converted many M-10s and M-10A1s to carry the excellent 17 Pounder gun. These were called 17 Pounder Self-Propelled Achilles.
Employment
M-10s are still used by Denmark (Achilles) and South Korea.
M-36s are still used by Pakistan (M-36B2) South Korea, Turkey, Yugoslavia (M-36B2).

M-10 Tank Destroyer, this photograph was taken from the rear

M–18 Self-Propelled Anti-Tank Gun   United States

Armament: 1×76mm M-1A1 or M-1A2 gun, elevation $+19\frac{1}{2}^\circ$, depression -10°
1×12.7mm anti-aircraft machine gun
45 rounds of 76mm ammunition
1000 rounds of 12.7mm ammunition
Crew: 5
Length: 6.654m (including gun)
5.282m (excluding gun)
Width: 2.87m (see note)
Height: 2.57m (including A/A machine gun)
G/Clearance: .355m
Weight: 17,650kg (loaded)
16,120kg (empty)
G/Pressure: .83kg.cm²
Engine: Continental R-975-C4, 9 cylinder, radial petrol engine developing 400hp at 2400rpm **OR** Continental R-975-C1 developing 350hp at 2400rpm
Speed: 88.5km/ph (road)
Range: 240km (cruising)
Fuel: 625 litres
Fording: 1.22m
V/Obstacle: .914m
Trench: 1.879m
Gradient: 60%
Armour: 7mm–25mm

Note. The width of the vehicle depends on the tracks fitted.

Development/Variants

The M-18 was developed during World War II and its development designation was T-70. It was standardised as the M-18 in February 1944. A total of 2507 were built by October 1944 when production was completed. Production was undertaken by the Buick Motor Division of the General Motors Corporation.

The M-18 was often called the Hellcat. Its primary role was of tank hunting and the vehicle relied on its high speed to get itself out of trouble, its armour being very thin.

There were a number of variants on the M-18 chassis including the M-39 and M-44 armoured utility vehicles, none of which are known to remain in service. In addition there were many experimental vehicles.

Employment

Used by Nationalist China, South Korea, Venezuela and Yugoslavia.

M-18 Hellcat (World War II photograph)

Self-Propelled Anti-Aircraft Gun System

Armament: 2×40mm cannon M-2A1 with 480 rounds of ammunition
1×M-1919A4 7.62mm machine gun with 1750 rounds
Crew: 6
Length: 6.356m (including guns)
5.816m (excluding guns)
Width: 3.225m
Height: 2.847m
G/Clearance: .438m
Weight: 22,452kg (loaded)
G/Pressure: .65kg.cm^2
Engine: M-42 has Continental or Lycoming AOS-895-3, M-42A1 has a Continental or Lycoming AOS1-895-5, 6 cylinder, air-cooled, supercharged petrol engines developing 500hp at 2800rpm
Speed: 72km/ph (road)
Range: 161km (cruising)
Fuel: 530 litres
Fording: 1.016m
V/Obstacle: .711m
Trench: 1.828m
Gradient: 60%
Armour: 10mm–32mm

Development/Variants
The development designation was T-141 and

the prototype was built at Cleveland, Ohio. It uses many of the components of the M-41 light tank family.
The 40mm cannon are mounted in a power-operated turret and have a traverse of 360°, powered elevation is from −3° to +85°. or from −5° to +87° manually. The guns have a cyclic rate of fire of 240 rounds per minute and a maximum effective range of 4700m.
The M-42A1 has a fuel injection system fitted to its engine. This increases the power of the engine to 525bhp as well as a small extension in its operating range.
In the 1950s an M-42 was fitted with a radar system on the right side of the guns; this, however did not enter production.
The crew of six are seated four in the turret and two in the front of the vehicle.
Employment
Used by Austria, Germany, Japan, Jordan, Lebanon, South Vietnam and the United States.

M-42 of the Austrian Army

M-88

United States

Armoured Recovery Vehicle (Medium)

Armament: 1 × 12.7mm machine gun M-2
1500 rounds of 12.7mm ammunition
Crew: 4
Length: 8.267m (including blade)
Width: 3.428m
Height: 3.22m (including machine gun)
2.921m (excluding machine gun)
G/Clearance: .457m
Weight: 50,800kg (loaded)
G/Pressure: .74kg.cm²
Engine: Continental AVS1-1790-6A, 12
cylinder, air-cooled, supercharged petrol
engine developing 980bhp at 2800rpm
Speed: 48km/ph (road)
Range: 360km
Fuel: 1685 litres
Fording: 1.625m
V/Obstacle: 1.066m
Trench: 2.616m
Gradient: 60%

Development/Variants

Design of the M-88 (development designation
T-88) commenced in 1954. The vehicle is
based on components of the M-48 tank series.
By February 1959, three prototypes had been
built and these were found to be satisfactory.
Production of the M-88 was undertaken by
Bowen-McLaughlin-York Incorporated at their
Bair facility. The first production M-88 was
completed in 1961, the first order being for
498 vehicles. Production continued until 1964
by which time about 1000 had been built.
A hydraulically operated dozer blade is
mounted on the front of the vehicle. This can

be used for dozing operations or for supporting the vehicle when the boom is being
used. The boom has a capacity of 6078kg
without the support of the dozer blade, and
25,400kg with the use of the dozer blade.
The main winch has 60.96m of cable and a
maximum pull of 40,823kg at 8.3m per
minute. The hoist winch has 121.9m of cable
and a maximum capacity of 22,680kg (bare
drum, low speed). The winch and hoist are
hydraulically operated.
The M-88, when built, had a cupola-mounted
12.7mm machine gun. Most have had these
removed and replaced by an unprotected
machine gun mount.
Trials have been carried out with deep fording
equipment. This has not however been adopted
for service.
In 1973 trials were underway with an M-88E1.
This has many components of the M-60
series, including a diesel engine and a diesel
auxiliary power unit. If trials are successful,
all in service M-88s will be rebuilt to this new
standard. The new designation will be
M-88A1 or M-88 PI (Product Improved).

Employment

In service with Austria, Israel, Germany,
Norway and United States Army. It is
scheduled to replace the M-51s still used by
the United States Marine Corps by FY 76
with M-88A1s.

*Rear view of an M-88 Armoured Recovery
Vehicle of the Austrian Army*

M–578
Light Armoured Recovery Vehicle

United States

Armament: 1 × 12.7mm machine gun M-2 500 rounds of 12.7mm machine gun ammunition
Crew: 3
Length: 6.42m (including crane) 5.937m (hull only)
Width: 3.149m
Height: 3.00m (without machine gun)
G/Clearance: .47m
Weight: 24,470kg
G/Pressure: .71kg.cm² (loaded)
Engine: GMC 8V71T Detroit diesel, liquid-cooled, 8 cylinder, turbo-charged, developing 425hp at 1700rpm
Speed: 59.5km/ph (road)
Range: 725km (cruising)
Fuel: 1137 litres
Fording: 1.066m
V/Obstacle: 1.016m
Trench: 2.362m
Gradient: 60%

Development/Variants

The M-578 (development designation T-120 and later T-120E1) uses the same chassis as the M-107 and M-110 self-propelled guns. The first production M-578 was completed by FMC Corporation in October 1962. Later the vehicle was manufactured by Bowen-McLaughlin-York Incorporated and the Pacific Car and Foundry Company. Other trials versions were the T-119 and the T-121.
The vehicle has a hoisting capacity of 13,620kg, with the crane turret traversed to the rear and the spade in position. The tow winch has 70.10m of .03m cable with the following capacities:
Bare drum, 27,240kg, 6.10 metres/minute, low gear.
Bare drum, 6724kg, 24.38 metres/minute, high gear.
Full drum, 17,343kg, 14.33 metres/minute, low gear.
Full drum, 4290kg, 58.52 metres/minute, high gear.
The turret has a traverse of 360°. The hoist/winch capacity is the following (76.20m of .002m cable):
Bare drum, 6810kg, 9.14 metres/minute, low gear.
Bare drum, 1553kg, 40.23 metres/minute, high gear.
Full drum, 4159kg, 14.94 metres/minute, low gear.
Full drum, 944kg, 65.84 metres/minute, high gear.
A wheel lockout system transmits lifting forces directly to the ground.

Employment

In service with Brazil, Canada, Great Britain, Netherlands, Norway, Spain and the United States.

An M-578 Armoured Recovery Vehicle of the Royal Netherlands Army, note that this vehicle has smoke dischargers mounted on the crane turret

SK–1 Armoured Car   East Germany

Armament: 1 × 7.92mm MG 34
Crew: 5
Length: 4.00m
Width: 2.00m
Height: 2.80m
G/Clearance: .28m
Weight: 5400kg (loaded)
Engine: Model 30K, 4 cylinder, in-line, petrol engine developing 55hp at 2800rpm
Speed: 80km/ph (road)
Range: 350km
Fording: .85m
V/Obstacle: .40m
Track: 1.50m

Wheelbase: 3.77m
Armour: 8mm

The SK-1 entered service in 1954; it is not used by the East German Army but is used by para-military units. The vehicle is based on the East German Robur Garant 30K 4×4 truck. The SK-1 is very similar in appearance to the Soviet BA-64 armoured car. The East German SK-2 is a six-wheeled armoured water cannon. The East Germans have modified T-34s and SU-76s to their own requirements. Refer to their resepctive sections for full details.

Egypt

Egypt has built a number of 4×4 armoured personnel carriers called the WALID. This is very similar in appearance to the Soviet BTR-40 vehicle and is powered by an air-cooled German Deutz engine. They are in service with Algeria, Egypt, Israel and the Yemen. Egypt did have a number of Sherman tanks fitted with AMX-13 turrets. As far as is known none of these remain in service; they have either been destroyed in combat or captured by Israel.

India

India builds the Vickers MBT Mk 1 in a new tank factory near Madras. For full details of the Vickers MBT and the Indian production of the tank refer to the page on the Vickers MBT Mk 1.

Italy

Oto Melara S.p.A. of La Spezia have built 200 M-60A1 tanks for the Italian Army and over 3000 M-113 APCs for the Italian, Libyan and Turkish Armies. They have also fitted the main armament to M-109s supplied by the United States. M-109s have been supplied by Oto Melara to Italy and Libya. Oto Melara has overhauled many M-47s to overseas countries. Refer to M-47 page for details of the M-47 rebuilt by Oto Melara. Oto Melara are building 600 Leopard tanks for the Italian Army. There is a separate page for the new Fiat wheeled armoured vehicles.

South Africa

South Africa has built over 800 AML armoured cars under licence from Panhard, although some components are still imported from France. Some Panhards have been supplied by South Africa to Rhodesia. Early in 1973 it was reported that South Africa was building an armoured car called the Eland; whether this is a name given to the Panhard or whether it is a new vehicle is not known. South Africa also has in service the Cactus surface to air missile system; this is called Crotale by the French. The South Africans paid for the initial development of the system. In 1969 it was reported that South Africa was testing two heavy tanks. Since then nothing more has been reported and these could well have been Israeli tanks under test. More recently it was reported that South Africa was testing a new light tank.

Some World War II Marmon-Herrington Mk IV/F armoured cars are still used in Cyprus. They are armed with a two pounder gun and a 7.62mm machine gun.

Yugoslavia

Up to 1965 the only known Yugoslav postwar armoured fighting vehicle was their version of the T-34/85 tank, very few of which were built.

M–590 Armoured Personnel Carrier

Armament: 1 × 12.7mm machine gun
Crew: 2 + 10
Weight: 9500kg
Length: 4.44m
Width: 2.69m
Height: 2.37m (including machine gun)

This was first seen in 1965 and the details below are provisional. The vehicle is amphibious and there is a trim board at the front of the vehicle. Some models have been seen with a shield for the machine gun and firing ports in each side of the hull.

Turkey

Turkey is to establish facilities for the construction of armoured vehicles.

Other Armoured Fighting Vehicles

CATI	Tank Destroyer	Belgium	No longer in service
Chrysler Swat	APC	United States	Development stopped
Conqueror	Heavy Tank	Great Britain	No longer in service
G-13	Tank Destroyer	Germany	No longer in service
Hornet Malkara	ATGW Vehicle	Great Britain	No longer in service
Hotchkiss LFU	Light AFV	France	Development stopped
Hotchkiss TT A 12	APC	France	Development stopped
Hotchkiss VP 90	Light AFV	France	Development stopped.
LVTP-5 Family	APC (Amphibious)	United States	No longer in service
M-39	Utility Vehicle	United States	No longer in service
M-50(ONTOS)	Tank Dstroyer	United States	No longer in service
M-51	Heavy ARV	United States	A few are used by USMC
M-103	Heavy Tank	United States	No longer in service
PBV.301	APC	Sweden	No longer in service
YP-104	Scout Car	Netherlands	Development stopped

A Unimog Armoured Personnel Carrier of the Irish Army. These consist of a Mercedes-Benz chassis with a Swedish-built armoured body. A total of 17 (2 prototypes plus 15 production vehicles) were completed in Sweden for the Congo. These were never delivered. They were purchased by Eire and entered service in 1972, they are armed with a 7.62mm machine gun

Future Main Battle Tanks

At the present time there are a number of MBTs under development. Below is a résumé of these.

Leopard 2 Main Battle Tank   Germany

The Leopard 2 MBT is being developed to replace the 1460 M-48 tanks still being used by the German Army. By the end of 1973 a total of 17 prototypes had been built and were being tested. These prototypes have been built by Krauss-Maffei, who at present build the Leopard 1. The United States has purchased a Leopard 2 for trials purposes. Early in January 1974, the following provisional information was released on the Leopard 2: Armament consists of a German developed 105mm or 120mm smoothbore gun with a thermal shield; this is fully stabilised. It has a crew of four men. Length with gun forward is 9.74m, width with track skits 3.54m, height to top of turret roof 2.49m, battle weight 50,000kg. It is powered by a Type MB 873 Ka-500, 39.8 litres, V-12 multi-fuel engine developing 1500hp at 2600rpm. This gives the vehicle a maximum road speed of over 65km/ph and a power to weight ratio of 30hp/ton. The suspension is one of the 'tube over bar' type and gives improved road and cross-country performance.

FMBT-80   Germany/Great Britain

There is a project called FMBT-80 (Future Main Battle Tank for the 1980s). This will replace the Leopard 1s and Chieftains at present in use in the very early 1980s. In late 1973, trials were conducted in Germany by the British Army with a quantity of Swedish S tanks to test the turretless tank under NATO conditions. The prime contractors in Great Britain would probably be the Royal Ordnance Factory at Leeds and/or Vickers Limited Elswick Works. In Germany Krauss-Maffei would probably be involved. It was reported from Germany in late 1973 that five German companies including Krauss-Maffei, MaK and Rheinstahl (these two companies are at present involved in the Marder programme), have been asked by the German Government to study probable designs for this new tank. It was also reported that MaK, had, on their own initiative, produced a turretless tank armed with two 105mm guns and a very high road speed.

T-70 Main Battle Tank   Soviet Union

The new Soviet Main Battle Tank is the T-70. This was previously known as the T-64 or M-1970 and has started to replace T-62s in Soviet armoured divisions. The T-70 has approximately the same overall dimensions as the T-62 MBT but is slightly lower. Its main armament is probably the same 115mm gun as fitted to the T-62, although some reports have indicated that it has a 122mm gun/launcher that fires either shells or small missiles. The suspension is new and consists of six evenly spaced road wheels and four track support rollers, the suspension system is very similar to that used on the SA-4 GANEF anti-aircraft missile vehicle and the new tracked armoured minelaying vehicle, although they have seven road wheels. The hull of the vehicle is very similar to that of the British Chieftain MBT. The glacis plate on the T-70 is well sloped and the driver is in the centre of the vehicle. The turret is similar to the T-62. The infra-red light for the commander is now on the right turret hatch and the gunner's infra-red searchlight is on the left on the main gun, ie the reversal of that previously fitted. This would seem to indicate that the gunner is now on the right of the gun and the loader on the left. Loaded weight of the T-70 is about 40,000kg. No details of performance are as yet known.

XM-1 Main Battle Tank   United States

After the United States and Germany cancelled the MBT-70 the United States went on to develop the so-called austere version called the XM-803. This in turn was cancelled and Congress decided that the tank would be far too expensive. On 23rd January 1973, the Project Manager of the XM-1 Programme, located at Warren, Michigan, invited American companies to submit proposals for this new tank. As a result of these proposals the Chrysler Corporation (who at present produce the M-60A1 tank) and the General Motors Corporation (who built the now defunct MBT-70) received contracts to build prototypes of the XM-1. After trials one of these will be selected to undergo further development which in due course will lead to a production order. Armament will probably consist of a 152mm gun/missile launcher and a Bushmaster secondary weapons system, or a 110mm gun as main armament. Prototypes will be armed with the current 105mm gun. The XM-1 will be smaller than the M-60, lighter and much faster. The XM-1 will accelerate from zero to 32km/ph in less than nine seconds compared to 16 seconds for the Improved M-60 MBT. Unit hardware cost ceiling (excluding tooling and other investment non-recurring costs) is approximately half a million dollars.

Photo Credits

The photographs used to illustrate this book have been received from many governments, companies and individuals all over the world. The sources, where known, are listed below.

Alvis Limited. 66, 67, 69, 70, 71 (top), 76 (top)
Associated Press, London. 83 (top), 84 (top), 84 (foot), 98 (foot), 100 (foot), 102
Australian Army. 163, 165 (foot)
Austrian Army. 10, 136 (top), 143 (centre), 147, 183, 184
Belgian Army. 45 (top)
British Aircraft Corporation (GW Division). 74 (foot)
British Ministry of Defence (Crown Copyright). 57, 58 (top), 68
Bundesgrenzshutz (Federal German Border Police). 65, 131, 132 (foot)
Cadillac Gage Company. 158
Canadian Armed Forces. 156 (foot)
Central Office of Information (Crown Copyright). 58 (foot), 80 (foot)
E.C.P. Armées. 19 (top), 20 (centre and foot) 21, 23 (upper middle), 29, 31 (top), 38, 39, 41, 113, 143 (foot), 170, 179, 180
EMI Limited. 74 (top)
Fiat Company. 86
FMC Corporation. 151, 154, 161, 164 (foot)
F.N. (Belgium). 11
Finnish Army. 64, 119 (top)
GKN (Sankey). 77
German Army. 37, 48 (foot), 49, 50 (foot), 52, 53 (top), 54, 56, 140 (top), 141 (top), 145 (top), 172 (top)
GIAT (France). 19 (centre), 22, 23 (top and foot), 24, 31 (foot), 40
GMC (Allison Division). 146
Hägglund and Soner. 122, 124, 126, 127
Indian Army. 14, 95, 140 (foot), 148
Irish Army. 33 (top), 187
Japanese Self-Defence Force. 87, 89
Krauss-Maffei. 44, 45 (foot)
Lockheed Missiles and Space Company. 150, 152
Mercedes-Benz (Germany). 55
Mitsubishi Heavy Industries. 90
Messerschmitt-Bölkow-Blohm. 47, 53 (foot)
MOWAG. 132 (top)
Normalair-Garret Limited. 76 (centre)

Oto-Melara. 143 (top), 165 (top), 174 (top)
Panhard and Levassor. 25, 26, 27, 32, 33 (centre and foot), 34
Philco-Ford Company. 165 (centre left)
Rheinstahl. 46, 48 (top), 50 (top and centre), 51
Royal Armoured Corps Tank Museum. 61
Royal Netherlands Army. 23 (lower middle), 30, 62 (top), 63 (top and foot), 92, 164 (top and centre), 185
Saviem. 36
Short Brothers and Harland Limited. 72
Soltam Company. 83 (foot), 84 (centre), 85
Solartron Limited. 2
Steyr-Daimler-Puch AG. 9
Swedish Ministry of Defence. 121, 123, 125
Thomson CSF. 19 (foot), 42
United States Army. 133, 135 137 (top and centre), 141 (centre), 153, 165 (centre right), 166, 167, 173, 180, 182
United States Marine Corps. 141 (foot), 160, 169, 172 (foot), 176 (centre)
Vickers Limited. 59, 62 (foot), 80 (top and centre)
Volvo. 128 (top)

T. Bell. 130 (foot)
R. M. Bennett. 149
Robert J. Icks. 159
George Von Rauch. 12, 144
Stephen Tunbridge. 130 (top)
J. I. Taibo. 136 (foot), 139, 142, 168, 177
T. C. Lopez. 176 (foot)
Susuma Yamada. 91, 178 (top)
Christopher F. Foss. 20 (top), 53, 63 (centre), 71 (foot), 75, 76 (foot), 78, 97, 115, 145 (foot), 156 (top), 171, 175, 176 (top)

Index